AF567001

THE REVIVAL OF GREEK THOUGHT

1620-1830

THE REVIVAL OF GREEK THOUGHT

1620-1830

G. P. HENDERSON

STATE UNIVERSITY OF NEW YORK PRESS
ALBANY

Published by State University of New York Press
Thurlow Terrace, Albany, New York 12201

International Standard Book Number 0–87395–069–0
Library of Congress Catalog Card Number 75–112608

PRINTED IN THE UNITED STATES OF AMERICA BY
THE RIVERSIDE PRESS, INC., CAMBRIDGE, MASSACHUSETTS

To my wife, Hester L. D. Henderson, and
in recollection of friends, Greek and British,
who fought and worked for Greece in 1944 and 1945

Contents

Preface xi
1. *Introduction: The Phases of Greek Reeducation* 1
2. *Theophilos Korydaleus: A New Aristotelianism* 12
3. *The Mavrokordatos Family: Moralism and Political Propriety* 20
4. *Damodos and Anthrakitēs: The Pains of Rationalism* 28
5. *Eugenios Voulgaris: New Ideas in an Old Language* 41
6. *Voulgaris's* Logic*: A* Speculum Mentis 53
7. *Voulgaris on Cosmology, Astronomy and Religious Toleration* 64
8. *Theotokēs and Katartzēs: A Translator's Choices* 76
9. *Iosepos Moisiodax: "Sound" Philosophy and Educational Reform* 87
10. *Athanasios Psalidas: Antagonism to Voulgaris* 99
11. *Psalidas's* True Happiness*: Philosophy and Revelation* 106
12. *Benjamin Lesvios: The Confrontation of Nature* 117
13. *Benjamin's* Metaphysics*: Philosophy Come into its Own* 127
14. *Adamantios Koraēs: The Classics as Humane Studies* 142
15. *"Nomarchy": A Harsher Call to Reform* 159
16. *Philippidēs, Konstantas, Gazēs: The School of Melies* 170
17. *Doukas and Koumas: Archaism and Liberal Education* 183
18. *Epilogue: Liberalism not Victorious* 199
Index 209

Preface

My interest in Greek literature written during the Turkish occupation was aroused by the publication in 1953 of E. P. Papanoutsos's Νεοελληνικὴ Φιλοσοφία, Vol. I (1600–1850). This volume contained selections from writings by various Greek philosophical thinkers of the period indicated, and an informative and judicious introductory essay. Through it I was introduced to C. Th. Dimaras's comprehensive Ἱστορία τῆς Νεοελληνικῆς Λογοτεχνίας, and thence was led to take a wider interest in the recovery made by Greek thought, language and education prior to the setting-up of the Greek state in 1830. The present book is an attempt at an independent assessment of the intellectual value, and the historical, educational and social significance of a large body of literature to which the two studies named were introductory.

The expression "Greek thought" requires some explanation. My concern is with intellectual history, in a sense which excludes, on the one hand, poetry and belles-lettres, and, on the other, dogmatic theology and any kind of writing in which either piety or mysticism prevails over reasoned theory, speculative interest or systematic learning. I have tried to write not a general cultural history, but rather a history of intellectual effort, of a striving to understand, accommodate and operate with *ideas*, taken systematically and regarded as the means of achieving both knowledge and the power to develop the human condition in accordance with what is known. The emphasis on striving and on disciplined enquiry is what excludes dogma, piety and mysticism. The emphasis on systematized knowledge is what excludes those classes of "literature" (poetry and other imaginative work) in which the aesthetic side of things is of most importance. If a defense be needed for this limitation, it is that the intellectual history, thus narrowed-down, of the Greeks under Turkish domination is represented nevertheless by a large field of material; that that history has hardly begun to be adequately studied or critically discussed; that this is less true of other aspects of modern Greek culture, and yet that there is substance and dynamism in the reviving Greek "thought" such as to make it a noteworthy feature of the history of the Greeks before independence. The thinkers whose work I shall describe were attempting, in essence, to provide a prospectively independent people with knowledge and intellectual standards such as might both aid and befit that people's nationalistic aims. The nature of their methods and the degree of their success both challenge discussion.

The task of collecting or getting access to the printed work with which I have been concerned has not been easy; much of the material is very rare. In obtaining it I have been heavily dependent on the help and kindness of three people, my friends Dr. Papanoutsos and Mr. Dimaras, already mentioned, and Mr. A. Anghelou, himself a specialist in the Neo-Hellenic "Enlightenment." I must record especially, with great gratitude, the readiness with which Mr. Dimaras and Mr. Anghelou have kept me supplied with their own editions of or critical studies in work belonging to my field. While—as I must emphasize—I have tried to view all of this work with an independent eye, I have nevertheless been instructed and guided by the judgments of these scholars, who have been in the field for a long time and whose native knowledge of it a ξένος must respect. Throughout the book I have tried to indicate where I have been dependent on one or more of the three main authorities I have mentioned, either as regards matters of fact or in questions of judgment. Otherwise it can be taken that I am expressing an autonomous point of view of the literature studied. Dr. Papanoutsos has helped me considerably by discussion, by commenting on portions of the book in typescript, and above all by his constant encouragement. My indebtedness to him is very great indeed.

My acknowledgments are due also—and are warmly given—to the librarians of the National Library of Greece and the Gennadeion Library, Athens, for the hospitality of their libraries and the generous assistance I have been given therein. I am likewise indebted for help provided by the library staffs of the University Library, St. Andrews, and the University Library, Dundee, over many years. I must express my gratitude also for the friendly and kindly way in which I have been received in the various places in Greece which I have visited because of their association with persons described in this book. I should like to mention particularly the hospitality provided by Mr. Ioannēs D. Sakellariou, President of the Community of Melies, in 1959; the knowledgeable and energetic help given me by Mr. Vangelis Skouvaras in reviewing the contents of the library in that place; the generous and informative guidance, in Mytilenē in 1965, of Mr. Ioannēs Moutzourēs and Dr. E. Hadjiemmanuel; the hospitality provided in Mytilenē by the Society for Lesbian Studies; and the courtesy and helpfulness of the librarian of the Koraēs Library in Chios during my visit there in 1966. Finally, I should like to record my thanks to Mr. W. Sinclair Gauldie for his auditions of various portions of this book in draft, and to Miss N. M. R. Kay for her preparation of my typescript for the press.

It is a measure of the extent to which I have been involved with the work of Papanoutsos, Dimaras and Anghelou that I have found it best to adopt a simple numerical system of reference to it. The lists of books and papers pertaining to those three, which follow, enable me to avoid giving full citations in their case, and simply to refer to the number given to some item in these lists. Thus, "Dimaras 4" refers to item number four in the list relating to Dimaras. (Because of their general relevance and usefulness, one or two items are included in the lists even if I have not had occasion to allude to them in footnotes.) All other references are given in orthodox fashion.

I have introduced a fair amount of quotation from the authors studied; partly for ordinary reasons of exposition and criticism, partly in order to convey the somewhat unusual flavor of their writing. Quoted passages have invariably been given in translation, all translations being my own.

Works subsequently referred to by name and number as listed (with extras):

E. P. Papanoutsos:

1. Νεοελληνική Φιλοσοφία *A'*. Athens: 1953. (Reviewed by myself, "Greek Philosophy from 1600 to 1850," in *The Philosophical Quarterly* 5

[1955], and referred to extensively by Raphael Demos in "The Neo-Hellenic Enlightenment [1750–1821]," *Journal of the History of Ideas* 19 [1958]. I have reused some material from my own review in Chapters 1 and 18.)

2. Νεοελληνικὴ Φιλοσοφία *A'*. Second edition, revised. Athens: 1959.

3. Νεοελληνικὴ Φιλοσοφία *B'*. Athens: 1957. (Reviewed by myself, "Modern Greek Philosophy," in *The Philosophical Quarterly* 7 [1957].)

C. Th. Dimaras:

1. Ἱστορία τῆς Νεοελληνικῆς Λογοτεχνίας. Second edition. Athens: 1954.

2. Ἐκλογὴ Ἐπιστόλων Ἀδαμαντίου Κοραῆ. Ed. with notes. Athens: 1952.

3. Ἡ Φωτισμένη Εὐρώπη. (Repr. from Νέα Ἑστία, 15 February 1952.) Athens: 1952.

4. Ὁ Κοραῆς καὶ ἡ Ἐποχή του. Selections, ed. with introduction. Athens: 1953.

5. Γύρω στὸν Κάλβο καὶ τὸν Κοδρικᾶ. (Repr. from Ἀγγλοελληνικὴ Ἐπιθεώρηση, 1953/4.) Athens: 1954.

6. Δ. Καταρτζῆ. Ἐγκώμιο τοῦ Φιλόσοφου, Μακαρισμὸς τοῦ Ὀρθόδοξου, Ψόγος τοῦ Ἄθεου, Ταλάνισμα τοῦ Δεισιδαίμων. Ed. with notes. Athens: 1955.

7. Ἕνας Διώκτης τοῦ Νεοφύτου Δούκα, Σαμουὴλ ὁ Ἄνδριος. (Repr. from Ἀφιέρωμα εἰς τὴν Ἤπειρον.) Athens: 1955.

8. Δ. Καταρτζῆ. Γραμματικὴ τῆς Φυσικῆς Γλώσσας. Ed. with notes. Athens: 1957.

9. Ἡ Σχολὴ τοῦ Ἁγίου Ὄρους στὰ 1800. (Repr. from Ἑλληνικά 15.) Thessalonikē: 1957.

10. Ψυχολογικοὶ Παράγοντες τοῦ Εἰκοσιένα. (Repr. from Σπουδαὶ τῆς Α.Σ.Β.Σ.) Athens: 1957.

11. Ἀδαμαντίου Κοραῆ. Τρεῖς Διάλογοι. Ed. with introduction. Athens: 1960.

12. Σατιρικὰ Κείμενα τοῦ Εἰκοσιένα. (Repr. from Διοικητικὴ Ἐπετηρὶς 1959/60 τῆς Α.Σ.Β.Σ.) Athens: 1960.

13. Φροντίσματα. Πρῶτο Μέρος. Ἀπὸ τὴν Ἀναγέννηση στὸν Διαφωτισμό. Athens: 1962.

14. Τὸ Πολιτικὸ Θέμα στὸν Κοραῆ. Μὲ Ἀποσπάσματα τῶν «Πολιτικῶν Παραινέσιων». Ed. with notes. Athens: 1963.

15. Ὁ Φιλελευθερισμὸς τοῦ Δ. Καταρτζῆ. Μὲ Ἀποσπάσματα ἀπὸ τὸ Ἀνέκδοτο «Γνῶθι Σαυτόν». Ed. with notes. Athens: 1964.

16. Ὁ Ἑλληνικὸς Διαφωτισμός. (Repr. from Ἡ Μεγάλη Ἑλληνικὴ Ἐγκυκλοπαιδεία, 1.) Athens: 1964.

17. Δημήτριος Καταρτζῆς (Σχεδίασμα Βιογραφίας). (Repr. from Ἡ Γενικὴ Παγκόσμιος Ἐγκυκλοπαιδεία Πάπυρος-Λαρούς.) Athens: 1965.

18. *La Grèce au temps des Lumières*. Geneva: 1969.

A. Anghelou:

1. Πῶς ἡ Νεοελληνικὴ Σκέψη Ἐγνώρισε τὸ «Δοκίμιο» τοῦ *John Locke*. (Repr. from Ἀγγλοελληνικὴ Ἐπιθεώρηση 7.) Athens: 1954.

2. Ἡ Δίκη τοῦ Μεθοδίου Ἀνθρακίτη. (Repr. from Ἀφιέρωμα εἰς τὴν Ἤπειρον.) Athens: 1955.

3. Πρὸς τὴν Ἀκμὴ τοῦ Νεοελληνικοῦ Διαφωτισμοῦ. (Repr. from Μικρασιατικὰ Χρονικά 7.) Athens: 1956.

4. Πλάτωνος Τύχαι. Athens: 1963.

5. Τὸ Χρονικὸ τῆς Ἀθωνιάδας. (Repr. from Νέα Ἑστία, Christmas 1963.) Athens: 1963.

6. *J. D. Carlyle's Journal of Mount Athos* (1801). Ed. with notes. (Repr. from Ὁ Ἐρανιστῆς 14.) Athens: 1965.

1

Introduction: The Phases of Greek Reeducation

There is sometimes point in emphasizing that from Homeric times to our own day Greek reflective thought has continued with relatively little interruption and, to a greater or lesser extent, can be studied directly, in its own literature.[1] Even the fifteenth century, it may be argued, represents no more than an intermission. This consideration has force against those who so romanticize antiquity as to forbid themselves, not merely to put a favorable value upon, but even to be curious about, Greek thought after Theophrastus. It still has force against those whose studies or interests extend as far as Psellos, Vlemmidēs or even Plethon but who, nevertheless, take it for granted that after the Ottoman conquest there is no Greek "thought" worth studying. The main purpose of the present book is to show that, from various points of view, this is not so.

Specifically, over the years between the early seventeenth and the early nineteenth centuries, there is a movement of thought, conducted by Greeks in Greek, which deserves examination by the historian of ideas, by the historian or philosopher of education, and by students of the interplay of cultural with general social or political history. The book will follow the course of that movement up to the War of Independence. This limit is chosen, not because it represents a complete halt in Greek intellectual history, but because at that stage the movement changes character and direction rather decisively. What may be seen as a continuous educational discussion and dialectic, extending from the first, tentative, revival of Aristotelian studies in the 1620's to the establishment of a whole spectrum of modern literary, philosophical and scientific studies by the 1820's, faltered in consequence of war and the establishment of new social and economic conditions; and when it resumed, proceeded in only partly the same terms as before. It was, however, a distinctive and extended enough phase on its own to support the idea that Greek thought has, in a way, never given up since it began.

That is one side of the coin. The other, with which this book is more concerned, is that the hiatus in Greek intellectual history which followed the Ottoman conquest of Greek lands was very serious indeed. From a shorter term point of view than that just adopted Greek thought did give up, in the sense that for at least a century and a half after Plethon (alternatively, after the fall of Constantinople) no fresh start was made. So far as Greek culture of a speculative kind was concerned, the later fifteenth and the sixteenth centuries were mere feeble survivals, in which Byzantine thought and philosophy, strong in the two centuries before the fall of Constantinople, withered away. Certainly in philosophy there is no trace of any originative writing in Greek (even including under that label new work of a "missionary" kind upon older ideas) during this period; and, as far as education was concerned, the seminary which then provided the highest level of teaching available to the Greeks under Turkish or any other domination, namely the Patriarchal Academy in Constantinople, progressed no further, in the more secular parts of its teaching, than a very few elements of dialectic, rhetoric and Aristotelian ethics.[2] The middle of the sixteenth century probably represents the lowest ebb in all Greek intellectual history. For one thing, Greek thought and education were receiving no invigoration from Greek scholars in exile. The more notable of these, during the centuries mentioned, did not write in Greek and may fairly be excluded from an assessment of contemporary Greek letters and education.[3] For another, the Orthodox church, left as the only authority in Greek cultural life, was in no position but to defend what it held. The hiatus in genuine Greek intellectual effort which was the consequence of these factors was complete enough and lasted long enough to create the following formidable problem.

When new ideas were at length introduced into Greek education, how were they to be accommodated? The language of the laity, in the seventeenth century, was simply unfitted, as it stood, to accommodate modes of thought belonging to either of the two possible sources of educational inspiration, namely Classical antiquity and modern Western literature, philosophy and science. The liturgical language of the clergy would require relatively little extension in order to provide for, say, a revived Aristotelianism, but for the re-expression of modern knowledge it was ill-equipped and, arguably, the wrong sort of diction anyhow.

The point thus put in terms of linguistic media might profitably be reput in terms of habits of thought. If Greek education were to revive after 1600, then the revival could not consist of a modification nor even a revolutionizing of habitual ways of thought. Through conquest, Greek lands had been excluded from that Renaissance to which Byzantine scholars had contributed so much. The Byzantine tradition itself, in philosophy, theology and other studies, was worn out. Whereas in Western Europe the most "revolutionary" of ideas could grow out of and preserve some connection with a context of thought, here such a context could come into existence only after a succession of new ideas had been received and, in some sense, come to terms with. The creation of that context could not but be gradual. Its form and content could well be the subject of long dispute, and in the end need not even be of a piece.

The main object of this book, then, is to follow the revival of Greek thought, regarded as confronting this complex problem. It will appear that the whole course of educational striving and controversy in which that revival expressed itself was an engagement with "philosophy." This word itself was the σύνθημα, the signal or watchword adopted by many of the great educators, and occasionally the term of anathema applied by their opponents to what they were trying to introduce. Now it is quite true that φιλοσοφία in this context, like "philosophie" in seventeenth and eighteenth-century France, means something more extensive than the logic, metaphysics, ethics and epistemology which, roughly speaking, represent its scope in academic usage today. It means, in general, a rationalistic mode of thought; one that is independent of superstitious or sheerly dogmatic elements in all fields. It extends very frequently to the physical or natural sciences, usually in such a way as to emphasize both their objectivity and their human significance. It extends sometimes to mathematics. At the other end of the spectrum it often covers what is, strictly speaking, theology, though theology professedly "natural" in its character. For all this generality in the meaning of the term, however, "philosophy" as introduced and fought over by the Greeks of the seventeenth, eighteenth and nineteenth centuries does include an astonishing amount of philosophy in the conventional, academic sense—astonishing, that is, in relation to the fact that in and through "philosophy," broadly speaking, what was being introduced was education, at least higher education, and critical culture as such. Education, it seemed, must have its apex: scientific knowledge remained continuous with philosophical, and the whole a unity. Even after the abandonment of Aristotelianism, therefore, the educational movement which we have to study has as its main representatives men who both valued philosophy (in the academic sense) and, for the most part, themselves introduced or worked out philosophical systems as a most important offering to Greek reeducation. These systems will not be my only object of study, but their origin, nature and value will be one of the main preoccupations of this book.

Who were these "intellectuals"?[4] Many of them went to schools or universities in Italy, Germany or elsewhere outside Turkish-occupied Greek territory. The majority of them eventually became ecclesiastics, and founders of, or teachers in, Greek schools working in occupied territory under the immediate supervision of the Church. Accordingly, even the more freethinking of their works tend to preserve a certain theological aspect. Most of the writers, sooner or later, express a firm assurance of the existence of God, the immortality of the soul and the prospect of future reward for virtue. Many speak as if the ultimate tendency of their writings were and ought to be to show these things, and only occasionally does any question arise in one's mind as to the sincerity of the arguments which they employ in order to do so. At the same time, it is the rationalist strand in their works which provides their main interest: considering how easily this could be misinterpreted, it was a very real hostage to ecclesiasticism. If we consider the Greek Church's not-unsullied record in the matter of persecution, it is clear how careful teachers working within its ambit had to be. There was no question of torture or killing, but men were not left unaccused, free to teach and secure in their positions if their orthodoxy was at all in doubt. A fair proportion of the writers to be mentioned in this book suffered in some degree for their "philosophical" independence and integrity. For all that, Greek thought up to the War of Independence shows an increasing secularization. Its main fascination, in fact, is twofold: the desire which it exhibits to work out a territory for philosophy and science in face of a well-established dogmatic theology; and its very great concern to show that the pursuit of such knowledge in unsettled and uncertain times is justified—that it will both restore the Greek people to its dignity and be a most real condition of its ability to live independently.

What were the basic means by which Greek reeducation was able to progress, before that independence was achieved? First, there came into being a series of schools for "higher education," increasing in number as time went on. Those which many of the Greek intellectuals attended "abroad" were themselves Greek schools. They were to be found in the Greek communities established in great mercantile centers like Venice or Vienna, or in the Turkish satrapies of Wallachia and Moldavia, containing sizable Greek administrative communities in Bucharest and Iaşi; or, not unimportantly, in the Ionian islands. Their existence, the degree of their activity, and the standard of their teaching were determined by one or more of three factors: the energy and human concern of the Church authorities in that place; the patriotism, foresight and generosity of private benefactors; and the presence and dedication of a suitably equipped teacher or group of teachers. Other schools which provided part at least of a higher education[5] for some of the men whom I shall describe were to be found in occupied territory itself. The Patriarchal Academy in Constantinople and schools in Ioannina and on the coast of Asia Minor were the most notable.[6] These "internal" schools became a focus for the activity of Greek thinkers and teachers, many of whom came in from "abroad" (presumably at some sacrifice) to educate and enlighten their countrymen, particularly those who might become clerics, administrators, teachers or doctors. The schools attracted benefactions, not only money but also books and equipment, from individuals or groups of people, very often expatriates who had some special connection with the place where the school was located. Such endowments were not, in general, lavish, but in some places, notably Chios and Melies, book collections were made which remain, to this day, remarkable. Hence these schools, both as centers of intellectual activity and as the objects of educational and patriotic benevolence became, more or less, emblematic of Greek regeneration.

It is noteworthy that the great majority of the "internal" schools were to be found at the periphery, and not at the ancient center, of Greek lands: in the Ionian Islands, Epirus, and Asia Minor, and not in Attica, or the Morea. No doubt the causes of this fact are complex. However, since Padua, Venice, Vienna, Leipzig and other European cities served for so many Greek scholars as sources of enlightenment or places of publication, it is reasonable to suggest that nearness to and ease of communication with Greece's hinterland was important in determining that the establishment of schools should be on its northern and eastern fringes rather than in its more central parts.

Interestingly enough, it does not seem as if the schools which were established within Turkish-occupied territory suffered direct repression from the Turkish authority. The removal of that authority was, at bottom, one of the main reasons for their existence; but in what eighteenth-century teachers, for example, write about their educational circumstances and hopes one finds an absence of complaints about day-to-day interference, by the Turks, in their affairs. The social and political significance of Greek reeducation, it would seem, was not appreciated by the Turks; and to begin with, certainly, that reeducation proceeded so much under the wing of the Church that in Turkish eyes it may not have differentiated itself significantly from the Orthodoxy, which, in their fashion, they were prepared to let live. Anyhow, it is mainly the general poverty of their circumstances, the lack of educational resources, and their differences with other Greeks, by which various of the Greek intellectuals who write of their misfortunes declare themselves to be afflicted.

So much for the schools as institutions. The next question is how provision was made for books and for scientific equipment. As regards the latter, it is only towards the end of the period under review that the problem of providing instruments and materials for scientific demonstrations is aired. Even then, it is small in scale, and the answer to this part of the question is simply that for the few schools where experimental science was a possible part of the curriculum, individual teachers or outside benefactors brought in, from abroad, such equipment as they could.

The larger problem was that of the production of books, as textbooks strictly speaking or for background study. Here Greek education owes a great and, throughout the period, increasing debt to individual patrons, again for the most part wealthy Greek merchants, who, purely for the good of their countrymen, sponsored the publication of instructive literature. The Greek printing presses of Venice, Vienna, Leipzig, Halle and other places produced that literature on an increasingly large scale, in a great variety of subjects.[7] Besides a certain amount of more or less original writing, it comprised paraphrases, epitomes, compilations and straight translations from Western European work in all sorts of theoretical and scientific subjects; and latterly, as to some extent at the beginning, scholarly work on classical literature. Much of this material was distributed free to those who required it.

An instructed observer of and contributor to this whole process remarked at the beginning of the nineteenth century that if "Europe" were to relapse into barbarism, there were now enough Greek translations of "European" books and a sufficiency of educated Greeks to let *Greece* restore to Europe the fundamentals of what she had lost. Anyhow, he went on, in the last decade of the eighteenth century a greater number of instructive books in different subjects had appeared in Greece than during the whole previous period since the destruction of the Eastern empire.[8] The claim that an intellectual revival preceded the political revival of modern Greece rests importantly, then, on the existence of this large body of instructive literature. One of my main tasks must clearly be to describe its nature, and to assess its quality and its impact.

The whole movement may be divided into three distinctive, partly overlapping phases. The first, beginning in the 1620's, was one of humanistic revival, supported by the Church, and based largely upon the new Aristotelianism that originated from Padua. The most important of those who carried this study into Greek lands was Theophilos Korydaleus,[9] a scholar who was head of the Patriarchal Academy for some years up to 1640. Korydalism as a body of literature is in effect just the works of its founder, but its influence in Greek education lasted for a good hundred years.

Well before the end of that phase, indeed from about 1670 onwards, two not-independent developments are apparent, which may be taken to constitute the second phase. One is the rising influence of an administrative class, to be set alongside that of the clergy. The Phanariots, and notably the Mavrokordatos family, were both the sponsors of education and writers on their own account. As writers they were preoccupied with moralistic and worldly themes, showing a more direct literary concern about human affairs than contemporary scholasticism could provide, and, in the process, they were to some extent transmitters of Western European ideas into Greek thought and writing. The second development in this second phase is precisely that receptiveness. It is their awareness of contemporary philosophical and scientific culture in France and elsewhere and their distribution of some of its ideas that unite the Phanariots with other representatives of the period. By far the greatest of these other scholars was Eugenios Voulgaris, a cleric, and a teacher of very wide knowledge and accomplishments who at one time or another transmuted into Greek much of the thought of Descartes, Locke, Voltaire and many philosophers and scientists besides. The publication of Voulgaris's *Logic* in 1766 represents the climax of the second phase.

The third phase comes into being partly as a reaction against the authority which Voulgaris, taking his turn after Korydaleus, had built up. He had done so even while being a philosophical and scientific eclectic and an exponent, within broad limits, of freedom of thought. He had done so, in a somewhat different way, through the attitude he adopted towards the problem of finding a Greek scholarly language suited for contemporary purposes. His extreme archaism in this respect represents one polar position in a debate that is not yet settled, and of which I shall take notice from time to time in what follows.

The third phase, we may say very roughly, comprises the last quarter of the eighteenth century and the first of the nineteenth. It displays a quite phenomenal increase in intellectual activity and an awareness in many of its representatives that their thought and teaching were dynamic, contributing to the Greek nation's coming-to. At the same time their writing, particularly in philosophy, shows a certain degree of professionalism and a tendency in the authors to be intrigued by intellectual problems for their own sake. Athanasios Psalidas and Benjamin Lesvios may be named as two writers who display some integrity in this sense. The professionalism extends to scholarship as well as to direct theorizing. Adamantios Koraēs' editing of the classics and his exegesis of them in the interests of a modern education are one clear illustration of it.

The third period, however, also brings to light two deep, and deeply related, divisions amongst the Greeks. First, the Church as a sponsor of education becomes both less influential, and steadily more restrictive and old-fashioned in its policies and practices. And secondly, the language question comes more and more to the forefront. The main protagonists in argument concerning it are Demetrios Katartzēs, Iosepos Moisiodax, Koraēs, and Neophytos Doukas, whose ideas I shall describe. In general, the possibilities are seen as an adaptation for scholarly purposes of the language of the people, the language of the people transmuted by the most extensive refinement and augmentation, and the readoption, more or less unmodified, of the Attic version of the ancient language. The Church's position in all this is inertial: it is neither interested in the possibilities of the popular language nor sympathetic to reform, and it has no initiative of its own to proffer.

Throughout the period the inflow of Western ideas continues. Locke again, Condillac and Kant may be mentioned for their special influence on particular writers, but we now have to take account of a whole host of "European" philosophers, mathematicians and scientists, presented to the Greek people in one way and another. In this connection, we can recognize for the first time the beginnings of another controversy, namely as to the place experimental, as distinct from book-learned, science should occupy in general education. Neophytos Doukas, already mentioned, and Konstantinos Koumas were two who took up this question, and they waged verbal war over it towards the end of the period. Koumas, without being a thinker of the first class, is worth this special mention here because he is emblematic of the whole third phase: he united in himself three of its main "progressive" tendencies, namely, a readiness to learn from the arts and sciences of "enlightened" Europe, a determination to write in a language which, while "refined," was basically the people's, plain and easy to understand, and an appreciation of the need to leaven the austerities of "grammatical," that is, linguistic and literary, education with some direct study of the surrounding world.

The words δουλεία or σκλαβιά ("slavery") tend to occur automatically in Greek references to the condition of the Greek people under Turkish domination. In many respects these terms are apropos, in some they are not. As a people speaking a language of its own, practicing its own religion, undertaking (even to a very limited extent) its own education, maintaining traditional habits, customs, and values, and preserving its folklore, its music and dancing and artistic *motifs*, the Greek people was not "enslaved." Various writers have commented, too, on the sustaining power of the popular belief that, reduced as they were, modern Greeks were continuous with and descended from the ancient Hellenes. One would want to say, therefore, that throughout the seventeenth, eighteenth and early nineteenth centuries the Greeks preserved and exploited a sense of apartness, indeed of uniqueness, and that of all the conditions making possible the educational revival which I shall describe, this was the most basic. Koraēs describes the situation without clichés: "Cette vanité [i.e., of descent from the Ancients], jointe à la différence de religion et de moeurs, et au traitement aussi indigne qu'impolitique que les Grecs essuyoient de la part de leurs conquérans, fit qu'une très-grande partie de la nation se regarda toujours comme prisonnière de guerre, et jamais comme esclave."[10]

Notes

1. Cf. B. Tatakis in É. Bréhier, *Histoire de la philosophie*, Fasc. suppl. II (*La Philosophie Byzantine*, Paris, 1949), p. 2.

2. See M. Gedeon, Χρονικὰ τῆς Πατριαρχικῆς Ἀκαδημίας (Constantinople, 1883), p. 67.

3. For an elaboration of this theme see Papanoutsos 2, pp. 7–8.

4. Διανοούμενοι is the usual Greek term for them.

5. This expression is, necessarily, vague. The school in Chios, to take one example, was described in 1803 as "une espèce d'université ou d'école polytechnique" (Koraēs, *Mémoire sur l'état actuel de la civilisation dans la Grèce* [Paris, 1803], p. 35). If one judges simply by the level of *aspiration* represented by most of the didactic works which I shall be discussing, one can see the point of using such terms in order to describe the schools in which they were used.

6. I do not know of any authoritative estimate of the number of such schools, classified by standard, at any particular period. Dimaras (4, p. 60) quotes evidence to show that in 1786 there were 35 "schools" operating in subject Greece, whereas by 1820 there were ten times that number of "middle or lower-grade" schools.

7. E. Legrand's *Bibliographie Hellénique ou description raisonnée des ouvrages publiés par des Grecs au dix-huitième siècle* (2 vols., Paris, 1918 and 1928), incomplete though it is, will give substance to this remark. Dimaras (4, p. 60) estimates that the output of Greek books written or produced by Greeks rose

from about 20 in 1790 to about 100 in 1820. (I shall refer to Legrand's eighteenth-century bibliography hereafter as "Legrand [XVIII].")

8. Koraēs, *op. cit.*, pp. 54, 61.

9. In transliterating Greek names, I subscribe to the principle enunciated by Gibbon: "In proper names of foreign, and especially of oriental origin, it should always be our aim to express in our English version, a faithful copy of the original. But this rule, which is founded on a just regard to uniformity and truth, must often be relaxed: and the exceptions will be limited or enlarged by the custom of the language, and the taste of the interpreter" (*Decline and Fall*, P.S. to Preface, Vol. V (chs. xxxix ff.), 1825 ed., pp. 3–4). Hence "Korydaleus" rather than "Korydalevs" or "Korydalefs."

10. *Op. cit.*, pp. 10–11.

2

Theophilos Korydaleus: A New Aristotelianism

The first great exponent, in modern Greek education and letters, of a humanistic way of thinking was Theophilos Korydaleus (1570–1646). Korydaleus was in several respects the Sir William Hamilton of Greece. He was a returned exile, having received the serious part of his education outside his own country. He was a scholiast of considerable learning and of an intellectual zeal which, in other circumstances, would have produced an authentic contribution to philosophy. He had a mission to teach, to enlighten. His philosophy represented both a fresh beginning and a dead end. His influence, however, lasted longer than did Hamilton's.

"Korydaleus" is an archaized form, adopted by Theophilos himself, of his family name "Skordalos" ("Lark").[1] The family lived in Athens, where Korydaleus was born and had some early education. In 1604 he went to the Greek Catholic College of St. Athanasios in Rome and in 1608 to the University of Padua, where he studied philosophy and medicine. The main feature of his studies there was his association with Cesare Cremonini (a colleague of Galileo), who brought him up in the new Aristotelianism that had distinguished Padua since the late fifteenth century. From the point of view of Greek education—the re-education of the Greek world, that is—this circumstance was most important, because through Korydaleus it made the long first phase of that reeducation revivalistic in character, with the recapture of ancient authority the aim, and the striving for authenticity and correctness in interpretation the great intellectual virtue. With Cremonini, Korydaleus was engaged not only on the direct text of Aristotle but also on the ancient commentators, striving for the true interpretation of Aristotle as for the truth. An education in philosophy and medicine may seem a queer, though not perhaps indefensible, combination of studies; but, in the instance of Padua, it is not so queer if one remembers the link provided by Aristotle's physical and other "scientific" works, which were studied there *inter alia*.

The new Aristotelianism was carried by Korydaleus into other Greek communities and into the Greek homeland itself. From 1609 to 1613 he taught, either at the Greek community or privately, in Venice. In the latter year, and apparently from patriotic motives,[2] he returned to Athens, where he taught philosophy, astronomy and geography. Then in 1620 he went to the island of Kephallenia, and from there in 1621 to Zakynthos, where he taught philosophy and practiced medicine. A year later he was ordained, but he abandoned his priesthood three years afterwards: neither then nor later does Orthodox priestliness seem to have sat easily upon him. The most important part of his teaching work began about the middle of the 1620's, when he went for three years to Constantinople, taking over the headship of the Patriarchal Academy. It was the enlightened and far from conventional Patriarch Cyril Loukaris who summoned him there, on account of his sheer philosophical resources, and the summons meant that Korydaleus's outlook then began to be transmitted directly to the central body of those priestly students on whom Greek culture at that time had to rely largely for its keeping, for he returned as head of the academy in 1636 and remained there until 1640. Between that year and his death in 1646, after a brief period as Metropolitan of Arta and Naupaktos, he taught philosophy in Athens once more.

Korydaleus's working life was one of almost continuous didactic activity. In the patriarchal academy he reorganized the teaching on the model of that given in Padua. A central place was assigned to philosophy (as distinct from theology); that is, to interpretation of and commentary on the main Aristotelian works. The result of such teaching was an educational attitude which has been called that of "religious humanism."[3] Systematic higher education, which was necessarily ecclesiastical in its general setting and its aims, had been secularized to some extent—it had become humanist in that it introduced its students to a method of thinking the standards of which were a product of human striving for insight, rather than "given" or divinely sanctioned, but of course it was humanism along narrow and easily conventionalized lines. Aristotelianism could not open the mind by suggesting powerful methods of enquiry to it. What it provided for seventeenth-century Greek thought was a relatively secure-looking corpus of philosophical knowledge (in a broad sense of the term "philosophical"). But, as Descartes saw, the possibilities of Aristotle's wisdom were confined pretty much to Aristotle's own range of problems: he illumined what he himself was preoccupied about, but neither for natural philosophy in general nor for metaphysical did he really provide an adaptable method. Aristotle too easily became an end in himself.

Seen through the eyes of Korydaleus he appears very much so. The two longish extracts from Korydaleus's work which Papanoutsos prints offer a fair sample of his style and method. The first is a Preface to Logic from a lengthy commentary called *Notes and Problems Pertaining to the Entire Logic of Aristotle*.[4] The book contains a discussion of Aristotelian logical concepts in general, notes on Porphyry's *Introduction*, and then commentaries on *De Interpretatione* and the *Prior* and *Posterior Analytics*. It is characteristic of Korydaleus to mention or quote Aristotle with unquestioning respect, and as being right. (The same is true of his work on rhetoric described below.) Aristotle is referred to often enough by name, but often too as "The Philosopher." Those who differ from him are often just failing to give proper attention to what he says. For instance, in discussing the subject matter of logic, Korydaleus develops the view that it deals with concepts, via significant sounds (φωναί), and that its business is to bring them into apodeictic relationships. The whole argument is a gloss on an untypically conceptualist passage at the beginning of *De Interpretatione*,[5] after quoting which Korydaleus says, "Certain people who hold fast to their own peculiar assumptions and pay little regard to the truth, either are completely blind (since they simply do not deign to recognize what Aristotle said), or else, in pressing their own points of view, see only to see wrongly."[6] The targets for this invective are obscure, but the attitude expressed speaks for itself, and is not confined to the particular disagreement that is in question here. In general, Korydaleus has a sharp way with dissenters. Defending the view (which he claims to find in Aristotle by inference) that logic is an art of construction, and not a theoretical science, he speaks of various opponents as being voicers of empty sounds, idle theorizers, precipitant innovators and purveyors of fable.[7] But it is no longer clear who these people are.

Korydaleus is not a figure of fun. His introductory treatise on logic, in its attempt to present the exact nature and scope of the subject, shows all the characteristics of a serious philosophical educator—a clear and careful (though archaistic) language, a methodical arrangement and systematic development of ideas, a willingness to raise problems (though, one might add, only to solve them) and a dialectical method of interpretation. This is not to say that his material—an inextricable mixture of epistemology, psychology, logic and semantics—has anything important to contribute to the theory of logic as the subject is now understood. In other words, he tries to construe the nature of logic from too many points of view.

An indication of this is provided by his definition of logical method as "an art instrumental to Philosophy, occupying itself primarily about the phenomena pertaining to the intellectual powers of our soul, and having as its proximate aim the knowledge and composition of proof, and as its more general one, reasoning."[8] He also holds that logic is, among other things, a ἕξις, a talent or accomplishment. But he raises the question whether, since we can both use logic and know it as a canon, there are not really two talents involved, a constructional and a theoretical, i.e., an art *and* a science. Korydaleus insists that there is only one (which, he insists, represents an art), because (a) if you know how sound arguments are put together you do not need another talent to enable you to argue soundly, and (b) if you can so argue you do not need another talent to appreciate how sound arguments are put together. (I suppose that all this might be true of a really intuitive mind of the sort idealized by Plato or Spinoza. Otherwise regarded it is sophistical and untrue. Students will testify that it is one thing to get a theoretical grasp of logical principles, another to evaluate specimen arguments.) But the question could have been discussed in so much clearer terms if the distinction between talking logically and studying your talk *quoad* logical had not been obfuscated by "arts," "talents" and the like.

It remains true, of course, that the study of logic (not least Aristotle's) is an intellectual discipline, and it requires no effort of the imagination to concede that Korydaleus's work on this subject had, educationally speaking, its point and value. The same cannot be said of his treatise on rhetoric, which provides the second sample of his work that Papanoutsos prints.[9] This, written in an involved and contrived style, seems to offer nothing that corresponds remotely to the needs of educable men in Korydaleus's time and circumstances. It deals with techniques of public speechifying. It raises few issues of philosophical or theoretical interest, but consists mainly of rules and precepts drawn from ancient example (which is often quoted) about the construction in detail of various kinds of speech and the sort of discourse appropriate to various different parts and purposes of speeches. It conveys nothing but an Oxford Union preciousness of two thousand years ago.

The work is worth mentioning, however, for two reasons. It is my first example of a recurrent antiquarianism which from time to time wasted the efforts of Greek reeducators, and which has been a distraction from the natural development of Greek culture and language down to modern times. And (the obverse side of this characteristic) it is an example, if an extreme one, of Korydaleus's unconcern with more recent Greek literary tradition and interests, an unconcern which signals his new beginning. The very remoteness of his piece on rhetoric expresses this. So also, elsewhere, does his bypassing of Byzantine thought and scholarship. Others have remarked that, in commenting on Aristotle, Korydaleus refers often enough to ancient scholiasts (such as Alexander, Themistius and Simplicius) and sometimes to Western commentators, but neglects the Byzantines.[10] Whether this was done from his own ignorance of the Byzantines, or in accordance with Italian fashion, or as a deliberate personal policy is not clear; but in any case its effect was the same—to recommend a peculiar and single-minded radicalism in educational policy.

What is one's proof of the influence of this philosopher in Greek reeducation? Two things may be mentioned: the distribution and longevity of his writings, and the fact that Korydalism became a tradition to be warred against.

Papanoutsos lists fourteen works of Korydaleus which have survived, seven of them in print.[11] Almost all are didactic, being commentaries more or less systematic on Aristotle's logic, his physics, the *De Caelo*, the *De Anima*, and so on.[12] Some of them were printed not once but several times, and in most instances the first printed versions did not appear until the eighteenth century. For example, besides that of 1624, editions of the *Rhetoric* appeared in Moscow in 1744, Halle in 1768 and Venice in 1786.[13] The logical treatise which I have described was first printed in Venice in 1729, and the commentary on the

Physics (a bulky quarto of [28] + 648 + [2] pages) at Venice in 1779. There has survived also a very large number of manuscript copies or versions of Korydaleus's works in monastery and other libraries in many places. For example, the Vatopedi Manuscript Catalogue[14] lists ten such copies. I myself have seen two manuscripts of the *Logic* in the old library at Melies, on Pelion, where half a dozen Korydaleus works in manuscript have been noted altogether.[15] Papanoutsos remarks that the largest collection of all is in the Rumanian Academy. Tsourkas reports that the libraries of this academy and that of Iași have more than a hundred and fifty manuscripts between them, mostly notebooks of pupils of the two academies.[16]

His works, then, continued to be printed and copied long after his death. But by the later part of the eighteenth century "Korydalism" had become a term of deprecation, a synonym for the sort of scholasticism that Theophilos's work had consecrated. The lingering influence of that work was referred to by the philosopher Moisiodax as "the yoke of servile Aristotelianism."[17] And not unjustly; for another nonconforming philosopher, Methodios Anthrakitēs, had been condemned by the Holy Synod in the 1720's "for deprecating and rejecting the doctrines of peripatetic philosophy" and had been ordered "in future to teach the peripatetic philosophy in conformity with the system of Korydaleus."[18] In his *Logic* some forty years later, Eugenios Voulgaris referred to Korydaleus as a "far from dim philosophical star amongst us,"[19] but in the first draft of that book he too had indulged in severe criticism of him,[20] and in the published version he went on to blame the restrictive influence of Aristotle for the barrenness of Greek philosophizing in recent times.[21]

The intellectual history of the Greeks in the seventeenth century is both thin and obscure, but it seems clear enough that Korydaleus was in a class by himself, as regards both scholarship and influence. Voulgaris's *Logic*, to which I have just referred, is a very discursive work, and it is interesting amongst other respects for a catalog of Greek achievements in philosophy and of philosophical scholars from the earliest times down to Voulgaris's own.[22] When it comes to the sixteenth and seventeenth centuries, all that it can offer us is a list of rather vaguely defined *savants*, men of general learning and of some proficiency in philosophy who may be said to have kept learning and education in Greek alive to some degree during those oppressive times.

Apart from Loukaris and Korydaleus, Voulgaris names twenty people who deserve mention for the seventeenth century. They include four particular associates of Korydaleus, but they are all ecclesiastics or teachers or men of affairs whose contribution to the survival of education in and through Greek was in giving or organizing instruction rather than in producing works of scholarship on their own account. Only one of them, Gerasimos Vlachos (1607–85), a Venetian Greek from Crete, is worth mention here, since he did produce, in fair quantity, studies in and commentaries on ancient philosophy, including a book called *The Definitive Harmony of Things According to the Greek Thinkers* (Venice, 1661).[23] His work, however, did not have either the intellectual quality or the influence of that of Korydaleus.

Korydaleus, then, was a teacher and scholar who provided the first frame of reference, available to Greek educators since Byzantine times, for the genuine cultivation and ordering of ideas. (That the frame soon became too narrow is another matter.) This work was accomplished in an ecclesiastical context. Although Korydaleus was not inclined towards the life of religiosity, and although he was subjected pretty continually to theological attack (having been accused in his time of both Calvinism and atheism),[24] it is broadly true that he taught under the aegis of the Church, and that his work was done in the Church's interests. In the phase next to be considered the context changes. The Mavrokordatos family who are its representatives come to express a new style of thought, and their educational ideas serve new interests. The setting of their writings is political, administrative and mercantile. While the educational principles characteristic of them are not at all antiecclesiastical, neither are they concerned specially with the interests or education of the clergy; instead they are rather markedly directed towards the upbringing of a certain class of "gentlemen." In the next chapter I shall be concerned with the style and the subject matter of writings addressed to this end.

Notes

1. For biographical details I am indebted to Cléobule Tsourkas, *Les débuts de l'enseignement philosophique et de la libre pensée dans les Balkans. La vie et l'oeuvre de Théophile Corydalée* (1570–1646), 2nd ed. (revised), Thessalonikē, 1967. (1st ed., Bucharest, 1948.) Tsourkas's paper, "Les Années d'étude de Théophile Corydalée au Collège Grec de Rome" (Thessalonikē (repr. from *Balkan*

Studies, 8), 1967) supplements Pt. I, Ch. 1 of the second edition, and settles some questions of dating.

2. In a letter quoted by Dimaras 3, p. 8 (and referring to this period) he speaks of having abandoned "the splendid museums and colleges of Europe" and of substituting "the yoke of tyranny for the sweetest of freedoms."

3. Dimaras 1, p. 65.

4. Εἰς Ἅπασαν τὴν Λογικὴν τοῦ Ἀριστοτέλους Ὑπομνήματα καὶ Ζητήματα (Venice, 1729). The book is a quarto of [20] + 499 pages.

5. 16a. And cf. W. D. Ross, *Aristotle* (4th ed., 1945), pp. 25–6.

6. *Op. cit.*, Introduction, §2 (Papanoutsos 2, p. 50).

7. *Op. cit.*, Introduction, §4 (Papanoutsos 2, pp. 55–6).

8. Ibid. (Papanoutsos 2, p. 56).

9. (In Papanoutsos 1 only.) The work is entitled Ἔκθεσις περὶ Ῥητορικῆς. The first edition of this was published in London, along with a treatise, Περὶ Ἐπιστολικῶν Τύπων (*On Epistolary Forms*), in 1625.

10. See Anghelou 4, pp. 58–9 (and Tsourkas, *op. cit.*, p. 269). It is not quite true that (as Anghelou asserts) he never mentions even Philoponos. (See *Logic*, Introduction, §4 [Papanoutsos 2, p. 54].)

11. Papanoutsos 2, p. 46. Fuller bibliographical details are given by Tsourkas, *op. cit.*, Pt. I, Ch. IV, and Pt. II, Ch. IV.

12. A painstaking account of these commentaries is given by Tsourkas in Pt. IV of his book.

13. Legrand (XVIII), nos. 317, 696, 1182.

14. Cambridge (Mass.), 1924.

15. A. Papadopoulos-Kerameus, Κατάλογος τῶν Ἑλληνικῶν Κωδίκων τῆς ἐν Μηλέαις Βιβλιοθήκης (Athens, 1901), nos. 25, 35, 57, 72, 91, 98. (Five of these are ascribed to the eighteenth century.) It is difficult to be sure that some other unheaded manuscripts listed here are not of works by Korydaleus.

16. Papanoutsos 2, p. 46. Tsourkas, *op. cit.*, 1st ed. (see my note 1), p. 61. I have not found the remark in the second edition.

17. Ἀπολογία (Vienna, 1780), p. 12.

18. Anghelou 2, p. 181.

19. Λογική (Leipzig, 1766), p. 41.

20. Anghelou 1, pp. 143–4.

21. Voulgaris, *op. cit.*, p. 44.

22. Ibid., pp. 1–45.

23. Ἁρμονία Ὁριστικὴ τῶν Ὄντων κατὰ τοὺς Ἑλλήνων Σοφούς. See E. Legrand, *Bibliographie Hellénique ou description raisonnée des ouvrages publiés par des Grecs au dix-septième siècle* (5 vols., Paris, 1894–1903; repr. Brussels, 1963), II, no. 443. For references to work on Vlachos, cf. V, pp. 408–9.

24. See Tsourkas, *op. cit.*, e.g., pp. 69, 77, 93.

3

The Mavrokordatos Family: Moralism and Political Propriety

Approximately seventy years separate the death of Korydaleus and the period when Nikolaos Mavrokordatos (1680–1730) was doing the most important part of his writing. Allowing that Mavrokordatos was as outstanding in his own time as Korydaleus was in his, we can see in him how Greek educational thinking moved and how it did not move during that comparatively long interval. Mavrokordatos was a ruler and not in the professional sense a teacher. But his writing is intensely didactic after its own fashion. It is also more fully fledged than that of Korydaleus, in that it deals with its subject matter theme by theme, independently of the order of thought suggested by any one particular guide (notably Aristotle) and without the corresponding exegesis. As a result the writing is somewhat more appropriate to the times than that of Korydaleus.

But in a different way it is just as restricted as the latter's. The themes, as we shall see, are dogmas, unanalytically put, and supported by constant reference to authority. The fact that the authority is distributed over Plato and other ancient writers as well as Aristotle, and over the Bible even more than these, makes no difference. Mavrokordatos cannot move unless surrounded by a cloud of witnesses. Consequently his educational theory and example remain otherworldly; they are conveyed in a "literary" style and manner which simply obscure fundamental thinking in the matters with which they are concerned. For all that, his work is interesting as serving a specific educational purpose at a specific time.

Nikolaos Mavrokordatos was a Phanariot, one of that class of Constantinople Greeks which provided many administrators, and sometimes high officers of state, for the Sultan's government. His family, indeed, was one of the "great" Phanariot families, and Nikolaos was not the first member of his kind, either as man of affairs or as writer. His father, Alexandros Mavrokordatos (1636–1709), was in so many respects a prototype of Nikolaos, that it is worth recounting here something of his life and activity.

Alexandros, unlike his son, was educated in Italy. He studied in Rome and in Padua—at the latter, the well-established combination of medicine and philosophy. Not unnaturally, he was an adherent of the philosophy of Aristotle. He held public office, being Grand Dragoman at the Sublime Porte, and earlier had taught in the Patriarchal Academy. Nikolaos himself speaks of his father as one of those who brought new life and breadth into Greek thought.[1]

Certainly, evidence of the range of his interests is to be found in his writings, published and unpublished, which include a *Synopsis of the Art of Rhetoric*,[2] a *Sacred History*,[3] a *Syntactical Grammar*,[4] a set of *Meditations*,[5] one of *Opinions*,[6] and many letters.[7] The *Meditations* is a collection of worldly-wise ruminations and admonitions, written in a classicistic but quite graceful and clear style. Papanoutsos[8] prints two very brief extracts from this work, worth mentioning because they express a spirit of discretion and compromise which continues to be evident in the more elaborate writings of Nikolaos. The first recommends acceptance of one's lot as the basis of true happiness and contentment (in contrast with the usual alternatives, bodily perfection, wisdom, authority, and possessions). The second recommends us not to neglect the *appearance* of virtue even if we aren't virtuous (except, presumably, so far as it may be virtuous to want to seem so) since the enemy to be suppressed is shamelessness, and, in any case, maintaining the form of virtue may engender the spirit of it. These sentiments express both the moderatism of a well-known ancient tradition and also a prudent, practical, temporizing moral outlook which, though it is given no philosophical support in depth, the ambivalent political position of the Phanariots renders intelligible.

The *Opinions*, another collection of counsels, was written by Alexandros for the benefit of his descendants, and it is an indication of the earnestness and also the conscious sense of importance that surrounded this family's educational upbringing. Both of these attitudes, certainly, were vindicated by the example of Nikolaos. In some respects he appears to have been a Greek J. S. Mill. By the age of eighteen he had, it is said, a comfortable knowledge of Ancient Greek, Latin, French, Italian, Turkish, Arabic and Persian. At that precise age he was able, not surprisingly, to succeed his father as Grand Dragoman at the Porte; and when a year younger he had written a *Dialogue on Life and Death*,[9] remarkable for the solemnity and portentousness, if not for the originality, which a youth of seventeen could bring to bear on that subject.

In 1709 Nikolaos became governor of Moldavia, and was the first Greek to hold that rank. Later he became governor of Wallachia, remaining in this office until his death in 1730. From 1716 until 1719 he was held captive by the Germans in Transylvania, but it was during this period of captivity that his main literary work was done. A series of conversations in worldly wisdom called *Leisure Thoughts of Philotheos*[10] was one item—it was not published until 1800 (anonymously, in Vienna), but at least half a dozen manuscript copies of it are on record. Another was a translation into Greek of the *Theatrum Politicum* of Ambrosius Marlianus, a treatise on the nature and limits of princely power, first published in Rome in 1631. The translation was printed in Leipzig in 1758, and a second edition published there in 1776.[11] The third and main item was the *Book of Duties*,[12] published in Bucharest as early as 1719. Of this work there were several reissues, not only in Greek but also in Latin and German translations. Apart from these items, the only literary activity of Nikolaos's which is worth mentioning here is his supervision of a *Summary Enumeration* of Greek men of letters during the seventeenth and the earlier part of the eighteenth centuries. The catalog was actually compiled by his secretary, Demetrios Prokopiou, for the benefit of Johann-Albertus Fabricius's *Bibliotheca Graeca*, then being produced.[13] It has been a quarry for subsequent writers on the literary history of these obscure times, including Voulgaris in the survey of previous Greek philosophy to which I have already referred.[14]

Mavrokordatos is much inferior to Korydaleus as a thinker. (I base my judgment mainly on the long extract from the *Book of Duties* printed by Papanoutsos.[15]) His method is undialectical, and since he raises few problems (in the sense of conceptual difficulties), what he has to say is almost void of philosophical interest. His work, though systematic in a sense, is a product of earnestness rather than critical study. He discourses on bravery, wisdom, justice, prudence and virtue, mainly in terms of praise and recommendation. Of course, one must not blame him for not doing what he did not set out to do. In a letter to Étienne Bergler, the translator of the Latin version published at Leipzig in 1722,[16] he makes it clear that the book was written to the glory of God and the advancement of virtue amongst the Greeks, not from motives of philosophical curiosity. Allowing all this, the nature of the doctrine put forward remains interesting.

The tone of the book is set, and maintained, by the sayings, "The first and principal task of man is to love and praise God," (62)[17] and "The foundation of practical wisdom (φρόνησις) is speaking with God as is due and making supplication for what is fitting." (87) It is paternalistic: in matters of duty "lofty souls are persuaded by reason, but the great multitude is led and brought along by rewards and punishments." (61) As well as being in accordance with reason, duty must be "in harmony with the divine law and appropriate to the agent's situation." (62) There is no argument to show that all these requirements are compatible or even what, in detail, they mean.

Considerable stress is laid on moderation (in an Aristotelian sense) as a pervasive virtue, and as one which carries with it the advantage of self-sufficiency. Mavrokordatos tends to speak of it in terms of seemliness, of a man's "not going beyond what is suitable to life's ideal." (74) Indeed, he makes a parade of the whole family of notions of what is becoming—propriety, orderliness, decorum and the like. He observes that what is good is always becoming,[18] but the whole trend of what he is saying is to show that what is becoming is always good. In a "philosophy" where *measure* is so dominant, other virtues tend to be conflated with it, and there is a corresponding conflation of the duties to which they lead. For example, echoing both Plato and Aristotle in an obvious way, Mavrokordatos describes justice, "the crown of the virtues," (79) in terms redolent of the ideas of propriety, seemliness, and minding one's own business. The following passage would have pleased Hobbes:

> When a just man is in a position of subordination, then he will maintain a spirit of agreement, will do nothing to destroy harmony, will bow the neck, will submit to the laws and to the orders of his superiors, will zealously proffer the service imposed on him, will be content with the situation in life to which he has been called, will have no truck with

wicked desires and impulses for the sake of obtaining honors, will not meddle in what does not concern him. (81)

The notion of liberty (ἐλευθερία), so far as I have read in this author, is conspicuous by its absence. And the following is far from revolutionary:

> In a civilized community . . . there must be no aping of the justice of war. For in any dispute the issue is resolved and justice restored either by argument or by force. But what befits a human being is to let things be put right by discussion; force belongs altogether to the beasts. It is only, therefore, when we necessarily cannot avail ourselves of the gentle remedy afforded by words, that we take to arms. We do indeed have to make war in order to enjoy peace without the oppression of insult. But after victory it befits us to spare our enemies. And a secure peace is always a state to be preferred. (82)

In spite of the humanity of this last passage it is difficult to be attracted by Mavrokordatos. He is too much in the grip of conservatism, compromise and tradition. He is on the side of the Church in a way which may be comprehensible in nationalistic terms but is not defensible in any other, for he affirms that the dogmas of the catholic Church must be regarded as unshakable and all innovation eschewed both in the articles of the Orthodox faith and in regard to ecclesiastical tradition.[19] From the point of view of Greek reeducation this attitude seems unpromising, but it must be remembered that in Mavrokordatos we are dealing with a ruler for whom the Church, as in a lesser degree even the Ottoman court, was a frame of reference to be taken for granted; that as regards these institutions he was in a position only to take advantage of their power; that this itself must have been a perpetual exercise in balance; and that from a man so placed there could issue—if for present purposes I may speak the language of historical determinism—culture and learning, but not inquiry. The education for the conduct of life to which both Alexandros and Nikolaos Mavrokordatos are committed, therefore, is strongly moralistic; and the conservative, unrevolutionary nature of their thinking is one indication of the political contradiction in which their class found itself.[20]

What then did Mavrokordatos have to offer to Greek intellectual advancement? The picture of him as a rather time-marking traditionalist which I have drawn requires modification in at least two respects. The first concerns his Platonism. To express his moralistic outlook he draws on ideas from Classical as well as Christian tradition, in a thoroughly eclectic way. But the point is that he derives inspiration, and a cast of thought, from Plato (notably from the *Phaedo*, *Republic*, and *Laws*) at least as much as from Aristotle. His general allegiance to Plato *is* new; and if Plato be counted a liberating influence, then Mavrokordatos did his best to open up Greek education in this respect. But, as things turned out, the allegiance was not carried on: this offering was not accepted. Anghelou puts forward the interesting opinion that the teaching of the *Crito*, in 1726, and the *Phaedo*, in 1727, by Georgios Trapezountios at Bucharest, is the only instance of the study of Plato in a Greek school during the whole of the Turkish occupation.[21] (Trapezountios, not surprisingly, was an associate of Mavrokordatos.)

The second qualification is that Mavrokordatos was at one time less unconscious of the value of contemporary Western thought than his set-piece didactic writings suggest. A passage from the *Leisure Thoughts of Philotheos* is worth quoting in this connection. The sentiments expressed represent more than lip service, though it is their sheer emphasis which suggests this, rather than the direction taken by Nikolaos's writing in general.

> But meantime I admire and never cease from praising and encouraging those Moderns who have penetrated to the innermost recesses of nature and who by their remarkable studies in every field of learning have made countless discoveries no less true than novel; so that often enough it occurs to me to say that if it were possible for the sage Aristotle to come to life again he would confess himself to be defeated outright in both physics and theories of morals and character, and would gladly become the pupil of such men.[22]

Succeeding generations of the Mavrokordatos family, up to the War of Independence, were notable for their continued concern with culture and education, but not for literary work of their own. In their general cultural and educational attitudes they came and went between modernism, or support for innovation, and conservatism. Nikolaos's son Konstantinos (1711–1769) followed his father as a trans-Danubian governor, but his literary interests and his models in education were French, of the Enlightenment, and neither Aristotelian nor Platonic. Another Alexander (1742–1812), who was himself for a time governor of Moldavia, appeared on the side of the conservatives in a notorious educational controversy in the early years of the nineteenth century.[23] Yet another, the Alexander who was one of the Greek leaders in the War of Independence and who ultimately became Prime Minister of Greece, was a Westernist in outlook and, it seems, in educational practicalities also.[24]

Notes

1. Anghelou 4, pp. 66–7.

2. Σύνοψις Τέχνης Ῥητορικῆς. Vatopedi MS Cat., no. 22.

3. Ἱστορία Ἱερὰ ἤτοι τὰ Ἰουδαϊκά (Bucharest, 1716). Legrand (XVIII), no. 105.

4. Γραμματικὴ περὶ Συντάξεως (Venice, 1745). Legrand (XVIII), no. 327.

5. Φροντίσματα (Vienna, 1805).

6. Γνῶμαι. On this see Anghelou 4, p. 123, n. 63, 2.

7. Vatopedi MS Cat., no. 21. A collection of letters was published in Trieste in 1879 (cf. Dimaras 3, p. 13, n. 22).

8. 2, p. 19.

9. Διάλογος περὶ Ζωῆς καὶ Θανάτου (unpublished). See Anghelou 4, pp. 67–8. (I am indebted to Anghelou, *op. cit.*, pp. 63 ff. for other biographical details concerning Nikolaos.)

10. Φιλοθέου Πάρεργα. See Anghelou 4, pp. 66, 124 (n. 66, 3).

11. Θέατρον Πολιτικόν. Μεταγλωτισθὲν ἐκ τῆς Λατινικῆς εἰς τὴν ἡμετέραν ἁπλὴν Διάλεκτον παρὰ τοῦ ... Νικολάου τοῦ Μαυροκορδάτου. Legrand (XVIII), nos. 517, 858.

12. Περὶ τῶν Καθηκόντων Βίβλος. Legrand (XVIII), no. 126. See also nos. 146, 161, 260.

13. Anghelou 4, pp. 64–5.

14. p. 17.

15. 2, pp. 61–89.

16. Legrand (XVIII), no. 146.

17. Page references to the Papanoutsos version are given at the end of each of the quotations in this paragraph.

18. *Op. cit.*, p. 74.

19. *Op. cit.*, pp. 63–4.

20. Cf. C. M. Woodhouse, *The Greek War of Independence* (London, 1952), pp. 27, 41.

21. Anghelou 4, p. 68. This whole study of Anghelou's is an attempt to

assess the failure of Platonism to be a serious rival to Aristotelianism in Greek reeducation.

22. *Op. cit.* (Vienna, 1800), p. 54. Quoted by Anghelou 4, p. 70.

23. That concerning Benjamin of Lesbos, of which mention is made on p. 140. For the identification, see Anghelou 3, p. 79, n. 36.

24. Anghelou, ibid.

4

Damodos and Anthrakitēs: The Pains of Rationalism

The work of Korydaleus had become the substance of a rigid, doctrinaire form of "official" church education. That of Nikolaos Mavrokordatos, cultured and aristocratic, was adapted for the education of officialdom in another, complementary sphere. Neither philosopher spoke to the people, as it were. Neither of them came to terms with the living Greek language of his day but rather, for reasons which I have tried to indicate in discussing Korydaleus, archaized consciously and of set purpose. In addition, neither of them employed any "method," in the Cartesian sense of the term, in their philosophizing: that is to say, neither attempted to provide rules, relatively simple, relatively comprehensive, but adaptable and fruitful, which could lead to philosophical discovery, even if the discoveries were to be only a recognition of what is problematic. Instead they left their readers with doctrine, such as to be learned, not developed: some of it instructive, no doubt; much of it edifying; but much also merely precious. Of course a *new* method in philosophy is also a revolution, and a revolution presupposes a solid philosophical tradition to be rebelled against. But the very concept of method is absent from the work of these thinkers: the sort of philosophy which they taught was not capable of taking over from others, far less of germinating on its own a central, dynamic rule or set of rules of the kind just mentioned.

I labor this point because in the work of the philosopher to be introduced next we get the faintest glimmering of the notion of rule-inspired philosophy, as well as—and this is not faint but unmistakable—the expression of philosophical ideas in a language which is familiar and uncontrived and hence ready to invite judgment by the hearer or reader on what it says. Our expectations, however, must not be too high. The philosophy which I am about to describe is eclectic, naive, over-reconciliatory and "improving." But it does mark some advance in the establishment of philosophical standards, and it does not smell of the lamp.

Vikentios Damodos (1678 or 1679–1752) was born a year or so before Nikolaos Mavrokordatos and outlived the latter by twenty-two years.[1] He was a native of Chavriata in Kephallenia. He went to school at the Flanginian Institute, a Greek community educational centre in Venice, and then studied law, along with some literature, philosophy and theology, at the University of Padua. Eventually he returned to Kephallenia, to the practice of law; but (for conscientious reasons, it is said) he gave this up and devoted himself instead to the teaching of philosophical and other subjects in his native village. Not that he remained a mere local sage. Pupils (including, it is said, Eugenios Voulgaris) came to him from many Greek communities and two of his works, an *Epitome of Aristotelian Logic* and an *Art of Rhetoric* were well enough known to be published in Venice seven years after his death.[2] The list of his unpublished writings is formidable. Papanoutsos[3] mentions ten items, including further works on logic and rhetoric, several on theology,[4] a *General and Special Physics*[5] (on Cartesian principles), a *Metaphysics: First Philosophy and Natural Theology*[6] and a *Synopsis of Aristotle's Nicomachean Ethics*.[7] Two works were first printed long after his death, a *Practical Handbook of Rhetorical Constructions*[8] (Budapest, 1815) and a *Synopsis of Moral Philosophy*,[9] published for the first time in Athens in 1940. This last work is the basis for my own judgment of Damodos's intellectual quality.[10]

Damodos's account of the nature of moral philosophy contains *in parvo* many of the main characteristics of his general style of thought.

> Moral philosophy, then, is to be defined as follows: practical knowledge (ἐπιστήμη πρακτική), or wisdom (φρόνησις), which surveys human action correctively, in accordance with the rules of right reason (τοῦ ὀρθοῦ λόγου), for the enjoyment of eternal blessedness and happiness. (91)

The concept of ὀρθὸς λόγος is Platonic,[11] but the way in which Damodos thinks of it and exploits it is not. More will be said about it later, but here as elsewhere it intrudes itself interestingly amongst commoner classical and Christian terms. Broadly speaking, the conceptual basis of Damodos's philosophy is Aristotelian but the general idea Christian; in discussing the nature, subject matter and parts of moral philosophy he relies heavily on Aristotelian terms and modes of thought, but, as the definition suggests, he will discuss the *summum bonum*, the end of man which is also that of moral philosophy, in terms of eternal blessedness. The definition thus leaves us in no doubt that moral philosophy is to be firmly practical, and teleological. Yet such philosophy is also "reasonable," something self-justificatory, in a sense—this is what the appeal to ὀρθὸς λόγος seems to be trying to establish, so that already in Damodos's definition of the subject we feel a tension between two proffered ways of recommending moral philosophy. Finally, the definition tries to conflate two of the most tricky (one might say, prickly) notions in ancient epistemology, those of ἐπιστήμη and φρόνησις. Worse than that: in the explanation of terms which follows the definition there is added a third kind of "knowledge" (γνῶσις) which moral philosophy is or involves; and, more incidentally, a fourth (νόησις) as well.

He explains that moral philosophy is called knowledge in the sense of a science (ἐπιστήμη) "because it draws true and evident conclusions from certain and evident principles." (91) But it also involves knowledge of those principles.

> The knowledge (γνῶσις) which we possess by nature in these moral first principles is called a conservational knowledge, or conscience—a realization of when one is acting well or ill; it is called "conservational" in that, having this knowledge, the soul desires to conserve itself, that is to guard itself from participation in evil actions. (92)

So far, so clear. But moral philosophy is also practical wisdom (φρόνησις) "in that it considers what a man must do and what not do, for the enjoyment of happiness. For practical wisdom is principally knowledge (γνῶσις) of those actions which it is right to do." (92) What is confusing about this consideration is that if we *can* have γνῶσις of such actions as it is right to do, then γνῶσις has ceased to be the intuitive knowledge of first principles merely and has become much wider in scope, perhaps indeed equivalent to the whole of moral "knowledge" in its theoretical aspect. It may be noted also that yet another sort of knowledge (νόησις) has been invoked when Damodos speaks of conscience's "realizing" when one is acting well or ill. This variety of terms is unphilosophical, in a way which does not qualify for Hume's excuse. The introduction of the notion of conscience, however, is interesting. One wonders immediately what is its relation to that of right reason, and one discovers before long that it is as near identical as makes no difference. The identity, however, is to be inferred; it is not stated.

The identity seems to follow from the description of conscience which I have quoted, together with the following:

> The law of nature or right reason is that natural light and knowledge (γνῶσις) by which we distinguish good from evil, the right from the wrong. . . . This law of nature has been given us by God. Since it is God's eternal law and eternal decree, in accordance with which our deeds are denominated good or bad, it is unchangeable; furthermore, the decree is one which has been revealed to us by God from our birth. This being so, we cannot offer the excuse that we did not know the evil of what we have done and that that was why we did the thing. . . . (101)

(The admonition thus given is difficult to reconcile with Damodos's previous assertion[12] to the effect that one sufficient condition of an involuntary action is invincible ignorance.) Here we have another very great variety of terms for a crucial concept, namely that of an ultimate authority in moral judgment. We lack only "moral sense," though Damodos's theory could as well be called a moral sense theory as anything.

That the concept we are considering is ultimate comes out in another way when Damodos (circularly) tries to explain by reference to it the very nature of what is moral.

> In every action two things are to be considered, its material aspect and its moral. The matter of the action is the particular deed that is done: its moral aspect the agreement or disagreement of what is done with the rules of right reason, which is to say of rectitude (τοῦ δικαίου). For example, Peter commits murder: the deed involved, namely depriving the murdered person of his life, is called the matter of the action: in that that deed disagrees with and is contrary to right reason, since rectitude forbids our murdering someone, it is morally significant. . . . (92)

Finally, Damodos thinks of right reason, sometimes at any rate, as a kind of mean. He has been saying that it is not the passions of the soul as such, but the way in which we use them, that is good or evil:

> So that when we use the passions without sin, as right reason would have us do, then the passions are subject to the proper mean, that is they neither exceed nor fall short of what is proper (τὸ δίκαιον). (105)

When I suggested that in Damodos we had the faintest glimmering of a conception which would hold his philosophy together and make it live, it was this many-faceted "right reason" that I had in mind. It is true that Damodos wants to have it every way, that this ultimate authority is, as divine law, peremptory and, as individual conscience, insistent. But at least, if his favorite term means anything, the deliverances of that authority are also satisfactory to the intellect so far as we do think about what we are to do and what not to do. There are moral judgments, he holds, in which the intellect comes to rest as being "reasonable," in a strong sense of the term, and such judgments seem to be accessible in, at the back of, any moral perplexity, however complicated it appears to be. None of this is worked out, but there is little point in carrying criticism of Damodos's overhospitable scheme of thought any further. The interesting feature of it remains that he confronts the mind of his hearer or reader not only with learning but also with the burden of choice, with the realization that, whatever else may be true of moral attitudes, thinking *can* be involved in them up to the hilt.

Here then is a philosopher whose teaching is relatively open and offers something of a challenge. Whether the challenge was in fact appreciated is another matter. In spite of his renown as a teacher Damodos does not seem to have left any mark on subsequent Greek philosophical literature. In what I have read of the Greek philosophers of the next two or three generations I have not come across either commendation or criticism of his views: but it is certainly an adverse criticism of Voulgaris that he failed to include Damodos in the list of those who had something to contribute to Greek philosophical culture up to his own day.[13] This is the more ironical in that Voulgaris blames the recent barrenness of Greek philosophy not on the lack of natural talent but on the restrictive influence of Aristotle, and he contrasts its achievements with those of contemporary "European" philosophy, which relies on ὀρθὸς λόγος. The irony is complemented by an inscription which appears at the end of an eighteenth-century manuscript compendium of Damodos's metaphysics, in the library of Vatopedi:

> Rhetorician Damodos stands alone amongst many,
> As the labor of this book contributes to testifying.[14]

In Damodos's thinking the appeal to the individual conscience exists, but as something nominal. He gives us no criteria of what it is to be acceptable to right reason—unlike Descartes, for example, he provides no paradigm, no instance of a truth so pruned of other sorts of appeal that we cannot but recognize those features in it which compel our assent come what may. When "right reason" plays such a *formal* part as this in someone's system, it is not surprising if the content of that system remains entirely consonant with orthodoxy, right or wrong. This happens in Damodos's case: he just simply projects into philosophy a Christian theological point of view, and the philosophy is a compound of so many elements that no one of them, in particular the individualist, could become dominant—the potentially leading philosophical idea is not yet strong enough to prevent the philosophy from shading into the dogmas of revealed religion. Interestingly enough, however, we do not have to go beyond Damodos's own generation to find a more acute perception of the autonomy of philosophy.

In fact, this theme had to be pressed, on one notorious occasion, with some desperation. The philosophical teacher involved was Methodios Anthrakitēs (who was born about the middle of the seventeenth century and died about 1748) and the time approximately three years after Damodos had taken up systematic teaching in Kephallenia.[15] I shall describe his troubles in detail, but first it is desirable to give some account of the man and his work.

Anthrakitēs had studied in Italy, and before the period of his troubles had had a fairly varied career, including a spell towards the end of the seventeenth century as priest and editor of books in Venice. However, like Damodos, he appears to have been an educator first and foremost. He taught in schools in Ioannina both before and after his time in Venice, besides teaching in Siatista and Kastoria (in the latter place until shortly before the episodes to be described). His range of instruction included various branches of mathematics, and philosophy. What exactly he taught in philosophy is hard to make out. One writer [16] says that in Ioannina he expounded the philosophy of Aristotle and the exegesis of Korydaleus, but he undoubtedly knew the work of Descartes and Malebranche, from both of whom he is believed to have made translations, and it was precisely the neglect or the rejection of the Peripatetic philosophy of which he came to be accused. What does seem clear from his own testimony as well as from the reports of his opponents is that he strove for the authority of the individual judgment in matters philosophical and that he tried to represent philosophy as having no implications for matters of faith. At a relatively early stage in his career (1699) he had made a public criticism of certain standards of behavior amongst priests.[17] As to religious institutionalism generally, his accusers' accounts suggest that he had little respect for it.[18]

But exact information about Anthrakitēs, in this respect as in others, is hard to come by. Apart from a compendium of mathematics, published in Venice in 1749,[19] little of his work appears to have been preserved. An unpublished *Introduction to Logic*[20] survives in a library in Budapest, but, while it has other points of interest, it gives almost no indication of Anthrakitēs' personality, nor hint of peculiarity in his philosophical viewpoint. It is a dense compilation of scholastic logic, appears to be quite unoriginal, and, so far as it goes, bears out Koumas's reference[21] to Anthrakitēs as being a hander-on of Aristotelian–Korydalean doctrine.

The circumstances, form and content of this *Logic* are worth just a brief description.[22] The first page of the manuscript bears the title "Introduction to the Logic of Methodios" (Εἰσαγωγὴ τῆς Λογικῆς τοῦ Μεθοδίου), which suggests that the manuscript is not original but a pupil's notes. (The enormous number of orthographical and other, often naive, mistakes which it contains suggests the same thing.) It was in fact presented to the library of the Greek school in Budapest by its owner, Georgios Zaviras of Siatista, in 1778. (Zaviras himself became an annalist of early-modern Greek literature.) The general arrangement of the *Logic* is simple. Via the logics of terms and of propositions the student is led to that of the syllogism (and associated forms), representing "reasoning," the structure of which it is logic's business to elucidate. There is a good deal of rather tortuous detail, particularly in the logic of terms, where grammatical considerations, on the one hand, and metaphysical, on the other, frequently appear. Anthrakitēs' students were exercised in a long (and inconsequential) succession of ways of classifying terms into significant and non-significant, categorematic and syncategorematic, simple and complex, definite and vague, convertible and nonconvertible (this distinction introducing another, between synonymy, homonymy, analogy and paronymy), general and particular (involving a discussion of the five φωναί, the predicables and the categories), abstract and concrete, absolute and relative, distributive and collective, being of first and of second intension (with the doctrine of supposition); and into other classes less standard and more obscure.

This represents a fair specimen of the pedantry given rein throughout the expository part of the *Logic*. Further examples are not needed, either to make one wonder at the faith and expectations of students who, in a remote and heavily Ottomanized town of Northern Greece in the 1700's, could occupy themselves hopefully with such learning; or to engage one's respect for the aspirations of the teacher. The expository part of the *Logic* is followed by a series of *quaestiones*, argued out in the manner of medieval disputations, which, dull and labored as they are, do show some anxiety to make the study of logic seem realistic. Is logic necessary to the attainment of the sciences? (The answer, yes and no, is developed through a long series of objections and replies.) Is logical ability a purely acquired talent or not? How is the subject matter of logic related to that of other arts and sciences? Is logic itself an art or a science? Is logic part of philosophy or an *organon* thereof?

If one looks here for any trace of the philosophical modernism with which Anthrakitēs has been credited, one is disappointed, and worse. Large chunks of what he has to say in discussion of the *quaestiones* are absolutely at secondhand. In dealing with the question about logical talent, he wants to begin by explaining the notions of skill, experience, art, science, the powers of the soul, and talents; and this, he says, he will do "in accordance with what philosophers commonly hold."[23] What follows is the *ipsissima verba*, to all intents and purposes, of Korydaleus in the Preface to Logic of which mention has already been made. In each of the subsequent *quaestiones*, too, one comes across, without warning, quite long passages which are either transcriptions (with minor variations) from the same Preface, or slightly reduced or slightly puffed-out versions. Anthrakitēs was undoubtedly being impersonal after his fashion. To what extent the remaining passages, or for that matter the expository part of the *Logic*, are "received doctrine" in precisely the same fashion, I do not know. (The expository part, certainly, is simpler in style than anything of Korydaleus's which I have read.)

Very few names are mentioned in the course of the work, and the mentions are uninteresting, so that one gets no clue from them as to Anthrakitēs' allegiances. Oddly enough, the only reference to the Peripatetics brings in the only tart remark in the book, though the basis of the criticism seems pretty safe.

> Definition in the proper sense is of two kinds. The one is called natural, as comprising matter and form; for example, "man is an organic body informed by a logical soul," as the Peripatetic definition has it, even if in truth it is not so—for the body is material and extended whereas the soul is immaterial and nonextended—and they speak as if the nonextended can inform the extended, when the contrary is the case. . . .[24]

The position is, then, that we lack material such as would enable a proper firsthand judgment to be made about Anthrakitēs' views. For this state of affairs, it seems safe to suggest, his differences with the Church, which came to a head in 1723, were responsible. (These were the troubles, connected with questions about the autonomy of philosophy, to which I referred earlier.)[25] The main facts (in a very complicated sequence which has been patiently disengaged by Anghelou) are as follows. Anthrakitēs was condemned twice by the Holy Synod in Constantinople during the year mentioned. He was not present himself at the first meeting, to which he had been summoned, but remained at Ioannina, trusting perhaps in a letter which certain notables sent on his behalf to an influential member of the Synod, explaining that he was too poor and feeble to make the journey. At this meeting Anthrakitēs was unfrocked, was forbidden to teach and had his works condemned. The basis of condemnation was his hostility to the Peripatetic philosophy (by now deeply rooted in the Patriarchal Academy and other schools).

The second meeting seems to have surveyed the whole question anew; and this time Anthrakitēs was present. He did his best to avert a condemnation, declaring beforehand that he was willing to have his "notebooks" censored, and he was not without one friend at least, namely Chrysanthos, Patriarch of Jerusalem,[26] who tried to have the Synod limit its scrutiny to Anthrakitēs' purely religious orthodoxy. This plan failed. Anthrakitēs was forced to recant the whole basis of his teaching. There followed a burning of his notebooks and other persecution, and at this stage Anthrakitēs went into hiding.

The next definite information which we have relates to 1725, by which time the Synod was prepared again to regard him as a teacher—but on the stern condition that in future the teaching be of the Peripatetic philosophy and that Korydaleus be the guide. Those are the bare facts. It may be permissible now to bring out some of their flavor, because we do have available a long letter by Anthrakitēs (valuably published by Anghelou[27]) on the subject of the Synod's second arraignment, a letter which in any case expresses clearly his views about the relationship of philosophy and orthodoxy, and I should like to give it in paraphrase. The letter is addressed "from the sunless Goura in the city of Constantine" to those in authority in Ioannina, and is dated 30 November 1723.

Anthrakitēs says something of his experiences on arriving in Constantinople. The patriarch Chrysanthos gave him to hope that a confession of faith would be enough to secure a remission. Chrysanthos himself did not wish to examine Anthrakitēs in philosophical matters, but only in matters of faith or theology. At the actual meeting of the Synod Anthrakitēs began with a declaration of Orthodoxy, but then he was confronted, by his principal accuser, with notebooks containing his philosophical teaching. Anthrakitēs replied that if the books *were* his, the matter which they contained was not his own but "the opinions of different philosophers" and that if he taught those it was not as ecclesiastical doctrine but simply to satisfy intellectual curiosity and the demand for learning. He should be examined as a Christian and not as a philosopher. He goes on to say that this suggestion caused a turmoil, such that eventually Chrysanthos went back on his promises and proceeded to examine him without restriction. "I am being condemned, therefore, by the Synod not as a bad Christian, not in regard to any dogma of the Church, but because I philosophize differently from the Aristotelians."[28] He protested to the Synod that he did not commit himself to any philosophy or regard any philosophy as certain. Anthrakitēs indicates, however, that at this stage he became thoroughly afraid. Let them but receive his declaration of faith, he told the Synod, and they could do what they liked with the notebooks. The declaration was then accepted.

But what followed was lamentable indeed.

Can you imagine that it is zeal for the faith and the inspiration of the Holy Spirit that moves them to collect together logics and systems of physics and Euclid and other bits of mathematics and to set fire to them in the courtyard of the church . . . with a great rabble outside, of seamen (γεμιτζῆδες), cobblers and tailors, and doing it as if these were the Arian heresies or some kind of assault on the soul; books which the whole wide world studies, and which have nothing whatever to do with matters of faith?[29]

Then Anthrakitēs was brought a confession and declaration to sign, to the effect that his teaching was the inspiration of the devil, that he would thenceforth abjure teaching of any kind whatsoever, and that he would receive no Christian confession. Since he could not sign this conscientiously and had learned that he was going to be banished somewhere in any case, he had gone into hiding. He adds that "they" were planning to banish and persecute teachers all over Roumeli and generally suppress education. He himself had no desire to be heretical in his teaching, but as regards heresy it made no difference what philosophy one studied, whether Platonic or Aristotelian, whether old or new. Did not the Fathers themselves study their several philosophies? The indiscriminate burning of well-known scholarly books would make the authorities of the Church into a laughingstock everywhere.

So much for the story of Methodios Anthrakitēs. He no more than Damodos represented a "movement." He was an isolated teacher overcome by the only movement there was, if ossified tradition can be described by such a term. But he contrived to make clear that no more enlightenment, no further move forward in Greek reeducation, was to be expected from the Patriarchal Academy of the time. Here was to be found the set policy behind the Synod's attitude, the set Aristotelianism and resistance to European philosophy in any form, for which some of its teachers became well known.[30]

Interest lies now, not in the patriarchal establishment, but in the activities of dominies, like Anthrakitēs, who had settled in more or less remote places and had given themselves to instruction for instruction's sake. Damodos retreated to a village in Kephallenia. And other examples may be quoted. One is that of Anastasios Gordios, who died in 1729. He studied medicine in Italy and returned to his village of Vraniana in Agrapha (Thessaly), where he taught, wrote and corresponded (with, amongst others, Nikolaos Mavrokordatos, for whom he collected information about manuscripts). He was a "grammarian" and not a philosopher, and a man of strictly Orthodox outlook.[31] Another such teacher, perhaps the most scholarly of all, was Antonios Katephoros (born in 1685). He taught in Kerkyra, where he had Eugenios Voulgaris as one of his pupils. He, too, was educated in Italy. He was the author of a biography of Peter the Great,[32] was acquainted with Byzantine thought[33] and may be presumed to have introduced Voulgaris, though precisely to what extent is uncertain, to the work of various contemporary Western European thinkers.[34]

And in connection with some of these men we hear of "schools," established by private benefaction or by a community effort, of a kind which was to play an important part in Greek education from the later seventeenth century onwards. The Flanginian Institute in Venice is one example. In Ioannina, a school founded by Emanuel Giounma in 1677, and at which Anthrakitēs taught, is another. (It is a remarkable fact that this school functioned in addition to, and not in place of, an earlier one in Ioannina, and that a third, the so-called Maroutsaian school, was in existence alongside these two for a time.)[35] By the middle of the eighteenth century, then, there was a variety of educational currents to be collected; and collected they were in the work of Eugenios Voulgaris, who must be considered next, at length.

Notes

1. For biographical details I am indebted mainly to Papanoutsos 2 and Dimaras 1.

2. Ἐπίτομος Λογικὴ κατ' Ἀριστοτέλην καὶ Τέχνη Ῥητορική. Legrand (XVIII), no. 532. For the *Rhetoric* see also Legrand, no. 539.

3. 2, p. 90.

4. Other bulky MSS on this subject are listed in the Vatopedi MS Cat., nos. 99–102.

5. Φυσικὴ Γενικὴ καὶ Μερική.

6. Μεταφυσική. Πρώτη Φιλοσοφία καὶ Φυσικὴ Θεολογία.

7. Σύνοψις τῆς Ἠθικῆς τοῦ Ἀριστοτέλους πρὸς Νικόμαχον.

8. Πράξεις κατὰ Συντομίαν εἰς τὰς Ῥητορικὰς Ἑρμηνείας.

9. Σύνοψις Ἠθικῆς Φιλοσοφίας.

10. The passages I translate all appear in Papanoutsos 2, to pages of which the figures entered after my quotations refer.

11. See *Phaedo*, 73a.

12. *Op. cit.*, pp. 99–100.

13. Cf. his *Logic*, pp. 42–4.

14. Vatopedi MS Cat., no. 465.

15. For general biographical details I am indebted mainly to Papanoutsos 2. On the issue between Anthrakitēs and the Church my authority is Anghelou 2.

16. K. Koumas, quoted in Papanoutsos 2, p. 20.

17. See Dimaras 1, p. 110.

18. See Papanoutsos 2, p. 21.

19. Ὁδὸς Μαθηματικῆς. Legrand (XVIII), no. 375.

20. Εἰσαγωγὴ τῆς Λογικῆς τοῦ... Μεθοδίου Ἀνθρακίτη τοῦ ἐκ Πόλεως Ἰωαννίνων.

21. See note 16.

22. As late as 1959, it appears, no other copy of this work was available, nor had the MS been studied by anyone competent to judge it in modern terms (cf. Papanoutsos 2, p. 20, n. 1). Since then a microfilm copy has been taken and a typescript of this made available to me by the kindness of Dr. E. P. Papanoutsos.

23. MS, p. 178.

24. MS, pp. 98–9.

25. Pp. 33–4.

26. Otherwise Chrysanthos Notaras, an Aristotelian in outlook, who had taught both Nikolaos Mavrokordatos and his family, and who remained Nikolaos's friend and correspondent. See Anghelou 4, pp. 64 ff.

27. Anghelou 2.

28. *Op. cit.*, p. 171.

29. *Op. cit.*, p. 172.

30. For example, at this time, Iakovos Manos, another intimate of the Mavrokordatos family. See Anghelou 4, pp. 68–9.

31. Dimaras 1, p. 111; Anghelou 4, p. 74.

32. See p. 42.

33. Anghelou 4, p. 85.

34. The question is discussed in Anghelou 1, pp. 129–32.

35. Dimaras 1, p. 110.

5

Eugenios Voulgaris: New Ideas in an Old Language

In Monboddo's *Origin and Progress of Language* (1773) a version is adopted of the already classic distinction between ideas of sensation and ideas of reflection. Monboddo refers to the latter as "*natural-born* subjects of the state, not *naturalized only*, as the others [i.e., ideas of sensation] are," adding "but the *sensations* are altogether *foreigners*." In a footnote he says:

> This is an observation of a late author, very little known, *Eugenius Diaconus*, a Greek by nation, and a professor in the Patriarch's university at Constantinople; from whence the reader would not expect to hear of any book of science coming at this time of the day. It is a system of *logic* written in pure Attic Greek, printed at *Leipswick* 1766. The learned reader, I am persuaded, will be glad to see some specimen of this *living* monument of *antient Greece*; I shall therefore give his words, which I think are elegant. Speaking of the first class he had mentioned, viz. the ideas of reflection, he says, Οἴκοθέν τε, καὶ ἄνευ τῆς παρὰ τοῦ σώματος συνδρομῆς ἡ ψυχὴ καρποῦται· ἐπὶ δὲ τῆς τῶν δευτέρων ἰδεοποιΐας, (he means what I call the first class of ideas, viz. those formed from external objects), καὶ αἱ παρὰ τῶν ἐκτὸς αἰσθητικαὶ ἀλλοιώσεις τὸ παρ' ἑαυτῶν συνεισφέρουσιν. Εἴποι δ'ἄν τις εἰκάσας ἰθαγενεῖς ἐκείνας εἶναι τῇ ψυχῇ ἐννοίας, ταύτας δὲ οἷον πολιτογραφουμένας· αἱ γὰρ διὰ τῶν αἰσθήσεων ἀνεπιστάτως διαγειρόμεναι ἁπλῶς ἐπίλυδες p. 159.[1]

There is another acknowledgment of Eugenios in Monboddo's *Antient Metaphysics* (1779), in the course of a discussion concerning the precise relationship of genera and species. Monboddo puts forward the doctrine that the containment of species in genera and of individuals in species is virtual or potential, whereas that of genera in species and of species in individuals is actual; and he adds a footnote:

> It is a piece of justice which I think I owe to an author, hardly known at all in the western parts of Europe, to acknowledge that I got a hint of the solution of this difficulty from him. The author I mean is a living Greek author, Eugenius Diaconus. . . .[2]

Monboddo was right in drawing attention to the curiosity which, in the later part of the eighteenth century, Eugenios's Attic Greek represented. It did not occur to him, though, that the revival of this ancient language in so uncompromising a form might be a mistaken ideal. As it was, the author whom he thus introduced to "the western parts of Europe," although probably the most influential single figure in the whole history of Greek reeducation, did nothing for that re-education so far as its medium, language, was concerned, except make chronic a division in, an alienation (in the early Marxian sense of the term) of the Greek soul. What appears in the afterlight as more than a curiosity is the new material which Eugenios provided, in a great variety of ways, for Greek thought, and the example which he himself presented of an enormously learned man whose learning was not locked up but poured out in the interests of the public good—in other words, of a very great educator.

His *Logic* (1766) and some other works give the author's name in the style Εὐγενίου Διακόνου τοῦ Βουλγάρεως, but "Voulgaris" being the family name and "diakonos" merely that of an office, the usual way of naming him is "Eugenios Voulgaris."

Voulgaris had a long life, from 1716 to 1806. He was born in Kerkyra, of a family long established in the Ionian Islands, and was educated there by one man in particular who may have had much to do with his width of interest in ancient and modern literature. This was Antonios Katephoros (b. 1685), the author of a biography of Peter the Great published in Italian in 1736 and in Greek translation (in Venice) a year later.[3] Katephoros also edited a collection, which he translated into Latin, of the writings of Photios, but this work survives in manuscript only. Anghelou states definitely that he introduced Voulgaris to Byzantine literature.[4] A rather more interesting matter discussed by Anghelou, but about which he can only speculate, is whether Katephoros did not also introduce Voulgaris to the work of

Locke. Unfortunately there is no hard evidence about this, but only rather vague probabilities. It is possible also that Katephoros introduced Voulgaris to the natural philosophy of Gravesande.[5] If, in either case, Katephoros was the link, the matter is of some interest, because Voulgaris used both Locke's theory of knowledge and Gravesande's physics (as well as his philosophy) to a very considerable extent in his own teaching, besides making translations from each of these authors. It is clear from a reference in his *Logic*[6] that Voulgaris himself thought of Katephoros as a notable scholar. How much more to Voulgaris's education there was than his association with Katephoros is uncertain. Various writers speak of him as having gone "perhaps" or "probably" to the University of Padua to finish his studies, but the qualifying terms are depressingly in evidence.

In 1737 or 1738 Voulgaris was made a deacon, substituting at this stage the "Eugenios" for his baptismal name, "Eleutherios." In 1742 he became head of the Maroutsaian school in Ioannina, and in 1750 of a school in Kozanē. The Maroutsaian school was one of two or three institutes of "higher" education which were functioning in Ioannina at the time. It provided in its own fashion an education both in "grammar" and in a variety of theoretical disciplines such as mathematics, physics and philosophy. It represented a type of institution which, in the absence of Greek universities, did as much as could be done in a more or less high-school setting and with pupils whose basic education was varied and informal, to introduce some knowledge of the more important theoretical and speculative subjects, at a university level.[7] Voulgaris played his part in realizing these ambitious ideas. In Ioannina, as in Kozanē later, he taught various subjects, but most notably modern philosophy in several of its main branches, taking account of the ideas of specific philosophers such as Locke, Leibniz and Wolff, and in general providing examples of rationalistic, humanistic methods of exposition and discussion.

Voulgaris's teaching, however, was seldom left undisturbed for long. In Ioannina it became a cause of hostility on the part of more conservative teachers, including the head of the Giounma school, the mathematician Balanos Vasilopoulos. The tension between Voulgaris and Vasilopoulos, which brought about Voulgaris's withdrawal to Kozanē in 1750, was not ephemeral and not confined to philosophical attitudes: the two were in controversy over mathematical matters long after Voulgaris's period in Ioannina.[8] And, in general, Voulgaris seems to have been a difficult teacher to live with. The superiority of his knowledge, his unusual versatility and (in his earlier years anyhow) his eagerness to force the educational pace, plus his own readiness for controversy, were attributes which led him, and most notably in the next phase of his teaching activity, into a position of lonely hostility towards many of those amongst whom he worked and those on whom he depended.

In 1753 Voulgaris became head of the Athonite Academy, a school established only three years before under the aegis of the monastery of Vatopedi on Mount Athos.[9] The five and a half years which he spent there were in a way the most celebrated period of his teaching activity, in that the Academy had been founded with some *éclat*, under the highest auspices and with high expectations, and many of these expectations came to rest upon the person of Voulgaris himself; but this was not his most tranquil period, and it is far from clear how productive it was in an educational sense.

The Academy had been founded in 1750 (we may take the date of the Patriarch Cyril V's foundation bull as that of its effective inauguration); it enjoyed the moral and material support of the Patriarch and besides him of a specially appointed four-member ways and means committee in Constantinople. It had as an overseer on the spot Meletios, sub-prior of Vatopedi, who had taken the initiative in its foundation two years before the issue of the patriarchal bull. Its doors were open both to monks on The Mountain itself and to pupils from outside. Its program of studies was both wide and ambitious: it was to be a college of general education, but with logical, philosophical and theological studies the culmination. A special building was to house it, built on a crest adjoining Vatopedi, with three floors, about a hundred and seventy small rooms for students, accommodation for the teaching head, a library and lecture rooms; apparently this building was ready at least after a fashion when Voulgaris took over in 1753.

There were, then, many favorable conditions. It is true that the first head of the Academy, Neophytos Kausokalyvitēs, had made no great success of the undertaking during the first three years, having only twenty students at the end of that time. But Kausokalyvitēs, though he had studied in Constantinople, Patmos and Ioannina and was learned enough—he was the author of a *Grammar* and edited other grammatical work[10]—was a scholiast rather than a philosopher and too conservative in his educational views and methods to be a suitable academic head of a school which was intended not just to consolidate but to give a new impetus to Greek education. Voulgaris, one would have thought, offered just the right contrast to his predecessor.

And indeed he seems to have striven successfully in many respects. He began with about seventy students (which, as Anghelou remarks,[11] was already more than the average for schools of this level) and the number rose steadily until, by the end, he had close to two hundred. Though he employed other teachers or pupil teachers to instruct in so-called "grammatical" studies, he had at some stage to double the amount of instruction that he himself was giving in the so-called "philosophical," or general theoretical subjects, in order to provide for so many students.

The general arrangement of classes in the Academy is not without interest, as being fairly typical of schools of that category at the time.[12] There was a broad division between lower (grammatical) studies, for the neophytes, and higher (philosophical) studies for the more sophisticated. The grammatical course was itself divided into elementary and advanced, the elementary consisting of elements of grammar and parsing, and the advanced of composition and syntax. The philosophical curriculum, which was taught by Voulgaris himself (apparently alone), comprised philosophy strictly speaking and mathematics. The philosophical course consisted of logic, an introduction to philosophy, and metaphysics, and the mathematical of arithmetic, geometry, physics and cosmography. Some study of Latin was also undertaken at this higher stage, but how much is obscure.

The material which Voulgaris used in his instruction is also of interest, but this time as being untypical. As textbooks he used more or less epitomized translations, made by himself, of Western European philosophers, mathematicians and physicists, but besides teaching "from" these works he gave systematic courses on his own account (especially in philosophy). Manuscript versions of these courses, and of his translations as well, were made by pupils on Athos as elsewhere and circulated widely. It was not until many years afterwards that any of them were printed.

As to the translations, at one time or another Voulgaris translated

Locke's *Essay* (in part, and most probably from Coste's French version),[13] the *Elements of Metaphysics* of Antonio Genovesi, a *Logic and Metaphysics* from J. B. Du Hamel, a *Logic* from E. Pourchot, Gravesande's *Introduction to Philosophy*, a *Physics* by J. Fr. Wucherer, an *Elements of Arithmetic and Geometry* from Chr. von Wolff, the *Elements of Geometry* of A. Tacquet and some of the work of J. A. von Segner, under the heading *Treatises on the Elements of Mathematics*—to name only those of obvious didactic importance.[14] None of them was published before 1767, that is to say during the time when Voulgaris was teaching in schools, but there is evidence that many of them at least were done during what Anghelou calls his "translating period"[15] between 1740 and 1750. For example, a pupil vouches for the teaching according to Tacquet,[16] and in any case the title page of the *Elements of Geometry*, like that of the Gravesande, indicates that the work was for use as an explicit manual of instruction (πρὸς ἀκρόασιν τῶν παρ' αὐτῷ μαθητιόντων) during the time when Voulgaris was teaching in Ioannina, the Athonite Academy and Constantinople. As Anghelou argues,[17] the first draft of Voulgaris's own *Logic* shows that he knew Locke's *Essay* while still teaching in Ioannina; he probably also translated a large portion of the *Essay* during that time. And a work of slightly different character, but itself presupposing a large amount of translation, announces itself just as the Gravesande does. This is his *Universal System*,[18] a handbook of astronomy put together from different "philosophers" as a source of instruction for Voulgaris's pupils in his various schools.

The courses which Voulgaris gave on his own account are represented by his *Logic*, his *Elements of Metaphysics*,[19] and a volume of physics under the Plutarchian title *The Principles of the Philosophers*.[20] These books, too, were published only after Voulgaris had ceased from direct teaching. They all bring together an immense amount of doctrine from an immense variety of sources and must all have taxed the stamina and syncretistic powers of Voulgaris's pupils to the utmost —beyond the limit, indeed, of many of them if we are to believe Moisiodax.[21] Certainly Voulgaris himself, in his address to the reader, confesses (though the predicament is far from peculiar to him) that the publication of his *Logic* had to be undertaken because so many of his hearers and pupils in various places were relying on incomplete or inaccurate versions of his doctrines, while other versions were traduced by much copying.

Voulgaris, then, was teaching out of a plenitude of resources, but even this final favorable factor did not enable him to succeed in his teaching mission on Athos. There were too many difficulties, moral and material. Moisiodax thinks[22] that Voulgaris's own standards may have been too high for the immediate circumstances. In addition, many of the students were quite penniless and the material miseries of life in the school were considerable. Those factors by themselves would not have destined the Academy under Voulgaris to be a failure. After all, the number of his pupils did rise steadily, right to the end. What seems to have made his life impossible was, rather, faction, strife, jealousy and ignorance. The Patriarch Cyril, Meletios the overseer, and one of Voulgaris's own assistant teachers, Panagiotēs Palamas, all attracted to themselves factions which contended against Voulgaris and his supporters, either for the emblem of primacy in this great educational project, or else in more specific matters of administration and organization. Also, there is some evidence of resentment by monks on The Mountain at the attractiveness of the new philosophy and at its proselytizing dangers.[23] The upshot of all this was that Voulgaris, in January 1759, abruptly took his departure from the school.

The more domestic difficulties just mentioned are described in a bitter letter which Voulgaris wrote in self-defense to Cyril (by now no longer Patriarch) shortly after his departure.[24] In it he gives a detailed account of the disorder and dissensions in which he was involved and the zeal with which he himself taught, and he rehearses the unsatisfactory part played by Cyril himself in the whole matter, through coming to Athos and giving far too ready an ear to factious monks, undisciplined students and intriguers generally.

> Reckon the weight (he begs Cyril) of my conscientious labors over so many years: measure the sweat I have poured out: calculate the zeal and tirelessness of soul with which I have served the race. My statutory duty was to give two courses of instruction each day, but, as you know, I gave three or indeed four. I devised ways of teaching the students a double course, from two different manuals, and still they were not satisfied. I lengthened the lectures regularly to a point at which the students cried "Enough!" The school never came to a recess during seasons of work without the students begging me warmly to postpone it. . . . Whereas it was my statutory duty to pay the salary of one assistant teacher I paid for five or six. Though under no obligation to do so I took it on myself to introduce a course of study in Latin, paying the teacher myself, as you

> know. . . . Just lately, as you also know, I arranged for the introduction of an extra teacher of sciences, again at my own expense. As regards fees for instruction I never failed—and here the sub-prior and the students are my witnesses—to give part of my salary to help those who needed assistance. I even bought medical supplies and provided aid for students who were sick—all this too at my own expense. I gave my mind to every possible method of establishing my school firmly and of making it grow. To this end I committed my life, wore down my health and scattered my resources.[25]

Voulgaris's departure from the Athonite Academy was the signal for its downfall. From 1759 onwards it went into steady and then rapid decline, with numerous periods when it functioned not at all, until about 1812 the last of various efforts made to revive it came to nothing.[26] How effective Voulgaris's own teaching was during his time there, in the impact which it made on individuals, is hard to assess precisely. One can name various of his pupils who came into prominence in literature or education later in the eighteenth century. Iosipos Moisiodax was one, and at the other end of the political spectrum, as it were, Athanasios Parios (an educator who believed that all education was strictly and narrowly "within the faith" and who was head of the school in Chios from 1786 until 1813); another was the Aitolian Kosmas, a peripatetic free-lance educator who also founded a great many schools in different parts of Greece, and who was the author of the pleasant saying, "It is better, my friend, to have a Greek school in your territory than to have springs and rivers."[27] Yet another was Gavriel Kallonas, who translated (via Coste) much of Locke's *Some Thoughts concerning Education* as part of an educational manual of his own.[28]

Voulgaris himself, in the letter to Cyril already quoted, made the highest possible claim in general terms for the effect of his teaching, and there is little one can do but concede his claim in this form:

> I say nothing of those large numbers of men whom I enlightened to the best of my ability and who are now making their appearance and being heard in so many communities, and those others who soon will be appearing and will be heard; and I pass over in silence those of our men who are still teaching, after my departure, in the school itself. At some other time, if it is needed, I shall compile the catalog of them and demonstrate how much I labored at the school. . . .[29]

This catalog, so far as is known, does not exist.

The last phase of Voulgaris's teaching career (all of which occupied but twenty years in the earlier part of a long life) was spent in the Patriarchal Academy in Constantinople, to which he was appointed as a teacher in 1759. He remained there for only three years; but once again he was involved in strife, principally with the Patriarch Samuel Chantzerēs who was a fanatical Aristotelian and repudiated Voulgaris's modernism in philosophy. From an educational point of view there seems to have been nothing else of particular note about this phase of his life.

In 1762 Voulgaris left what might be called metropolitan Greece for "Europe," and he never returned. His literary activity and the ecclesiastical positions which he held during the next forty-four years, amongst Greek communities abroad, suggest a smoother and more comfortable existence than the rough-and-tumble educational field-work of the previous twenty years had afforded him. It might be argued that the publication of his works, which, with one minor exception, began with the *Logic* in 1766, was as important an offering to the education of his countrymen as had been his direct teaching of them. But, although these works are of considerable historical interest, and although some were published expressly as textbooks and others may have molded opinion in various controversial, mostly religious, issues, the bulk of Voulgaris's work was published at a relatively late stage in his life, by which time his critics were in the field, and others now were trying to find out for themselves what the philosophy and science of the West had to teach, so that his printed work probably made less impact and was less useful than if conditions had made possible the publication a generation earlier of that large part of it which even then existed in manuscript. The *Elements of Metaphysics*, for instance, was not published until 1805 (in Venice); the translation of Gravesande not until the same year (in Moscow); the compendia of physics and of astronomy mentioned already likewise appeared in 1805 (in Vienna). The fact that the teaching which these last two compilations, in particular, served had taken place some fifty years previously is an indication that the development of teaching materials and resources in these fields had been negligible, and suggests that an earlier publication of the volumes themselves might have encouraged progress towards more up-to-date work by the beginning of the nineteenth century. As it was, both of these large works were published by the Zosimas brothers for free distribution amongst aspiring, scientifically minded Greek youth.

The works, or at any rate some of the main ones, require a discussion to themselves, both for their doctrinal interest and for what they reveal of Voulgaris's character. Meanwhile, the tale of his exile is briefly told. After leaving the Patriarchal Academy he traveled to Halle and Leipzig, where he saw to the publication of various works, including the *Logic* and (in 1768) a translation (with elaborate commentary) of Voltaire's *Essai . . . sur les dissensions des églises de Pologne.*[30] In 1772 he became a librarian and adviser at the court of Catherine the Great of Russia. At some stage later than this he was ordained as a monk and then as an archbishop, and took over the newly founded archbishopric of Slavinion and Cherson in the Ukraine, but he resigned from it in 1779 and returned to St. Petersburg. Two years later he retired to a monastery, where he died in 1806. After 1772 the main books which he published were printed in Greek presses in Moscow, St. Petersburg, Venice, and Vienna, so that no fewer than six of the major Greek communities in "Europe" had supported him and put their publishing resources at his disposal.

The published work of Voulgaris which I shall take for discussion in the next two chapters belongs to the instructive and useful, rather than the elegant side of literature. The relatively detailed analysis of some parts of it which I offer is intended to show how varied were the sources, ancient and modern, on which Voulgaris drew, and the confident way in which he ranged over the great areas of knowledge whose products he transmitted. My stress, here as elsewhere, is on the sort of work which is addressed primarily to the intellect, and to the sensibilities only secondarily (if at all). Other times, other curiosities: "Of his literary productions one of the most celebrated is his translation of the Aeneid into Greek hexameter verse."[31] Thus Dr. Philip Hunt, on Voulgaris, in 1801 (and none of Voulgaris's other productions does he mention). But I think it is safe to say that Voulgaris's *Logic,* particularly, made more of an impact on the educational thinking and intellectual development of his countrymen than did this or any other example of his more belletristic interests.

Notes

1. Edinburgh (1773), I, p. 46. I have supplied a few accents missing from the Greek as quoted. In full translation the passage runs: "The soul garners [the first class of ideas] from within itself, and without the concurrence of the body; but in the formation of the second class a distinctive contribution is made by sensory changes derivative from the outer world. One might put it figuratively by saying that the former are natural-born ideas in the soul, but the latter are as it were naturalized; for those that are brought about through the senses without the intervention of the understanding are pure incomers." Monboddo, unfortunately, has misread his author, who was distinguishing here not between ideas of reflection and ideas of sensation but between two kinds of ideas of reflection. (See further p. 57.) The author, incidentally, was not still a "professor" as late as 1773. (I am obliged to Dr. G. E. Davie for first drawing my attention to Monboddo's reference.)

2. Edinburgh (1779–84), I, p. 479. This passage is quoted also by Hamilton in *Lectures in Metaphysics and Logic*, eds. Mansel and Veitch (Edinburgh, 1860), III, pp. 205–6.

3. *Vita di Pietro il Grande* (Βίος Πέτρου τοῦ Μεγάλου), Legrand (XVIII), nos. 235, 236. A reference on the title-page of an ecclesiastical *Oration* by Ioannēs Makolas, printed in 1717 (ibid., no. 108), indicated that then or previously Katephoros was head of the Flanginian Institute in Venice.

4. Anghelou 4, p. 85 and (on the Photios translation) note 85, 2.

5. Anghelou 1, pp. 129–32.

6. P. 43.

7. These schools worked under a variety of names which suggests the latitude of their functions: besides "schools" we find "academies," "lyceums," "seminaries" (φροντιστήρια), "museums" and "gymnasiums." The fact is commented on by D. Glenos, Ἡ Ἀξία τῶν Ἀνθρωπιστικῶν Γραμμάτων στὴν Ἑλλάδα (Athens, 2nd ed., 1945), p. 37.

8. The controversy is described by G. Ainias, in Συλλογὴ Ἀνεκδότων Συγγραμμάτων τοῦ. . . Εὐγενίου τοῦ Βουλγάρεως (Athens, 1838), p. xxxi.

9. The best general account of the Academy and of Voulgaris's part in it which I have come across, is given in Anghelou 5, to which I am indebted for many of the details that follow.

10. See, e.g., Legrand (XVIII), nos. 680, 1198.

11. 5, p. 94.

12. In giving these details I must again stress my indebtedness to Anghelou (5).

13. The translation was not published, but survives in MS in the National Library of Greece, under the title Ὑποτύπωσις ἢ ὑπόμνημα φιλοσοφικὸν περὶ τοῦ κατὰ ἄνθρωπον νοῦ ἐκ τοῦ Ἄγγλου Λωκίου. For further details see Anghelou 1, pp. 132–8.

14. The original (short) titles of these translations (with place and date of publication where applicable) are:

Στοιχεῖα Μεταφυσικῆς Γενουηνσίου (Vienna, 1806)
Λογικὴ καὶ Μεταφυσικὴ Δουχάμελ
Λογικὴ Πουρχοτίου
Εἰσαγωγὴ εἰς τὴν Φιλοσοφίαν Γ.Ι.Σ'Γραβεζάνδου (Moscow, 1805)
Φυσικὴ Φρεδερίκου Βουκερέρου
'Αριθμητικὴ καὶ Γεωμετρία Βολφίου
Στοιχεῖα Γεωμετρίας Τακουετίου (Vienna, 1805)
Μαθηματικὰ Σεγνέρου (Leipzig, 1767)

There is a bibliography of Voulgaris's works in K. I. Sathas's Νεοελληνικὴ Φιλολογία (Athens, 1868), pp. 569–71, and another (better) one appended to K. I. Dyovouniotēs' article on Voulgaris in vol. VII of the Μεγάλη 'Ελληνικὴ 'Εγκυκλοπαιδεία (Athens, 1929).

15. 1, p. 136.

16. I.e., Iosepos Moisiodax, in a passage quoted *infra*, p. 89.

17. 1, p. 136.

18. Περὶ Συστήματος τοῦ Παντός (Vienna, 1805).

19. Στοιχεῖα Μεταφυσικῆς (3 vols., Venice, 1805).

20. Τὰ 'Αρέσκοντα τοῖς Φιλοσόφοις (Vienna, 1805).

21. 'Απολογία (Vienna, 1780), p. 16 (quoted in Anghelou 5, p. 97).

22. *Loc. cit.*

23. See Anghelou 5, pp. 98–9 and n. 107.

24. Published by G. Ainias, *op. cit.*, pp. 54–64.

25. Ibid., pp. 63–4.

26. A relatively detailed account of these attempts is given in Dimaras 9. J. D. Carlyle remarked in 1801 that "the divinity college at St. Andrews even in vacation time is a place of bustle and business compared to the school at Batopaide. Its only inhabitant that we found was a solitary cock . . . ." (*J. D. Carlyle's Journal of Mount Athos* [1801], ed. Anghelou [Anghelou 6], p. 37.)

27. Dimaras 1, p. 134.

28. Παιδαγωγία (Vienna, 1800). See E. Kriaras, Γαβριὴλ Καλλονᾶς, Μεταφραστὴς Ἔργων τοῦ Locke καὶ τοῦ Gracián, Thessalonikē (offprinted from 'Ελληνικά, Vol. 13), 1954, esp. p. 295.

29. Ainias, *op. cit.*, pp. 60–1.

30. See *infra*, p. 69.

31. From "Mount Athos.—An Account of the Monastic Institutions, and the Libraries on the Holy Mountain; from the papers of Dr. Hunt," in *Memoirs Relating to European and Asiatic Turkey*; ed. from manuscript journals by Robert Walpole (London, 1817), p. 200. The reference is to Voulgaris's Αἰνεὰς Βιργιλίου (St. Petersburg, 1791–2).

6

Voulgaris's *Logic*: A *Speculum Mentis*

One can get a rough idea of the scope of Voulgaris's *Logic* by comparing its contents with those of the then still fashionable *Port Royal Logic* (though this is not to suggest any direct influence of the latter on the former). Voulgaris's work is the more massive of the two. His long introduction, beginning with the origins of philosophy and leading up to the subject matter of logic through the divisions of philosophy, has no counterpart in the *Port Royal Logic*. Book I of the *Logic* proper (on concepts or ideas) has ground in common with Part I of the *P.R.L.* (on ideas), though the order and development of topics are different. Voulgaris's Book II (on thinking) is concerned mainly with truth, falsity and probability and does not correspond to Part II of *P.R.L.* (on propositions), which has its counterpart rather in Book III (on judgment). Book IV (on reasoning, διάνοια) corresponds to Part III and covers very much the same ground. Book V (on method) is largely parallel to Part IV, though the latter's treatment of the subject is the more extensive.

Voulgaris's presentation of Logic, thus broadly interpreted, is avowedly eclectic. He links the two notions of freedom of judgment and eclecticism, and defends a free-ranging method by saying: "And this is not to innovate but to proceed in the most ancient way of all: for nothing is more ancient than the pursuit of truth."[1] And again: "Not according to our reckoning is the hunter after truth to be registered as a Peripatetic or as a Platonist, nor is any other such name, whether ancient or modern, to be attached to him . . . but only that of Philosopher. And to be this, he must be eclectic."[2] "Is the fact that some piece of perfectly correct discourse issues from a Scythian and not from a Greek to put it at the nadir of acceptability because of the person who utters it? . . . To Platonize, or to philosophize according to Aristotle, is to be a sectarian rather than a conformist to truth."[3]

Voulgaris's warnings against an undue reverence for antiquity and against undue submissiveness to Plato and Aristotle are in marked contrast to his attitude to the philosophical language of antiquity which, as I have remarked already, he was determined to adopt and have adopted, for "academic" purposes anyhow. Here is one, rather obvious, instance of tension in his general intellectual position. He was the first of the modern Greek philosophers to set himself against working in a tradition. He was a mouthpiece of philosophical and scientific ideas requiring a terminology for which Attic Greek could produce the matter rather than the form. But he refused to accept the possibility that the spoken language of the people could be enriched from that Attic source and developed into a means of handling difficult ideas with precision: on the contrary, it seemed to Voulgaris more suitable to call on the ancient language as being a relatively complete and sophisticated instrument and to supplement its vocabulary as necessary. Here, in the *Logic*, we are given his considered renunciation of the popular language. Its resources amount to what he calls contemptuously "philosophical wordlets," insufficient to broach the heights of knowledge, and leading only to an uneducated, superficial kind of philosophizing, in fact to mere juvenile inanity. "Those booklets, then, which profess to philosophize in the vulgar tongue, are to be whistled off the stage."[4] The subsequent history of Greek philosophizing has proved Voulgaris to be simply wrong in dismissing the prospects of developing a scholarly language "from below."

There is another tension in Voulgaris's position which comes out in the early, programmatic part of the *Logic*. He sees a close connection between the eclectic method, right reason (ὀρθὸς λόγος) and freedom of philosophical enquiry. However, he argues, there is such a thing as undue liberty in philosophizing. A sign of this is the mind's tendency to get into paralogisms (of which Voulgaris gives one or two not un-Kantian instances). The difficulty is posed by revealed truth, which philosophical enquiries, notoriously, have tended to controvert as much as to support. There is a point at which philosophical investigation becomes both impotent and an encroachment. Voulgaris is sensible of the difficulties in saying precisely where the limit lies, but he expresses a resolution always to proceed in philosophy in the closest accord with "right reason," thereby, he has us understand, avoiding having to profess any doctrine that is not in accordance with revealed truth as expressed in Holy Scripture.

Voulgaris gives examples of doctrines which one may not call in question. (The "may not" pretty clearly expresses a moral veto as well as an offense against right reason.) They are such as the Virgin Birth, the incarnation of the divine in human, suffering form, and the crucifixion, death and ascension of Christ (to name but the most familiar of very many examples which Voulgaris quotes). At the same time it is quite wrong, he holds, to suggest that God and the divine should be excluded from the purview of the philosopher. The general formula which governs philosophical speculation upon these subjects is that we may investigate those and only those features of the divine which *can* "be grasped in terms of our natural notions (ταῖς κατὰ φύσιν ἐννοίαις)."[5] This is plainly question-begging, and the onus is back on "right reason," which Voulgaris has quite failed to *prove* as preestablishing a harmony with scriptural faith. (The burden on this notion has not lightened since it was put to service by Damodos.) Voulgaris remained, as he himself put it,[6] a theological philosopher, and he did not mean by this merely a philosopher who, like Descartes or Leibniz, accepted the existence of God as a metaphysical truth.

In general, there continued to remain two sides to his thinking: his sympathy with "new" philosophy and experimental science, and his sympathy with Orthodoxy. It is true that as he became older the latter came to possess him more and more, as the history of his changing attitudes to Voltaire (shortly to be discussed) will show. But the other side never became insignificant. As a Marxist critic remarks, not unjustly, he was a curious amalgam of Byzantine Christian tradition and Western humanism.[7]

Voulgaris spends 144 pages (or one quarter) of his book on preliminaries—the preparation required for entering on philosophy and the qualities and qualifications demanded by its effective study; the main causes of malady in the intellectual powers (ranging from sensual distractions through failure to realize the misleadingness and limitation of the senses—a theme treated in a rather Lockeian manner —to the abuses of words); the classification of the intellectual powers, their ways of operating, and dispositions; the nature and divisions of philosophy; and the nature of logic in particular. In discussing this last topic he raises a number of the questions which so preoccupied Korydaleus and Anthrakitēs in their *Logics*—for instance, the distinction between "innate" and "acquired" logic, the question whether logic is an art or a science, and that of the uses of logic—and makes rather less heavy weather of answering them than those authors did.

In this part of the book, as in others, he uses numerous long footnotes to collect opinions about or cite work on the questions at issue from a great variety of authors, the more ancient of them comprising Byzantine as well as Classical writers, the more modern including Bacon, Descartes, Locke, Arnauld and Wolff. Elsewhere in the *Logic* he discusses views of Hobbes, Gravesande, Malebranche and Leibniz as well, thus taking account altogether of a fair range of "modern" writers in and around the subject.

The approach to technical logic is prolonged even further by Voulgaris's letting the subject develop out of epistemology. The relationship, for him, is really quite simple. The logic of terms is the logic of signs of ideas; hence a theory of ideas must precede the logic of terms. The logic of propositions is the logic of verbal expressions of judgments; hence a theory of judgment must precede the logic of propositions and a formal theory of reasoning. Furthermore, judgment is only one "phase" of thought, its most decisive and clear-cut. Hence the general subject of *thinking* may properly precede that of judgment. Moreover, thinking presupposes understanding or "apperception" (πρόσληψις), but in fact the theory of ideas with which we began amounted in part to a theory of apperception; and logic in the technical sense turns out to be not so much an *organon* as organically linked to other parts of philosophy. The amount of space which it gets in this so-called *Logic* is approximately two and a half out of the five main books, and in extent that is a good deal less than half of the entire work.

I do not propose to go into all the detail of how this ground is covered. The *Logic* is so diffuse that for present purposes a faithful summary is out of the question. A few indications of how Voulgaris proceeds here and there are all that can be given.

His indebtedness to Locke, but also his refusal from the beginning to let innovations in philosophy compromise theology, appear interestingly in the very first chapter of Book I. He offers an account of ideas as changes of state (ἀλλοιώσεις) in the soul and then explains that there are three sources of idea-changes. (The very notion of an idea as a change, involving as it does some reference to a cause of change, would seem to exclude the postulation of innate ideas, and in fact innate ideas are no part of Voulgaris's theory.) The sources are, first the Creator, secondly the soul's reflection on its own states, processes, activities and so on, and thirdly the body.

The ideas which proceed from the first source are ideas of revelation, or else of mystical experience, and are such as transcend philosophy. Voulgaris gives no precise examples of this class.[8]

The second class is obviously that of Locke's ideas of reflection, taken to include not only ideas such as those of judging, attending, remembering and other "operations" of the mind, but others to which changes that are due to the external senses make some contribution, for example those of existence, duration, power, activity, passivity, cause-and-effect, truth, falsity, pleasure and pain.[9] (These last are Voulgaris's "naturalized" as opposed to "natural-born" ideas and this is his rather clumsy method of reproducing and extending Locke's doctrine that there is a range of simple ideas "which convey themselves into the mind by all the ways of sensation and reflection."[10]) He prefers to classify them as ideas of reflection, but with the rather involved qualification as to their genesis which unfortunately misled Monboddo in his reading of this passage.[11]

The third class of ideas is that of ideas of sensation, "third in rank but first in common use," as he quaintly says.[12] There is a consistent echo of Locke in the account which he gives of this class, but nothing that deserves special comment.

On one very minor matter he takes issue with Locke.

> Locke's conjecture (Bk. II, Ch. I, §21), that the Foetus is wrapped up like a zoophyte and is altogether without comprehension or perception, swimming in the fluid of its mother's womb, seems to me hard to accept, especially if you take into account the fact that it comes to be completely equipped with sense organs. For animals when conceived are without perception but on being born are already naturally percipient; they do not just begin at the moment of birth to be subject to perceptual changes.[13]

This may seem a rather severe assault on Locke's mild suggestion, that "a *Foetus in the Mother's Womb, differs not much from the State of a Vegetable.*"

The remainder of Book I, except for the last chapter, which is on the import of terms—the transition having been made from ideas to signs of ideas—deals with a considerable variety of distinctions applicable to ideas, then with definition and division, topics and categories. The distinctions are explained regardless of whether they are more of "logical" or more of epistemological or metaphysical interest. It is hardly necessary to look at Voulgaris's footnotes to realize that the following list arises out of a great deal of mixed philosophy, modern as well as ancient: simplicity and complexity, clarity and obscurity, distinctness and confusion, adequacy and inadequacy, concreteness and abstractness, intensionality and extensionality, and particularity and universality.

Voulgaris's didacticism comes to the fore in the account which he gives of Aristotle's categories. This, though almost purely expository, is done at some length.[14] Voulgaris justifies himself by observing that even those who affect to despise them, make use of Aristotelian categories in other parts of their philosophy: hence the traditional scheme should be a standard piece of philosophical knowledge. The same didacticism is apparent in Voulgaris's classification of terms, and his account of their uses and significance. There is much passing to and fro between grammar and philosophy here, and a most elaborate set of distinctions is offered us, on these two bases, in describing kinds of terms and their employment. Many of these, however, are made with insufficient discussion of their significance, and the reader is offered no explanation of the principles governing the apparently chaotic classification of them.

This very dry section of the *Logic* is followed by a much freer effort in Book II, which bears the title "Thought." All the opportunities offered by this vague term are taken. We begin with a discussion of doubt and its propriety. At the outset, the cry of "Hands off revelation!" is renewed, but from that point onwards Voulgaris undertakes a sober enough discussion (sometimes in Cartesian tones, although here there is no explicit acknowledgment to Descartes) of the extent to which we may doubt of various sorts of thing. The trouble is that Voulgaris has not really grasped (or that, if he has, he has ignored) Descartes's master plan of letting degrees in the conceivability of doubt lead him to the discovery of a unique, paradigmatic *philosophical* proposition: examination of the characteristics of which enables us to reassess other philosophical propositions—this being doubt technically employed.[15] Instead Voulgaris is worried by the *reasonableness* of doubt in rather more everyday circumstances than those in which Descartes was putting himself, and he only answers that it would be "most unreasonable and improper"[16] to doubt any of the following: (a) immediate sensory reports, (b) clear and distinct ideas, (c) what he calls *epoptic* and *ennoematic* judgments (an example of the first being "milk is white" or "gold is malleable," and of the second, "man is rational"), (d) formally correct reasoning, and (e) certain kinds of testimony. Leaving aside the fact that the foregoing classification invites questions, one is reminded at this point more of Common Sense philosophy than of Descartes. The present chapter concludes with some purely psychological description of doubt in the forms of "hesitation" and of "suspicion" or "conjecture."

The next chapter surveys the notions of truth (in correspondence terms), falsity, certainty, probability (= credibility) and error. It is when we come to consider, in the following chapters, the different degrees of "probability" and how to reckon them that Voulgaris spreads himself most of all and adapts his *Logic* to some very odd purposes.

The fourth chapter is a general critique of criticism, or a survey of probability judgments in different subject matters. The remainder of the Book, in five chapters, works all this doctrine out. The general kinds of criticism are (a) the symbolical, (b) the logical and (c) the pragmatic. The first need not detain us, being techniques, if such they can be called, for the assessment of the inscrutable, like ancient monuments, or ceremony and ritual of various kinds. The "logical" is divided into grammatical, poetic, rhetorical, exegetic (or historical) and dogmatic. One can but observe that criticism of these kinds is "logical" only in a very, very general sense of the term. It has to be such, at any rate, as can be applied to rules for judging of good and bad versification and, in rhetoric, matters like tone of voice and correct deportment.[17] Rules for judging of certain virtues in historical writing, such as completeness, consecutiveness and consistency (all of which are mentioned here) are perhaps "logical" in a less strained sense of the term.

Pragmatic criticism, like logical, has five divisions: interpretatory, historical, political, practical and physical (or natural). Interpretatory criticism has to do with techniques of forming probable judgments regarding the meaning and intentions of other people, through the study of written material, its stylistic features, selection of subject matter, and so on. General rules for textual criticism are given under this heading, as much, one feels, for the sake of instruction as for illustration. The "historical" type of criticism which comes under the "pragmatic" rubric has to do with questions of verisimilitude, and extends to verbal testimony in general; in particular, it deals with such difficulties as the number and integrity of witnesses, their qualifications, background, and so on, and emotive reporting. (On the sifting of evidence Voulgaris quotes with approval from Voltaire, *Des mensonges imprimés*, referring to the author as being "of surpassing literary reputation amongst us" [ὁ καθ' ἡμᾶς ἐν εὐκλείᾳ τῇ ἐκ τῶν λόγων περιὼν Οὐολταῖριος].[18])

"Political" criticism is basically a matter of assessing the strength of habits and customs, inclinations and tendencies in the individual soul. Most of the chapter in which it is discussed is a treatise on psychological types, regarding which one must again remark that what is officially illustration is expanded for its own sake. The basis of the classification, Intellect and Will, and the activities and dispositions that each colors, is old-fashioned enough and there is frequent citation of Aristotle and Theophrastus. Much of the character-sketching is acute, though. There is an excellent paragraph on men of prodigious memory. These may be with or without judgment—without it they make the worst kind of boring raconteur; with a dash of shrewdness, and no more, they remain praters, chatterers and discoursers; but with judgment their speech becomes weighty, and they become historians, genealogists, geographers and philologists of the very best kind.[19] There are also interesting if undeveloped observations like one suggesting an association between material prosperity and religiosity,[20] but I have already made the point that all of this ought properly to be just illustration.

There remain under the head of pragmatic judgments of probability the so-called practical, and the physical or natural. The first are predictions of the probable results of present phenomena, either in the realm of natural events or in that of human activity. Voulgaris gives an elementary account of inductive reasoning in each of these fields. He does not raise a problem about free will, though he offers a rudimentary justification (on social grounds) of general psychological knowledge.[21] "Natural" judgments of probability are judgments which offer probable causal explanations of natural phenomena. (Voulgaris does not remark that there is any problem as to the dividing line between his "practical" and his "natural" judgments.) He deals here with the difference between mere observation and experiment, he contrasts genuine arguments from experience with apriorism and superstition, and he says something about hypotheses, their construction, coordination, verification and refutation. Here, of course, we come back to a more familiar subject matter of books on logic, which often enough take scientific method as well as induction under their wing.

Book IV is entitled "On Judgment." Voulgaris proposes to take "judgment" in a broader sense than does Locke, applying it to every kind of assertion which joins or disjoins two ideas, and not just to that kind which involves mediating ideas, in connections less than certain.[22] This enables him to take "the verbal expression of judgments" as providing the entire scope of the logic of propositions which occupies the remainder of the Book. Neither on this logic nor on the logic of the syllogism and related matters which occupies Book V do I propose to comment. Voulgaris presents the traditional formal logic in pretty fair detail, didactically, with some faults, but also with occasional suggestions of logical acumen. Here, for amusement's sake, are the Greek mnemonics corresponding to "Barbara, Celarent . . .":

Grammata, Thease, Sanidi, Technikos;
Thambenen, Grapsodo, Thenaze, Tenio;
Sabasi, Sarini, Spinthamin, Tetaso,
Terintho, Gorgado;
Gamarin, Thameten, Tenaso, Tenino, Simarin.[23]

(Unfortunately I have found no hint of connecting phrases like those which give such euphony to "Barbara Celarent . . .".)

The fifth and last book of the *Logic* concerns method, taken up more generally than at the end of Book III. A good deal of the subject matter comes only rather vaguely under the heading of "method," and is rather a collection of leftovers. However, we are given precepts as to definition, division, particularizing, generalizing, identifying axioms and postulates, and an account of the nature of theorems, corollaries, scholia and so on; also there is a longish explanation of analysis and synthesis (understood in a Cartesian sense) as different methods in demonstration. A chapter on method in studying, and in analysis and discovery, follows. This is a series of rules of method on Cartesian lines, although no mention is made of Descartes; the modern authors cited are mainly Leibniz and Locke. After this we have a return to the synthetic method, which is equated with that of exposition and teaching, and we are given rules pertaining to order, economy, illustration, clarity and other virtues. Method in discussion and controversy is the final topic. The difference between a Socratic question-and-answer method and other forms of dialectic is explained. The remainder of the Book, and of the *Logic*, consists of precepts as to technique and good behavior in discussion.

I have said a great deal, some of it caustic, about the range of topics covered in this extraordinary work. But who would wish to make his criticism of the book condemnatory? Its 586 pages were written in a language (I am thinking not of ancient Attic but of Greek as such) which had long since ceased to be a medium of new thought and discovery. It was written for students many of whom had come through nothing like a formal process of school education and whose educational ambitions were unsatisfied in a great many directions. These facts suffice on their own to explain why Voulgaris allowed himself to ramify the subject of "logic" so much. He was not making an original contribution to the subject but rather presenting it in its broadest possible setting to a generation which needed precisely this broad kind of introduction to logical thinking. The book was no monograph, nor did it set out to be one. In any case, where the break with Aristotle had taken place in modern philosophy was not (or at any rate relatively speaking not) in formal logic but in the general gnoseology or philosophy of knowledge of which that logic was thought, by others besides Voulgaris, to be an organic part. Hence if two tasks had to be done, namely, instructing in systematized logic and presenting at least a part of philosophy in the new, free, "eclectic" manner, the two could with some justification be undertaken within the compass of one book, especially in the absence of previous printed work, in the Greek language, on either subject. One takes for granted, in a way, Voulgaris's grasp, his knowledge of other languages and his learning. To transmute all these into a large, scholarly work in

Greek unlike anything that had been accomplished before was remarkable and important. But this itself is not a sufficient basis, in the end of the day, for praise of his *Logic*. The book was not a mere *tour de force*. What makes it admirable after its fashion is that it tries to do some justice to the principle that all learning is one, in the knowledge that this can sometimes be a painful truth rather than a comfortable platitude.

In thus defending the *Logic*, I am not unmindful of my previous argument that the relatively late publication of Voulgaris's books was something of a tragedy. At least the *Logic* had a pretty fair start on all the others.

NOTES

1. *Logic* (1766), p. 45.
2. Ibid., pp. 57–8.
3. Ibid., p. 102.
4. Ibid., p. 49.
5. Ibid., p. 66.
6. Ibid.
7. D. Glenos, Ἡ Ἀξία τῶν Ἀνθρωπιστικῶν Γραμμάτων στὴν Ἑλλάδα (Athens, 2nd ed., 1945), pp. 38–9.
8. See *Logic*, p. 158.
9. Ibid., p. 159.
10. Locke, *Essay*, II, vii.
11. See my note 1, p. 51.
12. *Logic*, p. 160.
13. Ibid., n. 1.
14. Ibid., pp. 227–38.
15. On p. 273 he criticizes Descartes for allowing himself a degree of doubt that is beyond even philosophical justification.
16. Ibid., p. 261.
17. See ibid., pp. 289–90.
18. Ibid., p. 311, n. 1.
19. Ibid., p. 316.
20. Ibid., p. 320.
21. Ibid., pp. 326–7.
22. See Locke, *Essay*, IV, xvii, §17. Voulgaris comments on this passage in a long footnote on pp. 339–40.
23. *Logic*, pp. 446 ff. Those for the first three figures appear also in Anthrakitēs' *Logic*. Anthrakitēs disdains to uphold the fourth.

7

Voulgaris on Cosmology, Astronomy and Religious Toleration

The Principles of the Philosophers (Τὰ Ἀρέσκοντα τοῖς Φιλοσόφοις) is a volume of cosmology and physics consisting of 432 pages of text, along with a large number of diagrams. The preface explains that the work is to some extent imitative of Plutarch—curiously without naming the (supposititious) Περὶ τῶν Ἀρεσκόντων τοῖς Φιλοσόφοις from which the title is derived and which is cited often enough in footnotes—but that it takes account of the principal modern writings on physics as well as ancient, and that it is not merely historical but rather philosophical in intent. The aim is systematic explanation rather than a mere record of opinions. The heavy philosophical bias of the book is not surprising; it is far from clear how much direct acquaintance Voulgaris had with experimental physics, and for that matter the readers to whom the book was directed would have little or no scope for experiment themselves. Consequently, the main interest of the work is to be found in the reading that lay behind it and in the multiplicity of the topics of which Voulgaris showed a comparative grasp.

In the Prolegomena, he considers first a number of alternative definitions of "nature" (φύσις), then gives an account of the subject matter of physics based on a selection from these definitions, and proceeds to define "physics" for himself in terms of a theoretical science of nature in certain of its aspects (which he has enumerated). The definition is of no interest except that it leads him to comment on the significance of calling physics a science, on aetiological as distinct from historical explanation, on the respective places of experience and reason in physics, on the uses of mathematics and on the sense in which we can speak of physical "certainty." He introduces some basic rules of Newton and some axioms of Rohault. He then proceeds, in the first chapter, to talk about the existence of bodies, still in general, philosophical terms. There is no "ontological" proof of such existence, he maintains. Instead we must rely on the testimony of our senses (taken in the context of a causal theory of perception). The possibility of our being systematically deceived as to the existence of a physical world is ruled out by an appeal (on Cartesian lines) to God's veracity.

The next chapter, again philosophical, is on the nature of body. Voulgaris explains and criticizes, successively, (i) various versions of the view that matter is extension (credited to Aristotle, the Scholastics, and Descartes), (ii) versions of the view that matter is "bulk" (credited to Demokritos, Epicurus, Plutarch and Gassendi), (iii) the view which he assigns to Leibniz and Wolff that matter is extension plus active and passive power. He finally is content with the agnostic conclusion of Musschenbroek that we have no clear idea *a priori* of the nature of body. He accepts a distinction between primary and secondary qualities, of each of which he gives a list.

Chapter III concerns the primary elements or "principles" (ἀρχαί) of physical body. Voulgaris observes that there have been three ways of arriving at such principles, first metaphysically, secondly by the power of imagination, and thirdly by perceptual means. Under the metaphysical heading he considers Pythagoras, Plato, Aristotle, the Zenonians and the Eleatics. These all, he judges, more or less fail to explain the nature of matter. Under the perceptual he describes the theories of Thalēs, Anaximenēs, Herakleitos, Hesiod (and Pherekydēs) and Empedoklēs. He regards their theories as being more or less crude, and unable to account for the phenomena. For this same reason, and for their pretentiousness, theorists of the "imaginative" class (of whom Anaxagoras and the Atomists are taken as representative) are criticized still more severely. After a brief notice of Maignan and Gassendi, Voulgaris then turns to the Cartesian physics, or, as he calls it, "archology and cosmogony,"[1] of which he gives an outline exposition and a criticism. The criticism is exceedingly crabbed. He apparently ranks Descartes, too, as a creator of phantasms—he talks of his cosmological hypotheses as sheer "trifling"[2] and speaks of "the man's superficiality,"[3] and further condemnation is promised for special contexts. As to Leibniz's and Wolff's views, Voulgaris wishes that he could give a favorable account of them, but he cannot. For one thing, he maintains against them a downright dualism, and he concludes, "to assert that in all circumstances the extension of bodies is phenomenal and not real is to be purposely blind and to fight off the plainest experience."[4] Voulgaris's own view is that a Newtonian-type theory of elementary particles is the correct one (and is theologically acceptable), besides being in conformity with what is held by a great many other modern physicists.[5] At the same time Voulgaris, as he himself says in effect,[6] is a physical pluralist.

Chapter IV discusses rather a miscellany of matters, the extension, form, divisibility and synthesis of bodies. Voulgaris discusses the question of infinite divisibility at some length, distinguishing a physical point of view (from which infinite divisibility is not possible) from a geometrical (from which it is). He ends with a rather inconclusive discussion of what "form" is.

In Chapter V the solidity, porosity, hardness, elasticity and inertia of bodies (with other notions belonging to that cluster) are discussed. Solidity is known not just by touch, but by meeting and overcoming resistance. Here, Descartes is criticized for making solidity consequent upon extension instead of the other way round. Far from giving an answer, however, to the metaphysical question, "What makes things solid?", Voulgaris himself is content to remain agnostic. In a somewhat Reidian passage he says: "It is better and more consonant to reason just to declare that solidity depends on the nature of bodies and that of this, as we have confessed already, no exact determination can be arrived at *a priori*."[7] He criticizes the Cartesian account of elasticity, as also those of Clarke and Musschenbroek, before approving that of Newton. He distinguishes between inertia (ἀδρανία), passivity (ἀδιαφορία) and resistance (ἀντενέργησις). He criticizes Newton, Keill, Clarke, Gravesande, Musschenbroek and others for not distinguishing clearly enough between passivity or passive power and a sort of "sluggishness" (νωθρότης) of matter, and letting both come under "the power of inertia."[8] The Leibnizians, however, he considers to have confused the three main notions mentioned.

Time, space and the void are dealt with next (Chapter VI). Voulgaris defines "time" in terms of duration and "space" in terms of extendedness. He distinguishes between absolute and relative time, as also between absolute and relative position. He discusses critically the Aristotelian and the Leibnizian concepts of space, and is aware of the Leibniz–Clarke correspondence. He reviews the whole historical controversy about the void, which he is prepared to say in some sense exists.

The next chapter (VII) is on motion and rest. It begins with a metaphysical discussion, taking its starting point from Aristotle's conception of motion as the actualization of the potential, and it goes on to consider such problems as whether rest is anything positive, and whether motion is "implanted" in bodies (or how communicated). In all of this discussion there is a host of references to the literature of the subject, not least to Cartesian and Leibnizian theories and those of Musschenbroek. The second and greater part of the chapter, however, consists of a purely "physical" discussion of laws of motion, the main references being to Newton.

Chapter VIII is on impact and fragmentation, and Chapter IX on mass and gravity. The earlier part of the latter contains the usual historico-philosophical discussion of the concept in hand. Special reference is made to the views of Aristotle, the Scholastics and Gassendi, and to Descartes's theory of vortices. Towards the end of this discussion Voulgaris suggests that it is not surprising if, after so much confusion amongst the physicists, people fall back on theological explanations of the phenomena; but it is much better and (as with Newton) a mark of philosophical integrity just to admit our ignorance.

Voulgaris's severity on the introduction of theological hypotheses into science is repeated in a later chapter (XV), on the attraction of bodies. There he castigates those who give an occasionalist explanation of the phenomena, as producing "the merest suppositions."[9]

By the end of chapter IX Voulgaris has virtually written out the historical and philosophical part of his physics. The remaining twenty-two chapters, accounting for some two-thirds of the book, are informative rather than speculative. That is, they give Voulgaris's version of modern physical theory, drawn largely but by no means exclusively from Newton and Musschenbroek, and presenting a special science whose special concepts are relatively well defined and not problematic. Consequently there is nothing to look for here but straight didacticism about a long list of subjects: the downward movement of masses upon an inclined plane, pendulums, the motion of projected bodies, centrifugal and centripetal forces, "electric bodies," attraction, density and cohesiveness, fluidity, hydrostatic forces, specific gravity, the earth, water, air, fire, light and its refraction, and vision (with certain other topics subsidiary to these).

The book called *The Universal System* (Περὶ Συστήματος τοῦ Παντός) published in the same year and by the same publisher in Vienna as *The Principles of the Philosophers*, is a handbook of astronomy. There is little philosophical discussion in this book, but a point of interest is that Voulgaris prefers the Tychonian to the Copernican system. In the fourth chapter he gives an account of the Ptolemaic, Copernican and Tychonian systems in turn, and then sums up:

> In the light of what has been said, it is not difficult to give a satisfactory explanation, should one have a preference for the third of the systems put forward for our examination . . . namely, the Tychonian. For if it is not against nature, like the Ptolemaic . . . nor against the pages of Scripture, like the Copernican . . . and it in itself is found to be particularly consonant with astronomy . . . then it may reasonably be adopted in preference to the other two. No one should suppose us, however, to be thus committed beyond recall to the view that the relationship of the heavenly bodies to one another is as Tycho suggests. We are not of that way of thinking; it is rather that we take the balance of probability to be on the side of his opinion, and we maintain that the proper thing to do is to adhere to it until such time as greater light is shed for us on these matters. . . .[10]

The book contains the usual encyclopedic references, this time to astronomers and astral theorists ancient and modern.

I have given an account of these two books because they are historical curiosities, because they indicate what Voulgaris taught or set himself to teach, in natural philosophy, during his "active" period, and because they show the astonishing range of reading and interests in which his own early education had issued. More than this it would be wrong to claim for them. They do not seem (and the reasons may be those which I have suggested already) to have set a tradition of thought and discussion in the subject. There is one passage in Benjamin Lesvios's *Elements of Metaphysics* in which he criticizes those who appeal to God's veracity in the attempt to find a foundation for our belief in an "external" world. Benjamin thinks, like the common-sense philosophers, that our awareness of the existence of body is such as to make this guarantee philosophically otiose; and he names "our Eugenios" in this connection.[11] He quotes no specific context, but it would be reasonable to think that he has the argument of Chapter I of *The Principles of the Philosophers* in mind.

The few other comments which I have found on controversial doctrines, in Voulgaris, of a cosmological or natural philosophical kind pre-date the two "manuals." Iosipos Moisiodax, in part of his *Apology*, attacks Voulgaris's intolerance of the supposition that there may be other inhabited planets besides this one or, in the well-known phrase, a plurality of worlds. But the occasion is provided by the *Logic*.

> The celebrated Eugenios, in many parts of his *Logic* and especially in §19 of the second preliminary dissertation, is not merely displeased with the hypothesis of the habitation of the planets or the plurality of worlds; he as it were convicts and indeed pillories those who argue for it, calling the hypothesis itself a piece of sheer silliness and saying of the philosophers who support it that they are committing a fault unworthy of the philosophical profession. Why? Because, this man of wisdom says, they are making a leap from part to whole or from possibility to actuality.[12]

Moisiodax goes on to show how many-sided is the analogical argument on which the supporters of the hypothesis rely, and he suggests that in this controversy it is virtually Eugenios against all the rest. There is also a note by Moisiodax, in the same work, on Voulgaris's classification of motion and time under the genus of continuous quantity (with a brief account of the argument for classifying them as discrete quantity instead). Here also it is the hospitable *Logic* to which Moisiodax refers.[13] All this merely indicates how general a source book for comment or criticism the *Logic* had become, and how it was in a position to draw out some criticisms which in other circumstances might have waited upon the later manuals.

To round off this sketch of Voulgaris's thought and opinions, some account may be given of a work of very different character from any of the foregoing. This is his translation of Voltaire's pseudonymously published *Essai historique et critique sur les dissensions des églises de Pologne* (1767). The dissensions about which Voltaire was concerned involved the rights in Poland of both Protestants and Orthodox Christians *vis-à-vis* Catholics. Voltaire wrote after Catherine II of Russia's army had arrived in 1767 to protect the dissidents and prevent civil war. His design was to further the cause of toleration by describing the facts. Voulgaris's version[14] was published anonymously in 1768, in

Leipzig (although no place of publication is given on the title page). It was supplemented by long historical and critical notes and by an essay of Voulgaris's own on Religious Toleration. The point of the notes was that they should be elucidatory, critical and corrective as necessary, and didactic; but Voulgaris had in mind rather the sort of audience that one would preach to than a class to be instructed in college, and it is for this reason that the language used throughout the work is plain and colloquial, in marked contrast to that of the *Logic*.

The notes reflect the moderate, balanced admiration that Voulgaris had for Voltaire at the time. After saying that Voltaire is often enough of the same opinion and sentiments as himself, he adds, "Voltaire is always Voltaire, interweaving the good with the bad in his writings, and mixing up what is worthy of acceptance and commendation with what merits only aversion and censure."[15] Voulgaris does not doubt that his translation and notes will rank him, along with Voltaire, as an object of offense to the papists. As regards the appended essay he explains that it gives in systematic form Voulgaris's own point of view about religious toleration and, in particular, he considers the question "What is the reasonable limit to and proper measure of this kind of forbearance?"[16] According to one interpreter, the very reactionary Athanasios Parios, the essay was written "against atheistic Voltairean indifference" and the preceding notes as a "detailed refutation of the sophisms directed by the supreme atheist Voltaire against our undefiled faith."[17] This seems to me to be a rather one-sided interpretation. It is true that according to Voulgaris toleration does not go so far as indifference, but with that major proviso he clearly thinks there is a lot to be learned from Voltaire about it and about religious differences in general.

Of course, Voulgaris's own position is not all that clear-cut, nor easy to maintain in practice. One of his long notes[18] takes up a theme already broached in his *Logic*, that there are some matters philosophical intrusion into which represents a certain kind of offense. Here he shows the sort of practical implications that this position has. He is discussing two connected freedoms, freedom of thought and freedom to read. Both of these are admirable at first sight and in a general way, but there must be some limit to each of them. Voulgaris makes one most important concession, namely, that so far as concerns the humanistic arts and sciences there can be complete freedom (in which it might be remarked that his own *Logic* is an exercise, and of which his impatience with theological explanations in science or metaphysics is a defense). "But in the divine and mysterious dogmas of the faith," he says, "freedom of thought is brazenness, since it is mere folly to seek reasons for what is beyond reason."[19]

Voulgaris does not comment here on the difficulty of maintaining a consistent distinction in practice between matters on which there is revelation (and on which we ought not to press philosophical enquiries) and matters which come within the scope of human reason. Instead he states dogmatically that when the soul attempts to see "in another light"[20] what the Holy Scriptures and the Church declare to be thus-and-so, it is necessarily blinded and wandering. Liberty of this sort should be conceded neither to oneself nor to others. Consequently the corruption of opinion is censurable, just as is the corruption of morals, and good and pious rulers should see that it is prevented.

As to freedom to read, Voulgaris hedges his position similarly. Freedom to read the Holy Scriptures and the works of the Fathers should be unrestricted—at one point he very nearly concedes that it would be appropriate to translate the Holy Scriptures into the vulgar tongue—but not freedom to read the productions of heterodox, frivolous or evil-minded authors, in which such little as may be good is mixed up with much that is bad. The literary scholar and the theologian may read them with discrimination (and the Church and its Fathers will provide guidance how to do so), but not the unsophisticated or the less educated.

The toleration which should be practiced by a defender of the faith is described in the *Essay* in rather less general terms, but still not without leaving a great deal of ambiguity. Religious toleration is described as "an attitude of gentleness and clemency in a pious soul," which will employ only "reasonable" means in the correction and prevention of error and will avoid tyrannical, cruel or inhuman means when guarding others against it.[21]

Notice that such toleration, according to Voulgaris, is not acquiescence but a method of conversion and safeguard. The tolerant man is a "zealot for piety"[22] and not indifferent. Voulgaris's emphasis, however, is on clemency. In a very Aristotelian paragraph[23] he places toleration as a mean between indifference and brutality. What degree of severity then is consistent with "tolerance"? He answers that persuasion, teaching and good example may be reinforced in the last resort by social ostracism or by excommunication, but not by persecution (διωγμοί),[24] physical force or torture. (One wonders what counts as persecution.) Not only are these wrong and inexcusable, but they are also disastrous and unprofitable. Force can make a hypocrite, but cannot compel assent. Within these limits such a degree of severity is required as befits the religious sickness of the patient: this is both for his own sake and because the salvation of others must not be endangered by him.

Voulgaris then discusses how these principles should be applied by (a) the individual Christian, (b) the Church and (c) the sovereign and the civil power. The individual must be a zealot, but not a quarrelsome, turbulent, bitter or abusive one. A different treatment is required for domestic backsliders and for those outside our own communion, either those of different persuasion or (confirmed) schismatics and heretics. In the case of a backslider we may follow up the Church's own sanctions by discontinuing social intercourse with him and isolating him. No question of this arises in the case of foreign unbelievers or of heterodox religious systems, though we must disown the principles they stand for and be continuously on our guard against subversive religious influences.

As to ecclesiastics, the code by which they are to be guided does not differ from that which applies to the ordinary individual, but of course their responsibilities are wider and are "professional." Voulgaris writes mainly of the ecclesiastic hedged round by other systems of religion, which of course was typical of the Orthodox situation in his day. There is never the slightest suggestion on his part that these other systems may be even *as* valid as his own ("the miasma of alien religion"[25] is one of his phrases), but, he says, memorably enough, "Repel unbelief and heresy and schism, not the unbeliever and the heretic and the schismatic; or, if you like, the unbeliever and the heretic and the schismatic, not the man."[26] For the ecclesiastic proselytizing is permissible, but as a secondary task and always by teaching and example only. There is no question of his having jurisdiction over anyone but members of his own communion: here, though, his *spiritual* jurisdiction is complete. And the penalties of the Church are always to be spiritual, never bodily. Voulgaris develops this theme at some length and he makes a sustained criticism of the Roman Church for its confusion of spiritual and temporal jurisdiction.

Finally, as to the responsibilities of rulers: Voulgaris contends against the view of Themistius that a sovereign ought to be indifferent to the form or forms of religion practiced by his subjects. He holds that a multitude of conflicting "witnesses," and ecclesiastical division, are simply bad, and he takes Voltaire to task for speaking (in this present work) as if they were not. "The faith consists in correct and true belief about God; God is one, correct belief about him is one—consequently the faith is one."[27] So the faithful king must be not indifferent but "tolerant," with all that this implies. Again, though, the tolerance is to be limited to *persons*, regarded in a rather abstract way—their activities may well be immune from it, since the kingly zeal may go so far as the destruction of places of worship and other facilities (for example, books) belonging to any of his subjects who, in effect, are guilty of religious sedition. Not even subjects such as these, however, may be chastised by means of torture or the shedding of blood.

The difficulties in Voulgaris's position pretty well suggest themselves. There is a clear element of liberalism in his theory, so that much of what he writes in praise of toleration is attractive. But the destructive power of the Church's means of correction is greater than he allows, for the borderline between spiritual and bodily penalties is arbitrary. In any case, some things that the Church cannot do the Christian ruler may, and these include acts of what it is not too much to call persecution, short though they may fall of torture or bloodshed. It is interesting that a representative of a Church which was politically on the defensive could be so arrogant, but the smugness of Orthodoxy does color Voulgaris's essay. That the Church was in fact still the *labarum* of Hellenism may have something to do with this, as a motive, but if so it is not one which Voulgaris would naturally, or could with safety, make explicit.

As for Voulgaris's attitude to Voltaire, this changed and hardened quite extremely in later years. Neither in the *Logic* (which contained what may well have been the first written introduction of Voltaire's name into Greek thought), nor in the annotations and the essay just discussed, is any suggestion conveyed that Voltaire is other than a brilliant, stimulating representative of the Enlightenment, one whose views (it is true) have to be taken with circumspection but who can well and profitably be read by a critical ruler or under critical guidance. By 1790, however, Voltaire had become for Voulgaris "one of the great and famous names for impiety."[28] Thenceforth he was mentioned only to be condemned or confuted. This change is not excused but is to some extent accounted for, by general factors; the revolutionary events in France and conservative condemnation of the sort of "freethinking" which was associated with them. But in any case Voulgaris had long since confirmed himself as "an unbending defender and unshakable pillar of our Orthodox faith,"[29] and the wonder is that Voltaire got so long a run for his money as he did.

There is some poignancy in ending this sketch of Voulgaris with a *cri de coeur* which, although it, too, was written in 1790, expressed feelings that must have been familiar enough to him throughout his career, and particularly on those days when either wrangling or frustration made the instruction of the young and the transmission of European thought seem less exhilarating than usual.

> ... I take up and retake up one wretched book after another. The damnable thing is that I have no chance to digest those books that I really want to study, but can deal only with those that are forced on me by necessity, so that I have all the toilsome labor of continuous study without any of its delights and pleasures.[30]

Here was the more domestic side of the man described by his first biographer as being "like Aristotle uttering the most advanced principles of Newton, or Descartes Platonizing, in mind and in voice."[31]

Notes

1. *Op. cit.*, p. 31.
2. Ibid., p. 32.
3. Ibid., p. 33.
4. Ibid., p. 38.
5. Whom he names, p. 39, n. 1.
6. Ibid., p. 40.
7. Ibid., p. 61.
8. Ibid., p. 71.
9. Ibid., p. 179.
10. *Op. cit.*, §xcix.

11. Στοιχεῖα τῆς Μεταφυσικῆς (Vienna, 1820), p. 211 (Papanoutsos 2, p. 185).

12. ᾽Απολογία (Vienna, 1780), p. 110 (n. 1). "The celebrated Eugenios" translates the phrase ὁ κλεινὸς Εὐγένιος which became a familiar half-affectionate, half-derisive epithet for Voulgaris from the late eighteenth century onwards.

13. Ibid., pp. 118–9.

14. Περὶ τῶν Διχονοιῶν τῶν ἐν ταῖς ᾽Εκκλησίαις τῆς Πολονίας Δοκίμιον ... ἐκ τῆς Γαλλικῆς ... μεταφρασθέν.... Προσετέθη καὶ Σχεδίασμα περὶ τῆς ᾽Ανεξιθρησκείας. (For place of publication see Legrand (XVIII), no. 691.) Dimaras points out that it was Voulgaris who endowed the Greek language with the term ἀνεξιθρησκεία ("religious toleration") (15, pp. 10, 37).

15. *Op. cit.*, p. iv.

16. Ibid., p. 150.

17. Quoted by G. Ainias, *op. cit.*, p. xxiii.

18. *Op. cit.*, pp. 133 ff. (no. 173).

19. Ibid.

20. Ibid.

21. Ibid., p. 151.

22. Ibid.

23. Ibid., p. 153.

24. Ibid., p. 156.

25. Ibid., p. 170.

26. Ibid., p. 169.

27. Ibid., p. 197.

28. From a letter, quoted by Dimaras 1, p. 142.

29. Ainias, *op. cit.*, p. ix.

30. Letter addressed from St. Petersburg, 14 March 1790. Printed in Βόσπορος ἐν Βορυσθένει (a compilation by A. Mavrokordatos of poems and miscellaneous readings) (Moscow, 1810), pp. 359 ff.

31. Ainias, *op. cit.*, p. xxx.

8

Theotokēs and Katartzēs: A Translator's Choices

Voulgaris's letter of 1790 (quoted in the preceding chapter) was in effect his own formal renunciation of Voltaire. The reaction which he thus assisted was carried just about as far as it could go, in a literary context, by a preface written four years later by Nikephoros Theotokēs to his own translation of a French "refutation" of Voltaire's biblical criticism.

Theotokēs, who was born in Kerkyra in 1731, was, like Voulgaris, both an educator and a cleric. He was at one time head of the official Greek school at Iași and had some renown as a teacher of physics. He in fact published a two-volume *Elements of Physics* in Leipzig in 1766–7.[1] It was as an ecclesiastical orator, however, that he became best known.[2] He succeeded Voulgaris as Archbishop of Slavinion and Cherson for a period from 1779, after which time until his death in 1800 he remained firmly and exclusively an ecclesiastic.

Here, then, was a cultivated, accomplished, much-traveled and patriotic man, with a good deal of educational experience, who yet conveyed the impression that the culture which he represented was not, after all, robust enough to absorb Voltaire, that those restrictions on freedom of thought and its expression about which Voulgaris had written approvingly some twenty-six years before, now represented, more than ever, limitations on any further development of "religious humanism."

In 1794, in Vienna, there was published a work by Theotokēs (but not bearing his name), entitled *Demonstration of the Authority of the Books of the Old and New Testaments, and Defense of the Truth contained therein. Or, Refutation of Voltaire's Book called The Bible Now Finally Interpreted.*

Translated from the French, with Notes.[3] Voltaire's original work was *La Bible enfin expliquée . . .* , published in 1776. The "Refutation" translated carried the lengthy title given in Theotokēs' version, except that he substituted the full "Voltaire" for "Vxxx." It was by the Abbé Joseph-Guillaume Clémence, and was published in Paris in 1782. What gives Theotokēs' publication such interest as it has is not, one need hardly say, the theological content, but the tone of the translator's preface. This is remarkable for its unqualified condemnation of and bitter vituperation against Voltaire, and for its anti-intellectualism. Its justification of faith is on grounds not of abstract argument but of historical religious pragmatism and moral efficacy, which are held to rule out Voltaire's combination of mockery and sceptical analysis as simply insupportable. More important, the occasion is taken to issue a manifesto, as it were, on the methods and dangers of Voltairism: as if Theotokēs were trying finally to close an entry upon Greek culture that had been open for too long.

Voltaire is described in general terms as "a man who wears the cloak of philosophic reputation, but who in actual fact is nothing but an intellectual playboy, brazen enough to satirize the divine just as he does the human."[4] In blasphemy, impiety and general depravity he is well in front of all other antireligious writers. And, as the author of the "Refutation" has shown, neither his translating ability, nor his scholarship in general, with its eclectic method of criticism, its perverse and overliteral interpretations, and other faults, can stand up to examination. How then has Voltaire gained the position and the following that he has?

First, Theotokēs answers, it is because there are people who look for mathematical-type proofs in matters of faith and are misguided enough to be disappointed because they do not find them. Secondly, Voltaire's *worldly* attitude of mind appeals to the worldly prepossessions and tendencies which are uppermost in so many people. Thirdly, his easy, ironical style and apparently enormous knowledge seduce the ignorant and the uncritical. Fourthly, he and his followers have a special appeal to the vainglorious: "believers they address as simpletons and blockheads, but unbelievers as philosophers and men of strong spirit," and so they attract those who want to be known amongst their fellow-men as "lofty thinkers and Philosophers."[5] Fifthly, it is always easier to tear down than to construct. Voltaire knows better than to erect a polytheism (such as Porphyry's or Julian's), an atheism (such as Spinoza's), a fatalistic philosophy on the Epicurean model, or a blind unprovidential monotheism such as some of the moderns favor, and so he has confined himself to the criticism of the Christian religion. "He builds to destroy and it is destruction that he builds. He plays, he ridicules, he talks obscenities, he banters, he dissembles, he jests, he is merry; in appearance and reality he is another Lucian of the present age."[6]

This rather unnecessary polemic—to the best of my knowledge the original against which it and Clémence's commentary were directed was not itself available in Greek translation—raises the question what policy should be followed in translating works from contemporary foreign languages into its own by a society that is trying either to create or to re-establish a culture. Clearly, Voulgaris had had a policy, and there is no reason why some such policy as his should not be a matter of common agreement.

An attempt to lay down general principles governing the selection of what is to be translated and the sort of language to be used for translation was made, as a matter of fact, in 1787, that is, seven years earlier than the date of Theotokēs' publication, by Demetrios Katartzēs (c. 1730–1807) in a protreptic discourse devoted largely to this purpose. The essay, called in full *Exhortatory Address towards attaining Self-knowledge and the Common Education of the Race. Or, the Learned, the Half-Learned and the Unlearned*[7] (more briefly, *Know Thyself*), contains one principle which ought to rule out Theotokēs' efforts straight away. This is that the time for commentaries, whether of the Korydalean type on Aristotle or any other, except specialist exegetic ones such as are required to assist teachers in the interpretation of difficult texts, is past.[8] True, it is the interpretation of Biblical texts that is Theotokēs' concern: but one of Katartzēs' complaints against commentaries is precisely that they tend to take the place of the original, and, little as he himself would have liked the original Voltaire in this instance,[9] he could not but have regarded Theotokēs' efforts as misplaced, as being an insufficient presentation of first principles (even in the realm of Biblical criticism) and as having too little of didactic value to offer to the general education of the race.

It is not that Katartzēs regards ethical criteria as being irrelevant to the selection of foreign work for translation. "When he [the man of learning] sees the good things and the bad things which others have to offer . . . it will not occur to him to waste time in praise or condemnation of them, but he will try to obtain and secure the good for his own kindred and nation, and be concerned to get rid of the bad or to steer clear of it altogether."[10] Yet Katartzēs also contrives to convey the idea that such ethical criteria are of secondary importance. They concern a kind of writing which those who wish to exploit foreign learning in the interests of a re-emerging education should systematically ignore, not just by not translating it but by not spending time in reading it. The real principle of discrimination in the study of foreign languages and the reading and use of foreign books is that the languages should be those of well-developed modern "scientific" cultures and that the books should be instructional, so that questions of their moral goodness and badness hardly arise. "With the Tree of Knowledge in front of him like a sailor's binnacle he [the man of learning] will read those arts and sciences in which he aims to perfect himself; upon other writings, good though they may be, he will not direct his eyes; he will do so only upon didactic works composed in academies by their learned men."[11]

The same applies to some extent to the ancient Greek classics. Even estimable works like Plutarch's *Lives* or the *History* of Thucydides (both of which Katartzēs mentions in this connection) suffer from the fault of all "polite literature,"[12] in being too unsystematic, drawing on knowledge too haphazardly and being too imprecise. "Polite literature," taken alone, is good for nothing but the arid "grammatical" education which has satisfied most Greeks up till Katartzēs' time. If intellectual profit is what is wanted from it, however, literature should be approached *through* a knowledge of the sciences (broadly interpreted) and not directly or in the first instance. Didactically speaking, systematized universal history comes before Thucydides.

These interesting, bold, and far from ridiculous ideas are part of a general educational policy which Katartzēs introduces in terms very reminiscent of Descartes.[13] Granted that one takes the man of learning as one's model, then one should make a complete survey of one's ideas to decide which of them are authentic (that is, reflective of one's own direct experience) and which not. In other terms, one should sort out those which in their various ways are clear and distinct and advance only therefrom, keeping explicit standards of good reasoning before one as a constant concern.

Katartzēs, however, is not interested just in general educational theory. The vital question for him, as an eighteenth-century Greek, is how to apply that theory, how to develop a rationalistic type of education in a suitable Greek language. His own answer is that the Romaic, the natural contemporary spoken language, must be made to bear the burden. He has urged his "man of learning," previously, to regard the Romaic as continuous with Hellenic (as he calls ancient Greek) and the Romaic nation as having a parallel continuity. There is nothing wrong with the modern Greeks, he argues, such that they cannot converse with Philosophy, and there is nothing essentially wrong with their natural language so that they cannot do this face-to-face. The matrix in which Greek education is to develop must not be the ancient language. By and large, Katartzēs in effect says, to feel thoughts as your own you *must* do your thinking in your mother tongue, and for an eighteenth-century Greek it is not ancient Attic that is his mother tongue, although the continuity between it and his mother tongue is an advantage to be exploited.

So it is unrealistic to expect the development, natural and felicitous, of modern thought in an ancient Greek mold. One must learn ancient Greek, yes, but for the sake of the intellectual nourishment which it makes possible, and the resources offered by its vocabulary to a poorer generation which cannot naturally use but can naturally borrow from it. What all this means is that the new education "in ideas" implies a development of the Romaic from within, from a sense of inner necessity, and not the adoption or imposition of any other language.[14] And to come back to the task of the translator whose mission is to serve this type of education—what he must do is first introduce and then grow the tree of knowledge in Romaic soil.

Appropriately enough, this essay itself is written in an experimental "Romaic." Unquestionably the whole text of it is more natural and more lively than anything to be found in, say, Voulgaris or Theotokēs, but it does present some special difficulties to the modern reader. One comes across unexpected syntheses of more or less familiar terms, turns of expression that no longer occur, at any rate in more scholarly forms of demotic, words that have become very rare, at any rate in the senses in which Katartzēs employs them, and terms borrowed from ancient Greek which have not made good their places in the modern language.[15] The essential vigor of the style, however, is in no way diminished by these features, and the text is of great philological interest, especially when read as an illustration of Katartzēs' own systematization, elsewhere, of the grammar of "natural" Greek.[16]

If one likes the savor of "contradiction" in historical affairs, then one will appreciate Dimaras's observation[17] that Katartzēs' work exemplifies one facet of a general historical law, a law which insists that certain kinds of social order, as manifested in a certain characteristic kind of activity, contain the seeds of their own destruction. Katartzēs was a Phanariot.[18] The Phanariots were a ruling class, well established. That class had virtual control of Greek education in several important places. But the more "popular" that education and, not least, the more "popular" the language which was to be its medium, the greater the threat to the exclusive power and authority of its sponsors. Clearly, Katartzēs' program was for a development of education far broader in its subject matter and offering far more promise to the people than had been contemplated by Nikolaos Mavrokordatos seventy years earlier.[19] It is unlikely that Katartzēs himself would have been worried by any "contradiction" in his position, but from the "class" point of view it could fairly enough be said that in his educational thinking was implicit a new political and social system, the prospect of which would be accepted more complacently by some than by others.

As it was, Katartzēs' linguistic convictions ran him into trouble. His main writing, conforming to his own linguistic theories, was all done between 1783 and 1791. In 1791 (in circumstances which seem not to be known precisely) he was constrained to abandon his attempts to put these theories into effect: indeed, he then proceeded to transcribe his previous work into a sort of simple *katharevousa* ("purified" language), more official and more "eligible" than the original Romaic. He explains himself that he did so against his convictions, but simply and solely in order to be as helpful to his countrymen as conditions would allow.[20]

The account which I have given of the essay *Know Thyself* might perhaps suggest that Katartzēs was more of a rationalist (in Lecky's sense of the term) than in fact he was, and what has been said in particular about his educational theories might suggest that he was a more radical thinker all round than in fact he was. The balance may be corrected by reference to another curious and interesting essay of his, called *In Praise of the Philosopher, Blessing of the Orthodox, Censure of the Atheist and Deprecation of the Superstitious.*[21] What sort of philosopher, or philosophy, does Katartzēs have in mind? He is prepared to praise what he calls frequently in this essay "sound philosophy" (ἡ ὑγιεινὴ φιλοσοφία).[22] This is in fact philosophy which has all the important questions begged in its favor, in other words, philosophy which, by definition as it were, is nonatheistic. (One may recall again the cognate idea of "right reason" to which both Damodos and Voulgaris ascribed a providential sensitivity to religious truth.) Thus, for Katartzēs, "the philosopher" is able to deduce such things as the existence of the soul from his experience of "its" activity, the existence of God from the presence of final causes, and (as he says most mysteriously) the eternality of God's thought from "his own soul, which thinks in time."[23] Also, according to Katartzēs, the philosopher does not waste time "looking for first principles of what is already first, and for proof of absolutely everything. He does not want his wisdom to be nothing but a scholastic's endless talk."[24] He is guided by a kind of common sense which draws its light partly from the consideration that philosophy is not just a theoretical activity, and he devotes himself to moral questions as matters in which his speculation vitally affects the practical life. He distinguishes, according to philosophical canons, good actions from bad, but he also *does* the good because it is good. The pursuit of truth is one pleasure: a greater one is the deliberate pursuit of what is in various ways proper, in the expression of feeling, in action and in speech. The philosopher is a man with an educated conscience as his mentor.

It is in simple conformity with this sketch of the philosopher that Katartzēs should draw a close parallel between philosophy and Christianity (that is, Orthodoxy). The Orthodox Christian (as such) takes his first principles from revelation, the authority of the holy scriptures, the patristic writings and, in the process, from his own inward light. He has the same virtues as the philosopher, but through his faith, hope, and love they are the more strongly motivated. The philosopher and the Christian both work on principles; neither acts without reason, and what they do is consistent with what they say. In respect for virtue against vice they do not differ, but the Christian lives in hope of a future life, whereas most philosophers preoccupy themselves with the happiness to be had in this one. (There is some recognition here of the autonomy of morality.) A Christian's salvation does not depend upon philosophy, and philosophy is required by the Christian only (as Katartzēs seems to say) for the defense of the faith, only (as he does say) if the Christian is going to be a teacher in the Church, a schoolmaster, or a leader of the people.

There is nothing very unusual in the point of view that a man can be a good and secure Christian without being a philosopher, even when a "philosopher" is as little of a free-thinker as he is allowed by Katartzēs to be. But is not some tension possibly to be found in Katartzēs' thought, when one considers how important a part "philosophy," in his estimation, should play in general education? Is Katartzēs not saying that a Christian needs little philosophy because he needs little education? If so, he is surely saying something that is very much out of keeping with everything said or implied about popular education throughout the essay *Know Thyself*, where only the total, congenital ignoramus is to be left lying by the educational wayside.

I doubt if such tension is more than apparent. "The philosopher" and "the Christian," as they are described by Katartzēs, are really abstractions rather than men in the round. What he is arguing is the apparently banal thesis that a Christian *qua* Christian needs no philosophy. On the other hand, there may be some tactical importance for Katartzēs in stressing the point. One way of taking it is as an assurance that "philosophy" makes no claim to usurp the place of religious doctrinal education. It gives no competing account of reality, and such principles as it holds in common with Orthodoxy are in any case adopted or held in the light of revelation with a greater sense of compulsiveness than when the natural light alone is the medium. (The special point of philosophy is not the establishment of *those* truths.)

There is no question but that philosophy is being in a sense "protected" by Katartzēs. But he has relieved it from the risk of confrontation by an *odium theologicum* only through an arbitrary redescription. The same arbitrariness is found in his account of the unbeliever, who, according to Katartzēs, can only be a gross, amoral, barbarous brute. As a contribution to the literature of "characteristics" the essay therefore unquestionably fails. Its accounts of the philosopher and of the unbeliever are each in their way grotesque: only the superstitious character rings true. Philosophy is not a "safe" discipline (as philosophers have pointed out before now),[25] and it does no service in the long run either to philosophy or to religious apologetics to describe it as if it were. Also, it is of no use simply exhorting the philosopher, as is done by Katartzēs, not to turn Pyrrhonian. Philosophy will decide for itself whether Pyrrhonism is a tenable attitude or not.

Indeed, one may well feel that Katartzēs was making so many concessions to Orthodoxy in this essay that he did too little justice to his own liberal educational ideas. So often he appears to be conceding, as pawns to an imaginary ecclesiastical opponent, the existence of various virtues, accomplishments or other facets of character in which a philosopher may be admirable but a Christian may excel. What is left to recommend the philosopher, who, after all, is the primary subject of consideration in this essay? The essay presumably sets out to do more than just represent the philosophic life as an important second-best to the Christian. But it leaves the special virtues of philosophy too much in the background. According to Dimaras[26] its theme is the greater fulfilment of the Christian through philosophy rather than the enrichment of the philosopher by Christianity. Granted that we are talking about "the Christian" as an individual, all round, this is probably a fair inference from the way the philosopher is accommodated in the structure of the essay, together with Katartzēs' obvious anxiety to represent him favorably. But the aim is carried out rather timidly. The enrichment of the philosopher by the advantages of Christianity is described with relative fervor, and there is a disturbing remark that the Christian's philosophy "is to him but a mere embellishment."[27] Here, as elsewhere, however, Katartzēs may have fallen victim to his own abstractions.

It is very hard to say how influential either this essay or the rather more straightforward *Know Thyself* was. Everything that Katartzēs wrote between 1783 and 1791 remained unpublished during his lifetime and very little indeed was printed until quite recent times. The opposition to Katartzēs' linguistic theories (granted that there was such) would suggest, if nothing else did, that there was some circulation of his work in manuscript. But his influence is better attested by the fact that he created around himself in Bucharest, where he lived, a circle of *littérateurs*, including Moisiodox, Daniel Philippidēs, Gregorios Konstantas and Regas Pheraios, whose contributions to

Greek intellectual life and literature in the late eighteenth and early nineteenth centuries were all of them more than ordinary. Both Moisiodox (the subject of the next chapter), and Philippidēs and Konstantas (of whom an account is given in Chapter 16) belonged to the "modernist" school of Greek educationists. Each of those men made it his mission to absorb and transmit ideas from contemporary "European" culture, and each believed that the language in which those ideas should be communicated to his fellow countrymen ought to be basically his fellow countrymen's own; none of them subscribed to the view that what was wanted was a "purer" language drawn down from some Hellenic heaven. Regas, who is best known as a poet, falls outside the scope of the present study, but he, too, was one of the great "naturalists" (in a certain sense of the term) in early Greek linguistic controversy. Katartzēs' circle, then, held a pretty consistent view of how the content and the medium of Greek education should develop from then on.

Notes

1. Στοιχεῖα Φυσικῆς. Legrand (XVIII), no. 652.

2. Several of his orations have been edited and published by B. Tatakis in Σκοῦφος, Μηνιάτης, Βούλγαρις, Θεοτόκης (Athens, 1953). Further biographical details may be found either in this book or in Dimaras 1, pp. 141–3.

3. Ἀπόδειξις τοῦ Κύρους τῶν τῆς Νέας, καὶ Παλαιᾶς Διαθήκης Βιβλίων, καὶ τῆς ἐν αὐτοῖς Ἀληθείας Ὑπεράσπησις. Ἢ Ἀνασκευὴ τῆς τοῦ Βολτέρου Βίβλου, τῆς καλουμένης Τελευταῖον Διερμηνευθείσης Διαθήκης. Ἐκ τῆς Γάλλων Φωνῆς μεταφρασθεῖσα, ᾗ προσετέθησαν καί τινες Σημειώσεις.

4. *Op. cit.*, p. vi.

5. Ibid., p. xi.

6. Ibid., p. xiii.

7. Λόγος Προτρεπτικὸς στὸ Γνῶθι Σαυτὸν καὶ στὴν κοινὴ Παιδαγωγία τοῦ Ἔθνους. Ἢ Σοφός, Ἡμιμαθής, Ἀμαθής. First published (with omissions) in Dimaras 15.

8. *Op. cit.*, pp. 76–7.

9. In his Ἐγκώμιο τοῦ Φιλόσοφου (1785) he calls Voltaire "a learned fool" and treats him as abusively as Theotokēs does. See Dimaras 6, pp. 18–9.

10. *Know Thyself*, p. 64.

11. Ibid., p. 70.

12. The term is mine, not Katartzēs'. It seems an appropriate substitute, however, for his τὰ μὴ διδασκαλικά (pp. 70, 75 and elsewhere).

13. *Op. cit.*, pp. 58–9.

14. The idea of any language, ancient or modern, as a "mold" or "matrix" may seem philosophically disputable. Certainly a remark of Katartzēs' (quoted by Dimaras 1, p. 153) that no one "has any right to give a word a sense (πάθος) which it does not have in the mouth of the people" implies a respect for "ordinary language" such as was fashionable in but has now been partly repudiated by the pace-setters in postwar English philosophy.

15. For a more detailed analysis, see Dimaras 15, pp. 29–33.

16. See Dimaras 8.

17. 1, p. 153.

18. He was born probably in Constantinople and eventually had a high position in the administrative service of Wallachia. (For information about Katartzēs and for copies of various texts of his work, I am much indebted to the friendly interest of C. Th. Dimaras. Biographical details about Katartzēs are given compactly in Dimaras 17.)

19. See p. 24.

20. See Dimaras 15, pp. 27–8.

21. Ἐγκώμιο τοῦ Φιλόσοφου, Μακαρισμὸς τοῦ Ὀρθόδοξου, Ψόγος τοῦ Ἄθεου, Ταλανισμὸς τοῦ Δεισιδαίμων. Written about 1785. First published in its original form by Dimaras (6) in 1955.

22. The phrase ἡ ὑγιὴς φιλοσοφία is used, in a somewhat similar sense, by Moisiodax in his *Apology*. See Papanoutsos 2, p. 150.

23. *Op. cit.*, p. 12.

24. Ibid.

25. Cf. A. G. N. Flew, *Hume's Philosophy of Belief* (London, 1961), p. 242.

26. 6, p. 54.

27. *Op. cit.*, p. 15.

9

Iosepos Moisiodax: "Sound" Philosophy and Educational Reform

First Korydaleus, and secondly Voulgaris, gave Greek thinkers some heritage of their own to contend about. By the last quarter of the eighteenth century there existed in Greek a repository of philosophy, scientific theory of various kinds, and mathematics, large enough to let "domestic" criticism, which in the days of Korydalism had had to confine itself, by and large, to a polemic against one general style of thought, spread out and exercise itself on more varied and more particular matters. The two sharpest of Voulgaris's own critics were his pupil, Iosepos Moisiodax (c.1730–1800) and, a little later, Athanasios Psalidas of Ioannina. Each of these saw that Voulgaris, by trying to render new thought in antique modes of expression, could be at best a teacher's teacher, and between them they criticized his competence as an expositor of scientific knowledge, and as a mathematician, pretty unsparingly. In each instance, dissatisfaction with what Voulgaris had to offer led to the replacement of that material. Psalidas, especially, produced new didactic work on a large scale, and both he and Moisiodax justified their efforts with some characteristic educational or philosophical theorizing.

This disagreement with a tradition, however, did not indicate that Greek education could now be significantly more independent of outside help than it had been before. To provide detailed matter for classroom instruction it was still necessary in most subjects to translate or to epitomize Western European work. Both Moisiodax and Psalidas did so, leaving themselves relatively free only in the more theoretical, philosophical parts of their teaching. The difference between their situation and that of Voulgaris was simply that they, to a much greater extent than was possible for him, could think of themselves as reformers rather than as sheer innovators in providing the "matter" of education.

Moisiodax at an early stage wrote much more serenely about the Greek educational scene, and in particular about Voulgaris's place in it, than he was to do later. In 1761 he had published in Venice the first of two volumes entitled *Moral Philosophy, translated from the Italian by Iosepos Moisiodax, Deacon.*[1] (As is revealed only in the preface, the translation is in fact from a work of Lodovico Antonio Muratori [1672–1750]. The original, which Moisiodax does not specify, was *La filosofia morale esposta e proposta a i giovani* [Verona, 1735]. Muratori was chosen as a model because his approach to the subject of ethics was "simple, moderate and easily intelligible to everyone, or nearly everyone," and also because "he speaks here in no accents but those of an ethicist; as a philosopher, that is to say, and not as a theologian."[2]) The educational world to which Moisiodax contributed this translation was, he said, one in which "schools are multiplying, humane studies are flourishing, philosophy is taught and the voice of mathematics heard; the number of teachers grows—amongst them being some whom I should venture to describe as reviving the nobility of ancient times. A Eugenios Voulgaris in Byzantium, a Nikephoros Theotokēs in Kerkyra, a Nikolaos Zortoullios on Athos are men of the first distinction, all three of them fit to be authors as well as accurate teachers in every branch of knowledge."[3]

The geniality of these sentiments had been dissipated by the time Moisiodax composed his *Apology*, published in 1780.[4] Among other causes for disgruntlement he there picks on Eugenios's mathematics, at any rate that version of it which was exhibited in Voulgaris's rendering of J. A. von Segner's work, already mentioned.[5] Segner, he complains, is too difficult an author for Eugenios to have chosen anyhow for his particular purpose, and what he makes of him is just a hash.

> The reversal of correct order, overcompression everywhere, an excessively abstract way of putting things, the abbreviation of the proofs, the absence of examples, occasional defects in the figures employed, and on top of everything the language itself, a tortured instrument in general, and strained to conform with the Latin, all get in the way of understanding the aforesaid author. . . .[6]

It was in this same *Apology* that Moisiodax offered his sad verdict upon Eugenios's teaching in the Athonite Academy. Voulgaris had been relentlessly overambitious: "What was the fruit that we finally reaped from our unremitting toils? An imperfect idea of logic and, in some part, of metaphysics, a confused or superficial idea of arithmetic"—taught, he adds, according to the system of "the celebrated Wolff"—"and finally an acquaintance with one book only of Euclid's Elements, and not even that in full." He explains that Eugenios spent time out of all proportion on giving a variety of proofs, established or possible, of individual theorems (besides Euclid's, there might be Proclus's, for example, and Claudius's and Tacquet's and Eugenios's own), and that he would then supplement this teaching "with Whiston's corollaries, which were all very well in themselves but mostly were far beyond the powers we possessed at that time." [7]

Moisiodax is a man of enthusiasms, prejudices and great grievances. An undue proportion of his writing is self-defensive; his acuteness of mind all too frequently exercises itself amongst the refinements of suspicion. He is always having to protest that both what he writes and his manner of writing are for the common benefit, that he is dedicated not to his own advancement but to that of his kith and kin (τῶν ὁμογενῶν) and of Greece in general.[8] He is so sensitive about this that one wonders whether his own non-Greek or partly non-Greek origin (he was born in Cernavoda (Rumania) and the name "Moisiodax" means "Moesio-Dacian") had something to do with it.

But if his origin set him apart, the intensity of his outlook did so much more. There is no doubt that Moisiodax was, in educational outlook and practice, a radical: although himself a deacon he does not, except very rarely, speak as one in his writing. He is by no means a consistent enthusiast for "philosophical" studies in the narrower sense of the term, but believes absolutely in mathematics and "natural" philosophy; and he is the self-conscious exponent of a simple Greek style, the very antithesis of what his own master, Voulgaris, had prescribed.

For these reasons amongst others his career was restless and unhappy. He had sought education in many places, including Ioannina, the Athonite Academy and the University of Padua, and in 1765 he became head of the official Greek school in Iași. It is true that he remained in this place for twelve years, but it is also clear from his own account, in the *Apology* and elsewhere, that the educational program and methods which he tried to put into effect there brought about bitter contention between himself and the conservative-minded members of the Greek community. After his resignation from Iaşi in 1777 he taught no more—he wrote, and he published his main works within the four following years, but in the main he seems to have lived relatively inactive, unsettled and in ill health until his death in 1800.[9]

The nature of Moisiodax's radicalism can be ascertained from two sources mainly, the *Apology* already mentioned and a *Treatise on the Education of Children, or Pedagogy*,[10] published in Venice in 1779, the character and circumstances of which are of some interest. The work consists, in large part, of passages either completely translated or else paraphrased from Locke's *Some Thoughts concerning Education*, first published in 1693. Or rather, since Moisiodax was very much at home in French,[11] and there is no evidence that he knew English, they may have come from Coste's French version of the *Thoughts*.[12] The uncertainty may seem strange, but the fact is that Moisiodax simply does not mention his dependence on Locke, and it is a comparatively minor consequence of this that he does not cite the original from which he was making his translations. One may note the fact without moralizing; the main thing, after all, was to get the ideas concerned into Greek, and into Greek thought, and the συντεθεῖσα ("put together") which appears in the title (see note 10) is a pretty fair indication that what the book contained was *not* material all of which first sprang to life from the brain of Moisiodax.

Anyhow, Moisiodax does present many of Locke's basic ideas, sometimes in short, sometimes translated *verbatim*, and sometimes expanded, about both the parental upbringing of the child and the art and principles of teaching. He talks (and the order of topics is perhaps odd) about the dangers to children from servants and other regressive influences (Moisiodax, like Locke, is concerned here with the education of gentlemen [τοὺς εὐγενεῖς]), about the cultivation of self-respect, seriousness of mind and an obedient disposition, and about children's clothing (one of the few points of physical upbringing with which he concerns himself); then the choice of teachers and the relationships of parents with teachers; and then the business of teaching—how teachers must instil neither fear nor over-familiarity but respect, how lessons may be made attractive, how unruly children may be made to see sense, and how to deal with rudeness, untruthfulness and silliness.

These topics represent the Lockian portion of the book. But there are others, in which Moisiodax's debt to Locke appears in no more than occasional ideas. He is speaking mostly for himself when he recommends that children must sit at table with their elders but not take part in marriage celebrations and feasts, when he advises fathers how to deal with older children, vetoes their playing of cards in their children's presence, gives rules about the extent to which children may take part in hunting, and offers admonition about their protection against flatterers, parasites and similar agents of corruption. A longish section at the end, containing a detailed discussion of the teaching of grammar, syntax and essay-writing is likewise relatively independent of Locke.[13] Approximately half the book, however, is more or less concentrated Lockian doctrine.

Why call all this "radical"? The answer is that Moisiodax sees education to be the root of individual and social reform and that he expresses the autonomy of rationalist, secular education more sharply than any of his predecessors. Not that he has a particularly narrow, "intellectualist" view of education; for him it is a method of directing the temper and inclinations of children towards virtue, as well as of predisposing their spirit towards the love of learning. But he is on the side of those who stress knowledge rather than faith as the seat of virtue.

To realize how intense our need for education is, he bids his readers look at its only-too-manifest contrary, the ignorance which is spread out before us in "prejudice, frivolity, disregard for truth, irrational fears and insanities of many other kinds."[14] Let us look also at the combination of ignorance with depravity—and with power. When this happens we get a sort of procession of things into their opposites, of virtue into vice and vice into virtue. Ignorance is the condition characteristic of contemporary Hellenism, and its ally is complacency. "How many evil attitudes, superstitions, bad regimes and other insanities hold sway over us because of it (sc. ignorance), without our even being conscious of them?" Some people who ought to know better dismiss these anomalies as the inevitable result of misfortune, which prevents Greeks from setting up educational establishments and providing for them as they ought. But this same misfortune does not keep people from "superfluous spending on piety (ἱεροδοξίας), on such a scale that it would only take ten or twenty individuals, combining with their usual offerings, to set up a decent academy."

It may be noted in passing that Moisiodax was not the only Greek writer of his time to exploit *Some Thoughts concerning Education.* A straight translation of *Some Thoughts*, with the omission of upwards of a dozen sections dealing with the more bookish part of education, and a modicum of abbreviation in a few others, appears as the major part of another treatise on education[15] compiled by Gavriel Kallonas (1724–95), already mentioned as having been, like Moisiodax, a pupil of Voulgaris in the Athonite Academy.[16] So far as has been ascertained, this treatise was compiled independently of Moisiodax's.[17] Here, again, no acknowledgment is made to Locke (nor is any to Baltasar Gracián, the source of the moral tales and conversations which make up the remainder of the work): though it is fair to note that Kallonas's treatise was not published until five years after his death. In connection with this and with Moisiodax's effort one can but admire the capacity of Locke's common-sense ideas on education to attract and to survive.

Moisiodax's radicalism appears most expressly in his *Apology.* This is not a systematic book but a collection of lectures, addresses, specimen lessons, and apologetics. It leaves a very clear impression of the man's views and personality. It is best known as the source for Moisiodax's conception of "Sound Philosophy" (ἡ Ὑγιὴς Φιλοσοφία), which he described at the beginning as "the root of the tree of all knowledge"[18] and then as that indispensable and infallible guide through error and deception to which the late transformation of Europe is due.[19] Philosophy for Moisiodax is practical. If the term be taken as meaning "conceptual analysis" or something similarly limited, then Moisiodax cannot be said either to do any philosophy or to have any sympathy for it. He regards "sound" philosophy as having an explicit and relatively immediate humanistic purpose. It is "a unitary theory which investigates the nature of things with the constant end of providing for and establishing the true happiness which man, *qua* man, can enjoy on this earth."[20] It rejects scholastic conceits and empty concepts and allows no one, be he Plato, Aristotle, Leibniz, Newton, or anyone else, to be deferred to by having it said of him, αὐτὸς ἔφα. He allows that it contains five constituent disciplines, namely, Ethics,

Metaphysics, Physics, Mathematics, and what he calls "Critical Logic" (λογικοκριτική); but, of these, all but metaphysics are interpreted as practically directed enquiries.

Moisiodax's attitude to the traditional logic, and also on the whole to metaphysics, is very disparaging. Mathematics, he says, is incomparably more necessary to education than is logic. He blames Aristotle, or rather (as he concedes) Aristotelianism, for putting mathematics into eclipse, and praises Galileo, Descartes and Newton for restoring it. (He says amusingly of Descartes that he gives the impression of wanting somehow or other to transmogrify Nature rather than look at it, or of philosophizing about some other Nature and not about this one.) Even Voulgaris's logic is quite or almost irrelevant to mathematics and to natural philosophy. In general, he holds, both logic and metaphysics are too abstract to be of much interest or use.

Metaphysics itself he divides into Ontology, Cosmology, Pneumatology and Theology. What he has to say about theology is correct, brief and formal. (There are no open questions there; or to put it another way, reason can arrive at but one set of conclusions. That these conclusions are exempt from Moisiodax's previous judgment about metaphysics in general is presumably to be taken for granted.) Ontology and cosmology he describes without much interest. He rouses himself when he comes to pneumatology (a compound of the philosophy of mind and epistemology)—he is very severe on the subject as practiced.

> There is no more warlike sphere of thought than that of pneumatology. Hobbes, Lucretius, Locke, Arnauld, Bayle, Spinoza, all give battle, one against the immortality of the soul, another against its immateriality; all raise the standard of heterodoxy; and they struggle, albeit in vain, to overthrow the foundations of spiritual existence.[21]

This writing is not up to the level prescribed for "sound philosophy," but Moisiodax really has very little patience with any philosophy which, as it were, promises nothing in terms of personal and social betterment.

It is in keeping with his practical outlook that he should regard ethics as a first-order set of principles, a direct regulator of the main duties of man. Very optimistically, he describes the subject as providing "the exact instrument of measure designed to fix the level upon which a rational community conducts itself . . . the system of management which provides for and conserves happiness."[22] His words indicate an ideal conception of ethics rather than any actual system, though what he has in mind is an ethics of moderation in the Aristotelian sense, and also perhaps Stoicism, since he says that the point of studying ethics is that it reassures us against the excessive power of fear, jealousy and other passions. To a large extent, however, it is the liberating force of knowledge in general, including theological knowledge, rather than specifically ethical thinking to which he appeals in developing what he has to say about that protective function.

What Moisiodax calls "critical logic" takes the place of the scholastic which, he says, is of no further use. As little as ethics is this study to be undertaken merely for its own interest. It is concerned with the nature and classification of concepts and of propositions, but as aids to mastery of the sciences and of other bodies of doctrine. It deals with truth and falsity but so that one gains a useful knowledge of what guides the mind down the one route and misguides it along the other, and of a variety of particular matters ranging from the correct use of the senses to valid methods of identifying and interpreting the sacred books. Its discussion of the modes of reasoning, sophisms and related topics, of the analytic and synthetic methods of exposition and of the dialectic art is entirely relevant both to the acquiring of present knowledge and to the pursuit of new. Moisiodax's account of this "logic" is purely programmatic, but it is clear enough that what he has in mind is a substitute both for the scholastic logic and for the Rhetoric of older fashion, with something of the objectivity of the first and something of the functionality of the second combined in the interests of a new end, the assimilation of modern knowledge and the cultivation of the intellectual skills which it requires.

"Sound philosophy" includes also mathematics and physics; and "physics" is simply a name for the whole of science, from astronomy down to special sciences such as meteorology and oceanography, and including the organic, notably zoology, as well as the inorganic. Moisiodax gives a rhapsodical account of this range of studies, which plainly engages his enthusiasm far more than any of the philosophies narrowly understood. At the same time he does provide some specimens of his ground-level thinking in mathematical or scientific matters, namely, three lessons or portions of lessons in arithmetic; three in geography; a series of refutations of Aristotelian metaphysical conceptions (that of primary matter and others) done in a mathematical manner by means of complete proofs with scholia, and supplemented by argument (in a similar manner) to establish the credibility of an atomic theory; and lastly a series of four geophysical propositions, likewise proved in a mathematical manner, with the addition of scholia. He calls all this "philosophy," and his doing so is appropriate in that the greater part of the reasoning involved depends on purely *a priori* considerations.

But it remains true that what he is interested in is philosophy *of nature*, and it is this which provides him with the optimism and humanistic faith which are characteristic of him, even alongside the preoccupation with personal injustices and injuries which gives the *Apology* its motif (and which it would be merely tedious to enlarge on here). One ought to add that further evidence of his having done his groundwork in various fields is provided by two things: first, his own statement in the *Apology* that at one time he translated Tacquet's *Elements* up to and including the trigonometry and that he translated and taught (in Iași in 1776) the work of "'Ιωάννης 'Ανδρέας ὁ de la Caille":[23] and, secondly, his publication in 1781 of a *Theory of Geography*,[24] setting out the theoretical basis of that subject in an introductory but systematic fashion.

Moisiodax's position in the language controversy which has been part and parcel of the Greek struggle towards enlightenment is so explicit, and his belief in "the simple style" so coherent with his educational outlook in general, that this account of him may end appropriately with his own words on the question, taken first as a general one, and secondly, more specially, as a legacy from Voulgaris:

> Three principal reasons have led me to prefer the simple style to the Hellenic (i.e., to any restoration of the ancient language). The first is that the more simply a subject matter is set out, the more is it made clear. The second is that a subject matter, when set out simply, becomes comprehensible even to those who have had no contact with "letters." The third is that it would be a very good thing for Greeks themselves to write about the sciences or about anything else, and to do so by employing their everyday, common language.[25]

> If anyone is to be held to philosophize uneducatedly or to indulge in juvenile inanities, then it must be either someone who has no experience

of philosophy and philosophizes prematurely, or else someone who has a certain amount of experience but plays fast and loose with the subject in order to show off his cleverness. It will not be a person who, sticking to its proper tracks, writes about it in "vulgar" accents. For truth is common to all men without distinction, and consequently to every dialect without distinction; it is not bound fast and forever to one dialect only, the Hellenic. The Great Man, instead of whistling it off the stage, ought rather to sponsor our simple style and prescribe how it is to be standardized. He ought not to vilify it any more than the Scythian, to the present state of which forsooth he lends an ear. . . . What good does it do our young devotees of philosophy to be offered those fearsome constructions in which their fathers conceal themselves as in deep thickets, uttering what is apparently of great import, whereas often enough it amounts to nothing at all?[26]

It will be clear that in these matters Moisiodax's views are essentially the same as those of Katartzēs, though the latter's are the more fully worked out. In other respects also there is considerable sympathy between the two men. They both believe in the liberating power of knowledge in general and the potency of modern scientific knowledge in particular. They both tend to fence off theological knowledge from any very pressing enquiry, but Moisiodax gives the impression that it is he who is the more secular-minded of the two. His ὑγιὴς φιλοσοφία is "philosophy" insistent on its own standards and on freedom from dogmatic interference of all sorts. Katartzēs' ὑγιεινὴ φιλοσοφία, on the other hand, is "philosophy" content to remain within certain bounds, philosophy which restrains itself from entry into the field of religious dogma. The commitment of Katartzēs to philosophy is rather more expressly qualified in this respect than that of Moisiodax.

It would be correct to say, so long as the verdict were not misunderstood, that the main importance of Moisiodax lay in his pragmatism, his championing of the "natural" side of philosophy. But the fact is that Moisiodax's influence can have borne directly only on the *outlook* of those whom he taught or affected: granted the absence, so far as is known, of any experimental science worth the name amongst the indigenous Greeks of Moisiodax's generation, it is unlikely that he was able to teach his contemporaries how to proceed experimentally. Still, he does point a way, and it may be remarked that two successors of his, Athanasios Psalidas and Benjamin Lesvios (whose work will be described in subsequent chapters), succeeded in advancing, for however short a distance, along that way. It is quite possible, though, that the interest in experimental science possessed by those two thinkers developed independently of Moisiodax's exhortations.

Notes

1. Ἠθικὴ Φιλοσοφία μεταφρασθεῖσα ἐκ τοῦ Ἰταλικοῦ Ἰδιώματος, παρὰ Ἰωσήπου Ἱεροδιακόνου τοῦ Μοισιόδακος. The second volume was published, also in Venice, in 1762 (Legrand [XVIII], no. 566).

2. *Op. cit.*, pp. κβ′ and κθ′–λ′.

3. Ibid., p. ιε′. "Zortoullios" is a Hellenized form of "Zerzoulēs." Nikolaos Zerzoulēs was a Greek Vlach who at one time taught at Metsovo, and at another taught mathematics in the Patriarchal Academy in Constantinople. He succeeded Voulgaris as head of the Athonite Academy in 1759, but (contrary to what one might expect from Moisiodax's allusion) his tenure was not a success, and he withdrew after two years. (Some of this information I owe to Dr. E. P. Papanoutsos, some to Anghelou 5.)

4. Ἰωσήπου τοῦ Μοισιόδακος Ἀπολογία Μέρος Πρῶτον (Vienna).

5. See p. 46.

6. *Op. cit.*, pp. 35–6.

7. Ibid., p. 16.

8. See the preface to his book on Education (note 10 below), pp. 6–7.

9. For certain of the biographical details I am indebted to Papanoutsos 2, p. 147.

10. Πραγματεία περὶ Παίδων Ἀγωγῆς, ἢ Παιδαγωγία, συντεθεῖσα παρὰ Ἰωσήπου τοῦ Μοισιόδακος.

11. He published a translation, in Modern Greek and French, of Isocrates' exhortation *To Nicocles*, the French title of which is *Transformation de l'oraison d'Isocrate sur l'art de régner pour Nicoclés. Faite par Joseph Myssiodax, ou Chapitres Politics, traduits par le même en françois* (Venice, 1779).

12. *De l'Éducation des Enfans. Traduit de l'Anglois, par P*[*ierre*] *C*[*oste*] (first ed., Amsterdam, 1695). (Fifth ed., Amsterdam, 1744.)

13. A closer examination of the *Treatise* and particularly of its Lockian elements, can be found in E. Kriaras, Ἡ «Παιδαγωγία» τοῦ Μοισιόδακος καὶ ἡ σχέση της μὲ τὸ παιδαγωγικὸ σύγγραμμα τοῦ Locke (*Byzantinisch-Neugriechische Jahrbücher XVII* [Athens, 1943], pp. 135–53).

14. In the preface to the *Treatise*, pp. 3 ff.

15. Παιδαγωγία, περιέχουσα πάνυ ὠφελίμους νουθεσίας τε καὶ οἷον δὴ κανόνας περὶ τοῦ πῶς δεῖ ἀνατρέφεσθαι τὰ παιδία, συντεθεῖσα . . . παρὰ . . . Γαβριὴλ Καλλονᾶ τοῦ ἐξ Ἄνδρου . . . (Vienna, 1800).

16. See p. 48.

17. On this and other features of Kallonas's work, see E. Kriaras, Γαβριὴλ Καλλονᾶς, Μεταφραστὴς Ἔργων τοῦ Locke καὶ τοῦ Gracián (repr. from Ἑλληνικά, Vol. 13), Thessalonikē, 1954. I have profited from both this and Kriaras's earlier article (see note 13).

18. *Op. cit.*, p. vii.

19. Ibid., p. 98.

20. Ibid.

21. Ibid., p. 105.

22. Ibid., pp. 100–1.

23. Pp. 37–8. There is no indication that either translation was ever published. Voulgaris, too, had translated Tacquet. (I have been unable to identify this "la Caille.")

24. Θεωρία τῆς Γεωγραφίας, συντεθεῖσα ὑπὸ Ἰωσήπου τοῦ Μοισιόδακος . . . (Vienna).

25. *Theory of Geography*, p. x.

26. Ibid., pp. xi–xii. The references are to Voulgaris's *Logic*, pp. 49 and 102.

10

Athanasios Psalidas: Antagonsim to Voulgaris

Moisiodax is, to appropriate a Greek term, a "machetic" (fiery and aggressive) type of writer. His thrusts against Voulgaris, however, are not personal. It is always the work and not the man that he attacks. The same cannot be said of another broadside, published fifteen years after Moisiodax's *Apology*, namely, the *Kalokinēmata*[1] of Athanasios Psalidas (1767–1829). Yet it must be allowed that this manifesto also attacks Voulgaris's book in a more circumstantial and detailed way than any that Moisiodax achieved. Psalidas does single out at least one doctrine, Voulgaris's account of the threefold source of ideas in the human mind, for doctrinal criticism. I shall deal with this philosophical matter first before trying to convey the flavor of what Psalidas has to say against Eugenios either in more general or in more personal terms.

He complains here that Eugenios's description of the origin of ideas is not straight philosophy but a mixture of philosophy and theology. In this matter Eugenios would have done well to remember "the injunction of the philosopher, that there is nothing in the intellect which was not previously in the senses."[2] What is thus introduced is in fact an attack upon two out of the three sources (πηγαί) of ideas that Voulgaris had recognized.[3] In particular, Psalidas attacks his pronouncements about revelation. Revelation, he argues, can be regarded as neither a cause (αἰτία) nor a source of ideas (he means for philosophy; and he confuses the issue by arguing as if what Eugenios had held were that the content of revelation could be part of or overlap with the content of philosophy). He insists on the following points:

(i) Revelation is the discovery to an individual of certain truths which cannot be ascertained and expressed through reason, but the concern of philosophy and logic is with, and only with, man's natural mode of thought and the natural laws (including those of the formation of ideas) pertaining thereto.

(ii) What logic has to do with is "common" ideas, those which all men without exception possess or can acquire. Revelation's province is just different. Again, the ideas of logic are κατὰ λόγον καὶ ἔννοιαν, that is, can be reasoned about and made subject to standard classification, whereas those of revelation are "beyond" such possibilities. The former are based upon knowledge, the latter upon faith. To give any sort of expression to the latter, one needs to have been the subject of very special experiences, but what the elucidations of philosophy rest upon is common experience and the general laws of thought.

Psalidas concludes from these considerations that revelation cannot be called a source of our ideas. Incomprehensibly, he has been talking about "the ideas of revelation" throughout his discussion, but we get some help when he explains that revelation is not analogous to "an agent (αἰτία) such as produces immediately representations of objects." There is a special stress here on the word "immediately." Its use suggests that a "source" is to be a point of origination of certain things so far as these have features which cannot as such be traced back beyond that point. (According to classic theory, the mind would in this sense be the source of the ideas of secondary qualities.) And Psalidas proceeds to put the question, "Who ever obtained any idea immediately from revelation?", adding "unless perhaps some Prophet, as some would have it?"

The upshot is that revelation has no place in the considerations of logic but belongs to dogmatic theology. To show that some experience is revelatory it must first be shown that there exists a God, and this is the business of a study which not only does not precede logic but "comes after" ontology, cosmology, and psychology as well as logic. At this point Psalidas refers us for further elucidation to what he has said in his *True Happiness* (of which I shall be giving an account in due course).[4]

As a philosophical polemic, Psalidas's criticism is unfair. Voulgaris, in the particular passage attacked, does not discuss the *precise* sense in which revelation is a "source" of ideas and really says nothing on the subject incompatible with what Psalidas says. Furthermore, although he takes note, in his *Logic*, of revelation (and of mystical experience generally) as a source of "ideas," he is as far as Psalidas is from suggesting that the subject matter of logic includes a revelatory or any other kind of mystically given content—he says expressly that whatever belongs to the latter "transcends philosophy." So far as the immediate issue is concerned, Psalidas's vigorous discussion of revelation and its relation to philosophy is beside the point. It is true, of course, that Voulgaris uses the authority of revelation to keep a certain control of philosophy but, if this is what Psalidas is complaining about in the present discussion, one has to read between the lines in order to see it.

What is interesting, nevertheless, about his polemic is the anxiety behind it (a most common one in this generation of Greek intellectuals) so to mark out the boundary between philosophy and religion (or, more immediately, theology) in theoretical terms as to let philosophy be done securely in practice. In the instance of Psalidas it would be as appropriate to speak of a difference of level as of a line of demarcation—perhaps more so, because the limits to the competence of philosophy which Psalidas recognizes are drawn rather by his own Kantian philosophical outlook than by confrontation with theology. Of this I shall say more later. The fact remains, however, that Voulgaris in his *Logic* and Psalidas in his critical tract were, for all appearances to the contrary, up against the same enemy, the socially obstructive ecclesiastical reaction of a time and period.

The second of Voulgaris's "sources" of ideas which Psalidas discusses is "the soul itself" (to which, as I have pointed out,[5] Voulgaris ascribes the production of certain ideas without committing himself to a theory of innate ideas). Here, Psalidas simply challenges anyone to say *what* idea it is that the soul produces entirely by its own efforts. Any such "idea" would amount to nothing but a βλίτυρι, a meaningless sound. At this stage Psalidas lays down the following philosophical law:

> All our judgments, whether classified as analytic or as synthetic, have to do ultimately with ideas obtained through the senses from external objects; the analysis of them, that is to say, will have recourse either to categories in Aristotle's sense, that is to universal common properties objectively regarded, or to phenomena as Kant construes them, and therefore to categories taken, in his sense, as being in the subject, that is, as being those forms of perception and thought . . . through which all phenomena are constituted and so become objects of thought. . . .[6]

But in either case, Psalidas asks, how can the soul properly be said to be the source of ideas? One can only comment that Psalidas does less than justice here to the notion of "ideas of reflection," and that such ideas both are and are not due to "the soul itself."

In the rest of what he has to say about Voulgaris's *Logic*, Psalidas adopts a somewhat less measured tone. He complains about the general disorder and confusion of the ideas, and about the mystifying fanciness of linguistic style which makes the work unsuitable not only for pupils but for many teachers, and indeed for philosophers as distinct from rhetoricians. About Voulgaris's polemic against the plain style, Psalidas simply remarks that this has been disposed of already by Moisiodax, in the introduction to his *Geography* (from which I have already quoted).[7] He regards the long prefatory sections of the *Logic* as so much waste of time. If they were appropriately placed at all, they would be either too concentrated or not concentrated enough; but to a large extent, being more metaphysical than logical, they presuppose logic in the order of education and do not properly prepare for it. Voulgaris has conspicuously failed to be guided by his own advice that in philosophical thought what comes by way of preface and prelude should be a basis for the introduction and development of what follows. Psalidas is complaining, in effect, about a lack of philosophical professionalism in Voulgaris's work, and such a complaint is difficult to gainsay; but I have touched on this subject already in writing about the *Logic*[8] and will only remark here that Psalidas failed to see the need to turn a *Logic* into a *Speculum Mentis*.

All of this is still relatively sedate. But an extraordinary mixture of condemnations follows, beginning and ending with outbursts of what might by courtesy be called patriotic temper. Voulgaris is said never really to have wasted a moment's thought on helping his compatriots. His whole output displays "his vanity, his egotism, his pride and arrogance, and in consequence the emptiness of his reputation." In philosophy, mathematics, and history he should have done far less translation and far more composition. He compares unfavorably with "the worthy Theotokēs," who at least did well enough in physics for his day. Voulgaris wasted his time and impaired his vigor in "enslaving himself to an ancient Latin poet, namely Virgil, and a German mathematician, translating this man's thin, dry, and nurtureless arithmetic and geometry and that one's flight of Aeneas . . . and his

Georgics."[9] With his capacity and acuteness of mind, his power of memory and mastery of languages, Voulgaris could have been an original thinker and an intellectual liberator. As it is, there is a mistake in almost every line of his Virgil, and he makes terrible slips in mathematics too. One should look at page 9 of his *Logic*, where he explains that Pythagoras discovered that the hypotenuse of a right-angled triangle was equal to the other two sides. (It is true. In that particular place Voulgaris does say this.) On the same page he also says that according to Diogenes Laertius it was Thales who first recorded the principle of "the triangle in a circle," when it would only have taken a correct copyist to put down "right-angled triangle in a semi-circle." And Voulgaris fails as a man. "Despising his country and all his own race, he has taken himself off (on the slightest of excuses) to barbarous foreign lands, letting patriotism come second to pleasure and greed, and without putting either his life or his substance at risk for the sake of his people. . . ."[10]

It would be a pity not to set alongside this diatribe a note on Voulgaris written eight years later by Koraēs, who himself had "taken himself off" to foreign lands but whose influence as a patriotic mentor remained and became greater than that of Psalidas. The note at least serves to return us to urbanity:

> Ce respectable prélat est aujourd'hui le doyen des gens instruits de la nation. Il a été un des premiers qui ont contribué le plus efficacement à la révolution morale qui s'opere dans ce moment parmi les Grecs. Je lui paie d'autant plus volontiers ma part du tribut que la nation lui doit, que je me rappellerai toujours avec plaisir l'émulation qu'excita dans mon ame, jeune encore, la publication de sa logique, et à laquelle je suis redevable du peu de lumieres que je possede.[11]

Psalidas published *Kalokinēmata* at the age of 28, ironically enough before he himself had returned to the centre of Hellenism to work amongst his own people. He was born in Ioannina and educated there up to the age of 18. He then spent two years in Russia, but transferred in 1787 to Vienna, where he studied first medicine and then philosophy and science. Before he left there in 1795 he also saw to the publication of various writings—*True Happiness*, *Kalokinēmata*, an *Arithmetic*, translated for use in Greek schools from the original of G. I. Metzburg,[12] and a tract on a visit by Catherine the Great to the Greeks of the Crimea.[13] By 1795 he had composed in addition a very large amount of work which remains extant though unpublished, in grammar, rhetoric, logic, metaphysics, experimental physics, ethics, natural law, universal history, and geography.[14] His own *Logic*, for example, is referred to in *Kalokinēmata* as the source of his criticism of Voulgaris on ideas; the work is said to be "according to the system of the celebrated Feder, and the renowned . . . Kant."[15] In another acknowledgment to Kant a little later, in connection with his mention of categories, Psalidas says that a more extensive treatment of Kant's new system will be found in what he himself has already written on logic and metaphysics.[16] It was after an energetic period of authorship, then, and with *Kalokinēmata* already in print, that Psalidas returned from Austria to Ioannina in 1795. Within a few months he had begun a teaching career in that town which was to last, alongside other occupations, until 1820.

I shall say something later on about his didactic work and its influence. What obviously requires discussion first, however, is his *True Happiness*, published in Vienna when he was only 24.[17] This book is an extended piece of what may be called "authentic" philosophy, containing more straight argument and less impressionism (and less second-order discussion) than anything I have dealt with so far. True, it is heavily indebted to Kant, but Psalidas says that he is a deliberate mouthpiece of Kant no more than he is of anyone else. The impression he gives is indeed that he is exploiting Kant for his own purposes rather than that he is undertaking a missionary pedagogical campaign on Kant's behalf. The general theme of the book is the relationship between reason and revelation. This is treated in such a way that Psalidas can in effect say "hands off reason!"; and it may not be too fanciful to regard the book as an advance manifesto, serving notice that whatever its author may henceforth profess or teach in the name of "reason" is to be immune from ecclesiastical clamor. At the same time there is something enigmatic about the way in which Psalidas does fence off reason—the sincerity of what he has to say about revelation is not beyond all question, and it could be suggested that the book betrays too much cynicism to secure its ambitious aim. I shall discuss it, with these questions in mind, in the next chapter.

Notes

1. "Kalokinēmata" means, roughly, "Moves towards Progress." The full title of the manifesto is Καλοκινήματα, ἤτοι Ἐγχειρίδιον κατὰ Φθόνου καὶ κατὰ τῆς Λογικῆς τοῦ Εὐγενίου. The sub-title can best be translated "Weapon-in-Hand against Jealousy and against Eugenios's Logic." The original, now excessively rare, was published in Vienna in 1795, anonymously. A reprint, however, has been issued—in an edition of 50 copies—by A. Anghelou at Pestalozzi (Trongen), Switzerland (1951). My page-references are to this edition, a 16mo booklet of 32 pp.

2. *Op. cit.*, p. 11.

3. The reference is to Voulgaris's *Logic*, pp. 157 ff. (I have given a brief account of Voulgaris's doctrine on p. 57 of this book).

4. For quoted words or passages in the preceding discussion, see *Kalokinēmata*, pp. 15–17.

5. P. 57.

6. *Op. cit.*, p. 17.

7. See pp. 95–6.

8. See ch. 6.

9. A translation of the *Georgics* in heroic verse had been published by Voulgaris in St. Petersburg in 1786. See Legrand (XVIII), no. 1172.

10. Quotations in this paragraph are from *Kalokinēmata*, pp. 19–23.

11. *Mémoire sur l'état actuel de la civilisation dans la Grèce* [Paris, 1803], p. 16.

12. Ἀριθμητικὴ (τοῦ Metzburg) πρὸς κοινὴν χρῆσιν τῶν τῆς Ἑλλάδος σχολείων (Vienna, 1791).

13. Αἰκατερίνα ἡ Β΄, ἤτοι ἱστορία σύντομος τῆς ἐν τῇ ὁδοιπορίᾳ Αὐτῆς πρὸς τοὺς ἐν Νίζνῃ καὶ Ταυρίᾳ Γραικοὺς ὑπ'Αὐτῆς δειχθείσης εὐνοίας (Vienna, 1792).

14. For biographical details I am indebted largely to L. I. Vranousēs' Ἀθανάσιος Ψαλίδας ὁ Διδάσκαλος τοῦ Γένους (Ioannina, 1952)—an interesting though occasionally rather fulsome study concerned principally with Psalidas's political role and influence.

15. *Op. cit.*, p. 15.

16. Ibid., p. 18.

17. Ἀληθὴς Εὐδαιμονία ἤτοι Βάσις Πάσης Θρησκείας. Συντεθεῖσα ὑπὸ Ἀθανασίου Πέτρου Ψαλίδα .... εἰς τὴν ἁπλὴν διάλεκτον, καὶ ὑπὸ τοῦ Αὐτοῦ εἰς τὴν Λατινικὴν μεταφρασθεῖσα. Τόμος Α΄ (1791). A selection of passages from this book, in English translation, has been published by Raphael Demos under the title, "True Happiness, or the Basis of all Religion. By Athanasios P. Psalidas," in *Journal of the History of Ideas* 21, no. 4 (1960).

11

Psalidas's *True Happiness*: Philosophy and Revelation

True Happiness is an octavo volume of [48+] 408 pages, made up of the Greek text on the verso and a sometimes inexact Latin translation by Psalidas himself on the recto of each leaf. What we have is volume one only; Psalidas intended to publish two others but never did. Whether the remaining two survive as such in manuscript, I do not know, nor have I been able to find much indication of their contents, which Psalidas promised the reader would be "useful and novel, just like those of the first volume."[1] The subject matter of this one is, from a philosophical point of view, completely negative in its import. It consists in saying what philosophy not only may not decide, but may not even say. (In saying it himself, Psalidas is climbing up a ladder and kicking it away simultaneously.)

Psalidas's starting-point is that there are four truths at the basis of human happiness: the existence of God, the immortality of the soul, the reality of reward and punishment, and human freedom. He gives an intimidating account of what it would be like not to be sure of them (as if this were a much more unusual condition than it is or has been). True happiness, which consists in calm of soul and robustness of body, depends upon conformity with reason and subscription to the divine will, these two conditions meeting, as it were, in obedience to ascertainable natural law; and the settled individual polity which is thus described presupposes knowledge of the four truths mentioned. Can this knowledge, in which we have such a stake, be achieved "through reason without divine revelation"? No. Regarded as the product of reason, it is impossible, therefore. . . .

Psalidas does not consider what might seem to be the alternative conclusion, that what he is talking about is no "knowledge" at all, that the truths concerned do not represent any sort of "possession" and that no further question arises of our taking them seriously except in a pathological context. On the contrary, they are just too real to us to be ignored, he seems to be saying; we have them, and they impose their reality as truths upon us through the very feel of what it is to live, so that *this* is the primary thing—there is no question but that, once philosophy has been shown incapable of producing them, they remain with us. Revelation exerts its own, absolute and prior authority.

The interdiction upon philosophy from trying to determine anything whatever about God, immortality, freedom and the deserts of man is simply the outcome of an extreme, dogmatic empiricism. The "axiom" on which the whole work is founded is thus stated:

> All the ideas we possess we must acquire through the senses, and we could have no idea the object of which was not given to us through the senses, whether the object was simple (supposing that possible) or complex, whether limited or (supposing this possible) unlimited; whatever it was, the idea of it would have to be acquired through the senses, so long as what was presented was to be an idea and likeness of this thing at all.[2]

It does not take much philosophical imagination to make the transition from this "axiom" to Psalidas's conclusions about various traditional arguments for the existence of God. He stresses the truism that our minds are finite, and insists that whatever is represented in the way of idea must be definite in quantity and quality. Hence he allows us no ability to construct any sort of idea of an infinite object. The idea cannot be a direct sensory one; it cannot be abstract, for abstract ideas are strictly nothing but representations of terms standing for particular properties, and as such are derived from "experience . . . the foundation of human knowledge"[3]; and it cannot be innate, for as such too it could only be limited or finite and hence not representative of an infinite being.

In this manner Psalidas rules out the putative ideas of divine perfection and infinity. It is not that we have no "idea of perfection" at all: we do, but it is one which we form by reflection on experience, is relative only, and is insufficient to support any claim to form an idea of God. If we take the alleged contingency of the world, upon which another proof of God's existence is constructed, we are no better provided. What experience shows (so far as it goes) is that this world is a necessary being. (I cannot understand how Psalidas, according to his own principles, can allow himself to say that "the world" is anything at all: even, as it were, speaking provisionally in terms of "experience." He will not allow us to say, for example, that it manifests design. Sometimes he admits talk of the Whole, sometimes not.)

In the end, then, it has to be admitted that reason can provide us with no knowledge of a being existing outside the world of experience. Each of the main traditional arguments for God's existence—the ontological, the argument from contingency and the argument from design, can be shown to be sophistical because of the inconstructible nature of the concepts towards which it works.

At this point Psalidas enters on a long historical excursus, the aim of which is to show how philosophers, from ancient times to modern, have interposed "impossible" concepts between the human spirit and its recognition of God.[4] Their sin is fundamentally the worship of Analogy, whereby "they extract some likeness from that small stock of ideas which they acquire from surrounding objects and stretch it to infinity."[5] Hence they come to think of the world as a machine (constructed presumably without the aid of tools) or else try to describe its creation in other terms, all futile because derived from equally unadaptable models, that is to say, human manufacture regarded in one way or another. (The Spinozistic notion offered as an escape from such difficulties, namely that the world is *causa sui*, Psalidas finds simply unintelligible.)

Psalidas's critique of the remaining basic truths, regarded as philosophical propositions, proceeds in a similar style. That we are possessed of souls which are immortal he argues to be no more intelligible a philosophical proposition than that there exists a transcendent creator. The notion of immortality is bound up with the notion that the power of thought cannot be a property of matter but must be a property of some immaterial substance. Experience, however, furnishes no proof that thinking is irreconcilable with being material. (Psalidas quotes Locke at length on this subject.[6]) In the light of Psalidas's empirical "axiom" we are bound to say that the notion of spirit and its immortality can and does come only through revelation. The ideas of freedom and of recompense, which are bound up with one another, are in the same case. What experience reveals is that there is no action without its efficient cause; and mere *experience* suggests that virtue is very far from being appropriately rewarded, or vice punished. It cannot therefore make good either the idea of free human action or that of a perfectly just dispensation, which is to say, as Psalidas is inclined to do, that no such "ideas" are yielded by reason. It is the failure to accept this general fact that has accounted both for heresy, schism and faction on the one hand, and pantheism, atheism and polytheism on the other—in short that has so bedevilled men's minds that they have receded from rather than approached towards true happiness.

This outline of Psalidas's main arguments may convey the impression that what he has to say is brusque and over-general. As regards some of the topics he discusses (for example, the dangers of analogical argument in general and of extrapolation from specific kinds of experience in particular), such an impression would be unfair; as regards others, not so. Much of his philosophical workmanship is slipshod—he makes too much use of a few rather simple tools which very often cannot do the detailed work he wants.

I shall give one example. He defines "freedom" as "the power of a rational being to act without any external, efficient cause"[7] and on this basis finds it easy to saddle "reason" with the conclusion that no human action is free.

> Let us apply this definition, then, to actual human acts, so that we can see if they are endowed with freedom; let us take one particular example for analysis. It is obvious that when someone wishes to write he must have some representation before him in order so to wish: the wishing is a result of the representation. But that representation is an idea, and the idea, according to the axioms we have laid down, must be a likeness received from external objects. Hence, the external objects are the efficient cause of the writing. If, on the contrary, the person does not wish to write, he must again have a representation before him . . . so that for not writing, too, external objects are required. The individual, therefore, is himself the efficient cause neither of his doing nor of his not doing something, and when he himself is not the efficient cause, he cannot be called free. Our conclusion is that he can have no freedom, as defined.[8]

This argument depends heavily on the empiricist "axiom" which I quoted earlier; in fact over-exploits it grossly. Whatever we wish or choose to do, Psalidas is saying, we have to work on some idea received through the senses. The same holds for not-wishing, or rejecting a choice, and for any alternative wish or choice that may be open to us. But all that this particular application of the empiricist "axiom" has yielded is the admission that external objects are the condition of our being able to think about what we are to prefer or what choice we are to make. Granted that none of the ideas involved is produced out of a hat, the possibility of choosing between the alternatives that they represent is so far unaffected. A determinist needs to say much more than that any or all of the alternative ideas should *occur* to us. In any case they very often don't just occur to us. And the question is what happens once they are there, regardless of how they got there. Psalidas's axiom, here and in similar instances, leaves him well short of the conclusion that he professes to reach. Quite apart from its intrinsic defects, he invariably does not see how much supplementation it needs.

Further discussion of Psalidas's detailed arguments would be out of place here. What does need to be said, however, is how baffling the general result of his restrictions upon reason (urged in a multiply-directed polemic here and a concentrated one in *Kalokinēmata*) turns out to be. The brunt of his argument is that there are four truths—that God exists, that the soul is immortal, that there is reparation after death and that there is free human agency—the acceptance of which is necessary to happiness and to living effectively (which means, at the least, *not* in a state of nature in the Hobbesian sense). The relative "ideas" (of an infinite being, or a spiritual substance, and so on) exist. Psalidas never denies this. In spite of the apparently restrictive wording of his empiricist "axiom," he continues to talk quite happily of "the idea of God," "the idea of reparation," and so on. What he does deny is that "the mind" can either construct or understand such ideas, and *a fortiori*, either discover or demonstrate the truths into which they enter. It is not a question of the mind's constructing them and then being unable to give any coherent, defensible explication of them. Psalidas takes the strong line that it is not possible for it to *form* them. Yet there they are. And they are not innate: it would not be possible, he argues, for the mind to entertain them even innately. The only consequence to be drawn is that they are there by revelation, and that on this basis the appropriate "truths" into which they enter can be accepted.

But, now, what can Psalidas, when he speaks of ideas of revelation, possibly mean by "idea"? The very reasons which go to show that the idea of an infinite being, for example, cannot be formed and cannot be innate, ought surely to hold against revealed ideas also? What Psalidas tries to show by means of his "no derivation of the infinite from the finite" rule is that the "ideas" he is discussing are strictly unintelligible. Then how can they play the part of "ideas" at all? How can they function as constituents of acceptable and hence, in *some* fashion, comprehensible propositions? They ought to be nothing whatever but meaningless noises, in a sense of "meaningless" as strong as any positivist can ever have intended.

Psalidas is really in an impossible position. "The mind can neither acquire nor represent to itself the idea of an infinite being."[9] Yet it does have such an idea, by revelation. Therefore there is something wrong with the proof that it can't. If revelation stands, and if nobody can do better than Psalidas in his assessment of the powers of the mind, then the mind can only reflect upon itself with a repeating scepticism. It is not a question, for revelation, of supplementing the achievements of reason but rather, apparently, of making good what reason shows to be impossible. We are dealing with incompatibles. "Experience cannot possibly show that this world is contingent: on the contrary, indeed, it shows it to be necessary, a conclusion to which only divine revelation could refuse its concurrence."[10] And this is what revelation does: it actually teaches us the contingency of phenomena.[11] In this instance experience (and reason which interprets it) is not even perverse; it is just chronically and utterly, through no fault of its own, at loggerheads with the truth.

At such points Psalidas's philosophy collapses. His theory of knowledge in fact leaves no room for revelation, unless what revelation reveals is quite ineffable, and it is not at all Psalidas's attitude that this is so. In his Prologue, particularly, he not only formulates his four basic "truths" but also develops them with some modicum of logical interconnection, so that the concepts involved might be expected to lay themselves open to explication, and the propositions into which they enter to confirmation or denial, on the part of philosophy. The expectation fails, but not because it is shown unreasonable.

Psalidas's arguments are daring, though, and his attitudes interesting. His philosophical resources are very mixed, suggestions of Descartes, Leibniz, Condillac and Kant (amongst modern philosophers) being the most apparent. But the result is a rather individual piece of work, expressing a not very subtle, yet energetic and positive style of thought.

It is unfortunate that we have available nothing more constructive from Psalidas than what this first volume has to offer. Here he is bent upon emphasizing the restrictive implications of his vague dogma that our minds may traffic only in what has been received from sense. These are, in general, that "should we go beyond nature's limits, then we are to be accounted Enthusiasts, fanciful and foolish men."[12]

But he allows that there is also the contrary vice, that of falling short of these limits, of failing to exercise reason to its full legitimate extent. Should our position be on this side of the mean, then we are just "Sceptics, Prisoners of Caution and, again, foolish men."[13] For all his energy one is tempted to put Psalidas himself, in the absence of his second and third volumes, into this second category.

One may speculate in a general way why it was that Psalidas took such a hard-and-fast attitude to the relationship between reason and revelation. Is it possible to suggest that his commending of revelation and the life lived according to it was insincere? The surrender to revelation takes place so early and is so unqualified, in each of the questions discussed, that one wonders whether the whole piece of writing might not be taken as an ironical comment upon revelation and all its pretensions. How solemnly did he pen the words which conclude his Address to the Reader?

> Since you will see from what I have written in the first volume that these Truths have proceeded from God through revelation, you will be able to make sport of all the enemies of religion, like Rousseau, Voltaire, Helvétius and their fellows, and you will no longer hold them in honor as faultless intellects surpassing the rest of us in comprehension, but will judge them as being simply defective in self-knowledge.

If this and the whole treatment that follows were ironical, however, one would have to admit that the irony was overdone and also that its point would quite certainly be lost on those readers for whom Psalidas was writing in the first instance.

But perhaps—to take speculation just one degree further—its point was meant to be lost? Could Psalidas's ostentatious submission to revelation be intended simply to give him freedom of critical manoeuver in the teaching, for example, of "natural" philosophy, logic and those parts of general philosophy to whose problems religion, if not provoked on the larger issues, might remain insensitive? This is a possibility, but it would presuppose a deliberate calculation on Psalidas's part as to his readers' blindness towards what I have been putting forward as one possible issue of his line of thought—the deprivation of the notion of revelation of all meaningfulness, given the validity of Psalidas's philosophical reasoning in other respects. Why should his readers be granted the insight to follow his arguments but not to see this possibility (always supposing, of course, that Psalidas himself had it in mind)? It may very well be that his work was prophylactic in the way I have just suggested, but as regards the authority of religious revelation it is simplest and most natural to suppose that Psalidas was as submissive as an unsuspicious reader would take him to be.

From a historical point of view one could say, fairly enough, that Psalidas was simply adapting Kant's general results for Greek Orthodox readers. He was jettisoning, after all, that most difficult concept, practical reason; jettisoning it in that he was going straight to its results, the vindication of *God*, *freedom* and *immortality*, without requiring it as a means. It would be a concept very difficult to reinterpret in terms of the crude, sweeping empiricism that Psalidas professed, an unfamiliar notion which, in an Orthodox environment, could only be regarded as otiose if intelligible at all.

To what extent *True Happiness* was written deliberately to secure Psalidas's position against clerical interference is a matter of speculation. If the book was intended as a safeguard, then it was not in the event a very successful one. Part of the reason for this was a chronic scholastic rivalry within the town of Ioannina itself. The Maroutsaian school in Ioannina, to which Psalidas was appointed in 1796, was succeeded shortly afterwards by the Kaplaneian, and these two schools represented the liberal side of Ioannina's educational history. (It was in the Maroutsaian that Voulgaris taught from 1742 to 1750.) Another school, namely the Balanaian, represented the conservative, ecclesiastically-dominated side, and had done so at least since the days of Voulgaris. Its director for the long period from 1760 to 1807 was Kosmas Balanos (Vasilopoulos): his father, the mathematician and cleric Balanos Vasilopoulos, who had fought with Voulgaris, also taught there. (In Vasilopoulos's *System of Arithmetic*, published in 1803, the author is described with no nonsense as "teacher in the principal (πρώτης) school in Ioannina."[14])

Kosmas Balanos duly carried on the fight with Psalidas. In the Balanaian school he refused to introduce any of the new philosophical or scientific thought, even as rendered by Voulgaris; the "simple" language was banned; and, according to one account,[15] even the teaching of modern European languages was discouraged because these were vehicles of atheism. There is evidence of considerable rivalry between the two schools, and of a strengthening of the Kaplaneian, under Psalidas's direction, at the expense of the other. Not all of Psalidas's self-declaration and strenuous argument in *True Happiness* could prevent him now from being accused (by Kosmas Balanos and others) of atheism, Voltairism, and other forms of wickedness.

One of Psalidas's difficulties (but one which was also to some extent his protection) was his peculiar and carefully-maintained relationship with Ali Pasha, the Vizir of Epirus, to whom he stood as confidant and adviser, especially in foreign affairs and transactions with foreign visitors. Another was his teaching, the first to take place in Ioannina or (probably) any other Greek town, of experimental physics and chemistry, truly empirical science the results of which were received by some as magic and Satanism. In general, however, his difficulties simply expressed a tension, natural to a socially and politically oppressed and insecure community, between a certain untried order of things, namely freedom and experiment in and width of thought (the more dangerous when allied with energy and talent) and the anxious retention of older and more religious values, especially when such values have been tried and not found altogether wanting in the cause of nationalism.

The breadth and the ambitious nature of the educational program which Psalidas undertook may be gathered from information provided by Psalidas himself (in a letter) and by one of his pupils.[16] Psalidas describes the curriculum of three classes—lower, intermediate, and higher. The studies undertaken in the lower class were the elements of ancient Greek, arithmetic, catechism, and grammatical analysis. In the intermediate class they were ancient Greek spelling and syntax, comparative study of ancient and modern Greek, universal history, contemporary geography, and Greek archaeology. The higher class, also called the Greek Authors class, studied dialects of ancient Greek, poetics, rhetoric, epistolary style, mathematics, Latin, physics, and philosophy (logic, psychology, ethics and metaphysics). Psalidas's pupil describes an arrangement of higher studies belonging apparently to a class more advanced still. These were (a) the elements of philosophy according to modern European metaphysicians, Locke, Kant and others, (b) the elements of mathematics according to the system of Metzburg,[17] experimental physics following Horváth,[18] mathematical and political geography, and Latin. Some or all of the instruments used in Psalidas's scientific teaching (aerostatic, electrical, pneumatic, and optical equipment) were brought by himself from Vienna, and some of the teaching performed by means of them was done in public so that its nature should be made as plain and unmysterious as possible.

In 1822, which was the year of Ali Pasha's downfall, Psalidas left Epirus for Kerkyra. He spent the last seven years of his life there and in Levkas, to which he went as head of the *lykeion* in 1828. His time in Kerkyra was spent mainly in furthering, so far as he could under a neutral regime, the Greek cause in the war of independence. He acted as a liaison with foreign sympathizers, helped to organize the passage of volunteers to the areas of fighting, and argued and pled with the political leaders Mavrokordatos and Kapodistrias about various objectives—from the early establishment of an elementary-education system in the Peloponnese to the claims of Thessaly and Epirus for inclusion in the eventual Greek state. He had been a corresponding member of the first (French) Ionian Academy.[19] He became an honorary doctor of the second (Guilford's) but never a professor, although so far as knowledge and educational experience were concerned he could most completely have been one.

Unfortunately the philosophical promise shown in *True Happiness* was not further exploited; Psalidas's energies went into teaching and public affairs, and he became more and more a "teacher of the race," a self-consciously patriotic instructor and admonisher, as time went on. *True Happiness* had no sequel, either in Psalidas's own writing or in the comments of critics. It helped to produce the man, but there is no evidence that as a piece of philosophy it has been looked at seriously by any critic from his own day until recent times. At least one contemporary Englishman, it is true, had read it. The Rev. S. S. Wilson, on a visit to Kerkyra, mentioned it in a conversation with Psalidas, but, so far as his account tells us, his interest was in the style rather than the contents. "I remarked to Psalidas, that his work on *True Happiness* was written in a very ancient style, far beyond that of the mass in the present day, and asked him if he would adopt the same elevated style were he publishing it now. 'No, sir'; was his candid reply; 'I was very young when I wrote that work.' "[20]

Notes

1. *True Happiness*, Address to the Reader, *ad fin.* On p. 306 he says that he will be dealing in the second volume with the criteria of what constitutes "divine knowledge."

2. Ibid., p. 62.

3. Ibid., p. 58.

4. He takes special trouble with Spinoza. On pp. 236–49 he introduces his readers to some of Spinoza's main definitions and propositions, and criticizes them.

5. Ibid., p. 296.

6. Ibid., pp. 354–6.

7. Ibid., p. 378.

8. Ibid., p. 380.

9. Ibid., p. 56.

10. Ibid., p. 90.

11. See ibid., p. 12.

12. Ibid., p. 304.

13. Ibid.

14. Ἔκθεσις Ἀκριβεστάτη τῆς Ἀριθμητικῆς (Venice, 1803), p. 1.

15. By Demetrios Athanasiou (a follower of Psalidas), writing in the periodical Ἑρμῆς ὁ Λόγιος (Vienna, 1817) (quoted by Vranousēs, *op. cit.*, p. 43). For biographical information in this section I have drawn not only on Vranousēs but also on the following articles: S. D. Krinos, Ἀθανάσιος Ψαλίδας (Ἑστία VII, 1879), I. O. Kalogerou, Αἱ Θρησκευτικαὶ Πεποιθήσεις τοῦ Ἀθανασίου Ψαλίδα, and E. Sourlas, Ὁ Ἀθανάσιος Ψαλίδας ὡς Παιδαγωγὸς (both in Ἠπειρωτικὴ Ἑστία, 1952).

16. See Sourlas, *op. cit.*, p. 475.

17. The G. I. Metzburg referred to on p. 103.

18. Presumably K. J. Horváth (1732–99), who became Professor of Physics and Mechanics in the University of Budapest in 1777.

19. *Souvenirs de l'Aide-Major Lamare-Picquot* (1807–1814), ed. H. Pernot (Paris, 1918), p. 236.

20. *A Narrative of the Greek Mission* (London, 1839), p. 505.

12

Benjamin Lesvios: The Confrontation of Nature

A less crude philosopher than Psalidas, a well-educated physical scientist, a renowned teacher and enlightener, a cleric, preacher and "atheist"—a combination already not unknown to us in Greek eighteenth-century history—and a revolutionary in politics as well as in education, who took some part in the earliest Greek schemes of government and administration: such was the many-sided Benjamin Lesvios (1762–1824), with whom the map of Greek intellectualism now extends in a new direction. As his name indicates, this man was born in the island of Lesbos; his main work as a teacher was done at the academy of Kydonies (or Ayvalik) on the Asia Minor coast some twenty miles north-east of Mytilene; and although a school at Kydonies, another one (well known) under Athanasios Parios in Chios, and the "Evangelical School" in Smyrna were all in existence before Benjamin began to teach, it was his activity which in modern times first brought the eastern Aegean educationally to life.

There is some puzzle about his name. His family name appears to have been Γεωργαντῆς, but his original Christian name is not known.[1] He dropped it as well as the "Georgantēs" and assumed the "Benjamin" when he became a monk. The name that appears on the title-page of his books is "Benjamin Lesvios" (the surname not preceded by the definite article which, however, is often used in contemporary and later references to him) and this seems to have been at least a common signature of his. The explanation of the Βενιαμὶν Καῤῥέ with which he represented himself on a document in 1824[2] I do not know. "Benjamin" is clearly the safest appellative.

Benjamin's writings are not, like those of Psalidas, a young man's work. This applies certainly to his published books and also probably to the relatively finished drafts of those and of other material which exist in manuscript in various places. His thirst for learning may well be inferred from the long succession of places in which he tried to satisfy it. He left his native village of Plomari,[3] at some stage unknown, to go to the monastery of the Pantokrator on Athos. He was ordained there and sent, at about the age of 20, to Kydonies, where he studied for a year or so in the so-called "School of Oikonomos." Thereafter he pursued studies in Patmos, Chios and, after a brief return to Kydonies in 1790, in Pisa and Paris. He remained in Western Europe for about eight years, studying philosophy, mathematics, physics, chemistry, and astronomy, and was interested enough in the latter to visit London at one stage in order to see Sir William Herschel's telescope.

He was thus about 36 years of age before he returned finally to Kydonies to take up systematic teaching and writing. Within the following fourteen years he had compiled systems of arithmetic, algebra, geometry, physics and chemistry, metaphysics, and ethics; manuscripts of all of these survive.[4] His *Elements of Arithmetic, Elements of Euclid's Geometry* and *Elements of Metaphysics*, based on these versions, were published after he had left Kydonies.[5] The end of his teaching career there came in fact in 1812. His history after that year need not concern us for the moment; I shall return to it after giving an account of the scope and nature of the philosophy and of some of the general scientific ideas on which his teaching at Kydonies was based.

As a philosopher, Benjamin differs from Psalidas in that he is not just a man of one idea which is exploited in narrowly differing terms over and over again; his technique is less confined; also, he allows the subject a much wider scope, regarding it in this respect, as in others, far more from a Lockian than from a Kantian standpoint. Just as little as Psalidas, though, does he let philosophy (in the narrowest sense of the term) be a substitute for empirical science; he is as hopeful of empirical science as is the former, and in many respects his sentiments about it recall the enthusiasms not only of Psalidas but of both Katartzēs and Moisiodax as well. At the same time, he emphasizes the unity of knowledge: empirical science, to be valuable, must be mathematized, and mathematics is, of all disciplines, that which conducts us most surely to philosophy. Addressing the Reader of his

Arithmetic, he says: "Philosophy must be recalled to its native country, and we must not let the charm of letters preoccupy us to the exclusion of all else. The call is to issue from that very discipline which Xenokrates described as *handles of philosophy*; that is, from mathematics, in which the primary study is arithmetic." He goes on:

> Now it is mathematics and only mathematics that have inherited that label; rhetoric, poetics and so on serve only for man's embellishment and are, in a way, superfluous studies. In all of human learning and knowledge it is only mathematics that properly possesses either the depth or the breadth to be termed science (ἐπιστήμη). So it is only mathematics, and not rhetoric, poetics, or anything else that, along with experiment, will bring light into the investigation of nature's mysteries. Remove mathematics from the earth and you will behold man creeping upon the earth, unable to raise himself from its surface or to emerge from the situation into which he was born. Mathematics is so necessary to education that without it education must come to an impasse and, what is of primary consequence, must fail to find any way of penetrating the secrets of nature . . . .[6]

In the above recall to philosophy Benjamin is clearly using the term "philosophy" in a relatively comprehensive sense: what mathematics enables us to handle includes the investigation of nature in its relatively specific aspects; it enables us, in other words, to formulate a "natural philosophy." (Benjamin does not seem to be thinking in Plato's way of mathematics as the forecourt of philosophy.) But there is more to this than just a matter of terminology. "Natural" philosophy is for Benjamin continuous with what would ordinarily be regarded as metaphysics in one of its branches, namely, ontology.[7] When ontology is dealing with the nature of the qualities of matter or with the regularity, orderliness and intelligibility of natural processes, the data on which it is working are (or include) those suggested to us by physical science, and its interpretations of them still constitute, in the last resort, truths about the physical universe—albeit the most general that we can formulate—as distinct from truths about "ideas," discourse, propositions or theories; so that it concerns metaphysical philosophy in this direct manner whether natural philosophy reads nature mathematically or not, and mathematics opens upon metaphysics in an immediate and decisive-looking way. While all this is so, it remains true (as I suggested earlier) that Benjamin does observe a reasonable amount of distinction in principle between questions which should be solved in terms of a specific science and questions which are metaphysical, even if in practice some of the scientific hypotheses which he supports are relatively *a priori*.

His *Physics* (Φυσική) has not been printed, but its scope has been described and various of its more general arguments quoted *in extenso* by Stephanidēs.[8] "Physics," as used by Benjamin, comprehends not only physics in the conventional modern sense but also a certain amount of natural history, cosmography, astronomy and (most importantly, because of the novelty of the subject in a Greek setting) chemistry, for which he proposes the Greek name στοιχειακή ("science of elements") as being preferable, for semantic reasons, to χημική.[9] He was an admirer of Lavoisier, to whose work he refers from time to time. His exposition, however, according to Stephanidēs,[10] is that of a man educated enough in modern experimental science to be able to describe its procedures and results for himself; in other words, he is one who can quote and refer to original researches when necessary—he does not just translate, or compose a handbook on the basis of other handbooks.

Stephanidēs quotes enough of Benjamin's *Physics* to let us form some judgments about the author's scientific standpoint and capacity. Benjamin has a nose for merely verbal explanation, sometimes perhaps sensing verbalism when rather more is involved. For example: "Aristotle says that the prime mover moves all the heavenly bodies, but this does not differ from saying that they all move because we see them doing so."[11] "The notion of affinity (συγγένεια) is one that is altogether without significance; it enables us to say no more than that what has thus come about comes about thus. Oil, for example, will not mix with water, and the chemists say that this comes about because these bodies have no affinity with one another, which is as much as to say that these bodies don't mix because we see that they don't mix."[12] "For me to say that it is by a divine law that bodies tend towards the center of the earth would amount to saying that I don't know why they do so . . .. If we were to use *this* mode of explanation . . . we should leave nothing whatever unexplained."[13] "That bodies have been set in motion by the divine will, and that I don't know what set them in motion, mean just the same thing."[14]

He stresses the principle of maximum economy in scientific explanation. The following passage contains a rather dogmatic (or insufficiently pragmatic) statement of his grounds for doing so:

> The opinion of those who have had recourse to chemistry in order to explain galvanic phenomena is both complex and one-sided. . . . I, however, think that the dissimilarities they emphasize are apparent and not real, that the galvanic current does not differ from the electric at all essentially, and consequently that it was an unjust verdict on Galvani to accuse him of making a mistake in identifying the two. Nature is simple and its laws must be simple, so that it would be superfluous for it, when a certain effect could be accomplished by an existing agency, to create a second. The multiplication of instruments is proof of small knowledge in the artificer. . . . A nerve is quite a different substance from others; in other words, its particles are arranged differently from those of other bodies; consequently the electric current it contains is differently disposed from what it is in those others.[15]

Probably the most idiosyncratic of Benjamin's theories is his hypothesis of the Πανταχηκίνητον (a word of his own signifying a medium movable in all directions). He arrives at it by raising a question against Newton's theory of attraction:

> How is it possible for a body to operate at a distance? I throw a stone upwards, and it comes back down; the force, they say, which is accumulated at the centre of the earth, draws the body downwards. This is prodigious: the force is located in one place and acts in another. The same force, they say, is an inseparable property of bodies; a body is located in one place and its force exerted at another; and here we have a further marvel. This force, they say, has been so constituted as to operate in inverse proportion to the square of the distance. That is, a law has been imposed enjoining that this force is to operate at a place where it is not present, and in such-and-such a way in relation to such-and-such things.

He then affirms:

> The particles of matter do not possess this force at all; bodies (to speak loosely) do not have any active power. It is something else that acts, in the sort of situation we are considering. For the moment, let me just put forward its existence as a hypothesis; I shall enter upon the proof of it subsequently.

The hypothesis is that "there is a cosmic current which moves upwards, downwards and in every lateral direction; that it traverses and issues from matter inexhaustibly, on every side and from every point on spherical surfaces; and that it is proportional to the quantity of matter." It is to be called Πανταχηκίνητον (which I shall translate loosely as "universal motive element"). "The universal motive element comes to the earth from the sun, the planets, their satellites and the fixed stars; and it returns from the earth towards all these bodies."[16]

This hypothesis does at least provide Benjamin with a means of achieving unitary scientific explanations. Thus, he brings within its scope not only bodily motion and gravity, but also magnetism, electricity, light, and close-range attraction (under which he subsumes various chemical changes otherwise grouped as manifestations of chemical "affinity"). Bodies move, he holds, because they are borne along by the universal motive element which issues from them, the direction of motion depending upon confluences of that element from various directions; light and heat are produced by the reaction between the sun's motive element and that of the planets; there are explanations, in terms of the motive element, of centrifugal and centripetal forces; and so on.[17]

In the *Metaphysics* he uses the hypothesis in order to account for sensation and voluntary movement. He raises the question[18] how it is that bodies can work on the senses. Is it by the emission of imperceptible particles? Locke is quoted as a representative of the view that this is how it happens, and Hartley referred to as supporting a "chemical" variant of the same thesis. Benjamin refuses to follow either of them, largely on the ground that they do not provide an answer to the simple question where any replenishment could come from. He himself, however, has taken this question up.

> We ourselves have shown, in the *Physics*, that into and out of every body there flows ceaselessly and in every rectilineal direction, a certain current. . . . It must be a *current* that issues from bodies, because, as we already know, it cannot possibly be particles from them. . . . And since, if a current issued from olfactory objects without flowing into them, they would be qualitiless, that is would remain unperceived, and since this is not so, it follows that the same current must ceaselessly flow into them. This is what I call the universal motive element.[19]
>
> If, then, a current issues from every body, it must clearly do so from our own: so that, given that our soul, by means of the nerves, registers the impact of this current, this is sensation. It is clear, however, that we must

> suppose the nerves to be so fashioned by nature, that the current issuing from them will leave unaffected the disposition of the particles of the motive element issuing from the body that is making a sensory impact on us. But, someone might say, if what arouses *every* sensation in us is one and the same, why do we have five senses, involving the sort of differentiation of sensation that they do? Here is the answer. We have only to grant a difference in disposition of the particles of the motive element issuing from bodies; what comes from one will be arranged in one way, what comes from others will be arranged in other ways. It is precisely this difference that our five sense organs make.[20]

This is why we can say that one and the same thing (the motive element) works on one and the same thing (the soul) to produce one and the same result (sensation), and why we can also say that when the motive element proceeds from illuminated bodies the result is the sensation of light or color, when from resonant bodies, sound, and so on.

As regards our own initiation of bodily movement, Benjamin's account draws on the same factor. He holds that if the soul is not affected by bodies, except by means of the universal motive element, the soul must use the same means to bring about movement of the muscles. "As in magnetism and electricity, where I say that the current involved is one and the same, we see opposite motions taking place, so the extension and contraction of the limbs must be accomplished by the soul by means of one and the same current."[21]

Benjamin concludes this account with a very rationalistic methodological statement. Whatever this motive element he has been postulating may ultimately be, "right reason (ὁ ὀρθὸς λόγος) demands that it should be one thing and not two or many, even if its effects are both different and opposite."[22]

It would be easy to deride this theory but more appropriate to point out its virtues—its insistence on linking explanation in one scientific field with that in another and, partly through this, its laying itself open to empirical falsification (with the advancement of knowledge which the contriving of such falsification brings), the second of these depending, of course, on its making initial sense. Whether the hypothesis of the universal motive element does this is not for discussion here. Benjamin's confidence that it does allows him at least to demonstrate what it would be like to have available a colligating principle of the sort proposed.

The question arises, however, how much of Benjamin's teaching was of that rather lofty, theoretical, abstract kind to which his discussion of this speculative principle belongs. Was it concrete enough ever to suggest procedures which might put his hypothesis empirically and not just conjecturally or in imagination, to the test? That he does on occasion describe experimental procedures in detail is clear enough even from the passages quoted by Stephanidēs.[23] But it is not clear to what extent he was able to carry out actual experiments. Stephanidēs is able to suggest only that he "probably accompanied his teaching with experiments,"[24] and I am in no position to do any more. Lack of scientific instruments and material was certainly an impediment to the spread of scientific knowledge amongst the Greeks of Benjamin's time, and such equipment as existed was probably to be found only here and there. Psalidas, it may be recalled, brought a certain supply with him from Vienna to Ioannina, and Benjamin himself, in a speech made in Dacia in 1818, refers to the fortunate resources possessed, at that time, by the school in Chios. "One small island, Chios, possesses the most excellent scientific teachers, quantities of scientific books and quantities of experimental instruments, and yet a territory like Dacia has nothing, apart from two small geographical globes."[25] He makes no mention, unfortunately, of the school at Kydonies, either as it was in 1818 or in his own time six years previously.

Benjamin's thought is bold, and it is free-ranging. So much must be clear from the various passages quoted already. Let me add to them one or two *obiter dicta* (still from the *Physics*), both to reinforce this impression and to suggest why it was possible for some of his conservative opponents to apply the absurd label "atheist" to him.

> There are two reasons why the system of Copernicus has met and continues to meet with such resistance on the part of ordinary people, the egotism of mankind and the natural difficulty presented by the belief that the earth is in motion. As for the text of Holy Scripture, it is completely irrelevant to this question. When men of small ideas are unable to resist a man of education in terms of natural science, they abandon natural weapons and take up divine ones.[26]

In the same vein, he writes:

> Scripture is something communicated to us; it is not a system of philosophy. Human egotism and incomprehension, and nothing else, are what makes the earth be at rest.[27]

In this connection he warns us against putting philosophical weight on ways of speaking ("the sun has risen," and so on) that have come down to us from a differently circumstanced day and generation. Even professional astronomers, he points out, go on using ordinary language for many purposes. He is sympathetic to the idea of a plurality of worlds.

> There is no idea that suggests the infinite power of God in so lively a fashion as that of the inhabitation of the heavenly bodies: but man, apparently, is prepared to diminish even the glory of God if only he can increase his own.[28]

Notes

1. For various items of biographical information I am indebted to: G. A. Aristeidēs, Βενιαμὶν ὁ Λέσβιος . . . (Athens, 1880); N. D. Soterakēs, Βενιαμὶν ὁ Λέσβιος. Μέρος Α΄. Βιογραφία (Mytilene, 1939); I. Moutzourēs, Ἡ Λέσβος καὶ ἡ Ἑλληνικὴ Ἐπανάστασις (Mytilene, 1955); and Anghelou 3.

2. See Soterakēs, *op. cit.*, pp. 56 and 59.

3. Not the present village of that name, but what is now Megalochori or Kameno Chorio ("Burnt Village") some four miles inland from it.

4. In the library of the *gymnasion* in Mytilene, and there may be other copies elsewhere. According to M. K. Stephanidēs, Αἱ Φυσικαὶ Ἐπιστῆμαι ἐν Ἑλλάδι πρὸ τῆς Ἐπαναστάσεως (Athens, 1926), p. 30, there is (or was) another copy of the *Physics* in the "Benjamin" reading-room in the present-day Plomari. See also note 38.

5. Στοιχεῖα Ἀριθμητικῆς. Παρὰ Βενιαμὶν Λεσβίου. Τόμος Α΄ (Vienna, 1818). Γεωμετρίας Εὐκλείδου Στοιχεῖα . . . (Vienna, 1820). Στοιχεῖα τῆς Μεταφυσικῆς . . . (Vienna, 1820).

6. *Elements of Arithmetic*, p. θ΄.

7. The reason for this reserved way of putting the matter is that although Benjamin in fact brings ontological questions within the scope of "metaphysics," his official definition of this study ought to have prevented him from doing so. His own *Metaphysics* is for the most part epistemology and psychology.

8. *Op. cit.*, pp. 30–49.

9. See ibid., p. 34.

10. Ibid., p. 39.

11. *Physics* (section not given) quoted ibid., p. 41.

12. *Physics*, §591 (quoted ibid., pp. 48–9).

13. *Physics*, §36 (quoted ibid., p. 53).

14. *Physics*, §279 (quoted ibid.).

15. *Physics*, §674 (quoted ibid., pp. 44–5).

16. *Physics*, §36 *et alibi* (quoted ibid., pp. 45–6).

17. For further details, see Stephanidēs, *op. cit.*, pp. 46–7 (to which this paragraph is heavily indebted).

18. In Ch. 2.

19. *Metaphysics*, p. 39.

20. Ibid., p. 41.

21. Ibid., p. 44.

22. Ibid.

23. See, for an example, Stephanidēs, *op. cit.*, p. 37.

24. Ibid., p. 39.

25. The speech is printed by G. A. Aristeidēs, *op. cit.* For passage quoted see p. 53.

26. *Physics*, §193 (quoted by Stephanidēs, pp. 50–1).

27. Ibid., §194 (quoted by Stephanidēs, ibid.).

28. Ibid., §203 (quoted by Stephanidēs, p. 53).

13

Benjamin's *Metaphysics*: Philosophy Come into its Own

In philosophy proper, the same boldness as enlivens his *Physics* is characteristic of Benjamin's thinking. His *Metaphysics* is a compendium of epistemology, psychology, gnoseology, ontology and natural theology; but, whatever topic he is discussing, Benjamin seldom gives an impression of perfunctoriness, and never of speaking by rote. He is indebted to Locke, but not slavishly so, and he quotes or refers to other modern philosophers, such as Descartes, Malebranche, and Condillac, in an independent and critical way. There are certain large questions on which he is quite unsatisfactory. The problem of the relationship of soul and body is *not* satisfied by the account he gives of perception and voluntary movement in terms of the universal motive element, but he behaves as if the problem were merely one of ascertaining and describing some such mechanism. Some of his philosophical workmanship is careless: he comes and goes on the question whether ideas are "general" entities or not, after apparently taking his stand on the argument that they are. He has a fondness for conflation of a startling and confusing kind as when he declares that "idea," "concept," "form," and "phantasm" are synonymous terms.[1] Nevertheless his work is more thorough, subtle, interesting and original than any philosophy written in modern Greek up to his time. On most of the main topics he discusses he has arguments of his own to try out. He neither obscures what he has to say with historical wrappings nor (for the most part) presents it in an unduly didactic or handbookish fashion.

His indulgence in conflation, however, shows itself in the earliest sections of the book. "Metaphysics" appears initially as "the science of the rationale (τῶν λόγων) of each . . . of the sciences and arts"[2] (so that, as he notes, there can be a metaphysics of metaphysics—which turns out to be a knowledge of the soul and of God); it appears next as "the theory of the rationale of ideas, or of the intellectual powers of man."[3] This study of the intellectual powers can also be called ideology (ἰδεαλογία), general grammar, or logic, depending upon how you look at its subject matter.

Ideology studies ideas as such or in themselves (καθ' ἑαυτάς). What Benjamin believes is that this is the all-important first part (indeed, to judge by his own division of the subject, the greater part) of metaphysics, but for him it also leads naturally into ontology, or ideas taken in reference to their objects (ἐπὶ τῶν ὄντων). So that what metaphysics attains in the end is rather more than what either of the initial descriptions might lead us to expect, but this is because a "theory of ideas" both is and is not self-contained. This last point is implied in another way when Benjamin argues that what he calls psychology leads by a continuous movement of thought to what he calls natural theology. "Psychology" he defines as "the theory . . . of sensations, memory, imagination, thought, consciousness, will and self-authorization."[4] But the knowledge, thus ramified, of the nature of the soul involves as its obverse, so to speak, knowledge of the creator of things, which is natural theology. (The transition from the one sort of knowledge to the other is one of the themes of the last two chapters in the book.)

Benjamin's first main topic is sensation, but it is only towards the end of his discussion of this that he reaches any explicit philosophical problem. At the beginning, when he is describing the anatomy and physiology of the central nervous system and the brain, one such general problem is rather conspicuously ignored. After explaining that the "seat" (ἑστία) of both sensory experience and motor activity is the brain, he says, "That which receives sensations and that which moves the limbs are one and the same thing, which I call *soul*; sensation and volition are powers of one and the same entity"[5] (the argument for this being that in various ways these powers involve one another). The classic problem of the interrelationship of soul and body, an embarrassingly obvious one at this point, is bypassed, without promise of further treatment—and in fact there is no further treatment. What we are given instead is Benjamin's account, already described, of the interrelationship of external bodies and the senses (in sensation) and of the nervous system and external bodies (in voluntary movement), in terms of the universal motive element. Apart from some not very striking observations about the elementary and essential part which the senses play as a condition of "knowledge of things," and some fairly lyrical writing about the sense organs as wonders of nature, this remains the principal topic discussed until we reach the following problem:

What are we to say about the arguments of certain metaphysicians to the effect that colors are different for each person, for example, that given the same physical conditions what one person sees as red another sees as green?

It is curious that this piece of speculation is represented by Benjamin as if it were an attempt to argue a matter of fact, namely that the supposed diversity is the case, and not that, for all we know, it may be the case. The only way of showing that the supposed diversity is not the case is to dismiss the logical possibility of it, and it is the logical possibility that nags. We must show it to be objectionable on logical grounds, in other words find some incoherence in it, if we are to meet the sort of metaphysical scepticism that Benjamin has in mind.

Of his own four counter-arguments, three of them would seem to be relevant to this aim and one not. This one is the first. He points out that if the colors sensed were different in the way supposed then one could never prove this, for proof would involve entering into the person of others so closely as actually to sense through their sense organs. This type of consideration, it is true, can be and is employed as part of an argument to establish at least one respect in which we cannot know what goes on in the minds of others.[6] Here, however, it is of no use against the sceptical possibility which Benjamin ought to be attacking. Of course we cannot prove that people see colors in the non-uniform fashion suggested, but this does not rid us of the philosophical worry that they *may* thus see them.

Benjamin's remaining arguments, whatever their value, are in fact relevant to this possibility. The first is general, gnostic, and philosophically unconvincing. Human nature, he claims, is one and the same and not variable (he means in factors as general as those we are considering). If, as is the case, all men sense colors not through their ears, their feet or any organ or part of the body other than their eyes, there is no reason why the result should not be one and the same, i.e., that colors should not be sensed uniformly.

The second argument is more intriguing but also, unfortunately, more definitely unsuccessful. Everyone, he observes, finds green, for example in landscapes, a pleasing color. But the rays that yield this "green" account for the middle band of the spectrum. Those that account for the greatest pleasure, not just to one but to each man, can therefore be definitely located or plotted in this way. But, on the sceptical argument, this should not be possible. According to it, the most pleasing color need not be that which is associated with those median rays at all. However, as we know, it is; so the sceptical argument must fall. (Surely Benjamin's argument begs the question? One form of the question at issue is whether the same color-sensations always correspond to the same rays. If colors *were* rays it would be a different matter.)

The third argument is a less circuitous one than the second. Everybody hates black and tends to avoid it, except for mourning. But if my black were your green and his white, this would not be so. The argument invites the retort that it is what *we call* "black" that we hate (when fashion tells us to) and not necessarily what to anyone else is "black"; but with this move we reach the question whether, if no further differences whatsoever are associated with the one sort of difference that the sceptical argument postulates, the one sort of difference is really comprehensible—a forlorn question, perhaps, and one upon which Benjamin does not actually venture.

What can be admitted is that Benjamin takes (for his time and circumstances) unusual trouble with the problem considered as a mere intellectual challenge, and that he allows himself to be irritated by it with little ulterior motive, except that it gives him one more opportunity to indulge his emphasis on things being "one and the same."[7]

Benjamin makes a sharp distinction between sensation and perception, in that perception, unlike sensation, is an "active" power and involves a degree of recognition or "qualification" of whatever it is that is perceived.[8] The ability to "qualify" things involves "ideas," and such ideas are allowed to recur in memory and imagination. However, unlike Hume, Benjamin holds that certain ideas are independent of a perceptual source; he gives as examples (thinking, it seems, along Platonic lines) those involved in saying that the three angles of a triangle are together equal to two right angles, or that courage is a virtue. It is in this context that he ventures to pronounce "idea," "concept," "form," and "phantasm" to be synonymous terms. What in a perceptual setting we call "ideas" can also be found as "concepts" when it is "intellection" (νοῦς), or the power of the mind to deal in a certain way with things in absence, that we are examining. The same ability to qualify (and what might be termed the same "factors of qualification") must be taken into account in both settings.

At this point Benjamin feels it possible to take one step further in assimilation and to say that "quality, perception and idea are in reality one and the same, differing only relatively,"[9] and he seems to be committed well and truly to idealism. To what extent this is an accurate impression will be seen when we come to his discussion of qualities as such, and of the existence of bodies.

A certain vacillation in his handling of the term "idea," however, must first be pointed out. In introducing the term he says firmly that ideas are "general entities," in contrast to sensations which are individual or specific (ἀτομικά).[10] The assertion is repeated when he comes to discuss what he calls, disconcertingly, "the universalization of ideas."[11] (If ideas are already general, what can their universalization be?) He says, "Every idea is something general and every sensation specific. . . . Now, since nature has created no general entities but only specific things, ideas are the work of man's mind and not of nature, and therefore ideas are not (literally) got through the senses."[12] But a little later he proceeds to speak of "the specific idea of this olive-tree" and he contrasts this with the "general idea that represents the totality of olive-trees."[13] A little later still we find him speaking about the way in which "a specific idea acquires breadth of extension (πλατύνεται)."[14]

The same hesitation characterizes his doctrine of terms. If, he asserts, we examine the words belonging to familiar language and the ideas signified by them, we will see that very few are individual or specific, almost all general. The only individual names we have are for men and places, so that "one wouldn't go wrong if one said that all human ideas are general and none specific."[15] This is a laxer summing-up of what he has just been saying than can well be credited, especially since his final word on the subject is that ideas are classified into "general and particular, or universal and specific," and since he gives as examples of specific ideas "Plato" and "this man."

Benjamin's coming-and-going is hard to follow. One would like to think that he was on the edge of some interesting doctrine concerning a sense in which all our "ideas," even those of Plato and of this particular man, are "general"; but I am afraid that all he has succeeded in saying is that ideas by and large are general, and that the fact that some are general entails that all are constructions of the mind, that none is "given."

Benjamin's apparent idealism is nowhere stronger than in the pronouncements he makes about the qualities of bodies. "My own view is that the qualities of bodies are dispositions of our own souls, and not that they are found within bodies themselves." He proceeds to argue the matter in detail, leading up to the same conclusion expressed in a most provoking and paradoxical way.

> I open my eyes, and I see bodies of different colors. Now one of two things must be true: either these colors are found on the surface of those bodies or they are in my soul, for they could not possibly belong to both. But—what else is the seeing of something but a sensation in my soul? If the rays of the sun striking upon some body, on snow for example, did not by refraction strike upon my optic nerve, I should never see snow as white. So that what we call whiteness lies in me; that is to say, it is a disposition of my soul. It is not, as such, to be located within the snow. In a manner of speaking it is I who am white and not the body lying at a distance from me.[16]

A series of corresponding arguments follows for each of the senses, yielding conclusions of which "fragrance lies within me"[17] is one of the more pleasing instances. The qualities of bodies, he says summarily, are nothing but our sensations. (In the light of the contrast between sensations and ideas this makes nonsense of the conflation of "quality," "perception," and "idea" previously noted.) In calling bodies white, sweet, and so on, we transfer our own "dispositions" to whatever it is that causes us to be affected in these ways. But, he points out, we rather stop short of consistency in doing so. Why not call the rays of the sun hard because they bake mud hard?

It would seem, then, that according to Benjamin bodies are completely qualitiless, and that in this regard he is in a worse position, if possible, than Locke. Why not just give them up and let the external world *be* dispositions of soul?

Benjamin has in fact safeguarded himself against this question, at any rate after a fashion. Although he talks of qualities in the general way that I have been describing, he preserves the status of some of them, as it were, by taking them out of the category of "qualities" and in this way reinstating a version, of a kind, of the primary–secondary distinction. He introduces it, before embarking on the arguments I have just been retailing, in terms of the distinction between general or essential qualities and non-general.[18] This distinction he wants to question, because the general or essential ones—and he gives extension and inertia as instances—belong to all bodies whatever, make no difference in any, and hence are not really happily to be called qualities. Whatever they are to be called, it turns out, they do undoubtedly characterize bodies, thus at least preserving the notion of a physical world which is this rather than that; the admission of other such items (belonging to a class of what we might, for want of a better term, call primary characteristics) enables him in addition to assign some definite character to his universal motive element which, together with bodies, constitutes the external world.

What Benjamin does not do is see the difficulties of such a position as Berkeley saw them. What, if anything, is the difference between extension and sensible extension? How can primary characteristics not be absorbed by the sorts of argument about sensible qualities which Benjamin himself is putting forward?

As to idealism in general, Benjamin does disclaim it, in a chapter which he devotes explicitly to the question of the existence of bodies.[19] He there offers two general kinds of argument. The first is that idealism is self-refuting: if things that threaten my existence are really "phantasms," the soul depends on non-existent things, which is to say that it itself has no being. (This is obviously a hopeless argument.) The second is that my experiences of "resistance" and of interference in my transactions with the so-called physical world can only be interpreted as signifying the existence of "independent" entities; but this still does not involve the real external existence of "qualities." (The argument from resistance has had various exponents from Dr. Johnson upwards. Benjamin's is by no means a crude version of it.)

As regards the whole question of the qualities of matter, Benjamin's position is given most characteristically, I think, in the following passage:

> I have shown with sufficient cogency that there exists a certain current which arouses sensations in us. Since this current is one, uniform thing and its actions on each of the sense organs infinitely various, it follows that the differences in sensations are due to the bodies from which the current issues; that is, we must ascribe to each body a different texture, on account of which the particles of the current issuing from it are differently disposed and the differences in sensation accordingly produced.[20] . . . So that a quality of bodies is indeed something, namely that special texture of their particles by reason of which the particles of the universal motive element issuing from them are disposed precisely as they are.[21]

"Snow is white," then, means, "The texture of the particles of snow is such as to arouse in the spectator the sensation of whiteness." Alternatively, it means something like, "Snow has the same texture as lime, paper, milk, etc."[22] (Benjamin has no qualms about allowing philosophers to decide what it is that one ultimately "means" by what one says.) The problem of universals which is invoked by this last example he does not discuss until later.[23] It is clear enough from what he says then (and as one might expect from indications already given) that he is a conceptualist.

Benjamin's theory of knowledge takes in, as well as the topics I have discussed, self-consciousness, attention, memory, judgment, reasoning and various subsidiary matters. Many of his discussions, here as elsewhere, contain points of view of his own, or at least contrive to put some point in an engaging way, but are composed very largely of general psychological or old-fashioned logical considerations, and do not require further description here.

I pass to his discussion of language, the main features of which are of no special interest, but which happens to contain two points worth noting. The first is that Benjamin here complicates his theory about ideas still further by observing that "in general, every idea is . . . nothing other than a conclusion: or, if you prefer, it is the exposing (ἔκθεσις) of a conclusion of some piece of reasoning or analysis."[24] This is to stress the conceptual aspect of "ideas," on which Benjamin has already insisted in one of his conflations, and the truism that ideas are the work of the mind. It also presumably indicates that ideas are, as it were, the result of our successfully assigning something to a class or kind, so that an idea in a certain manner packs away a judgment. Benjamin's observation marks all of this rather imprecisely; the alternative version he offers us is certainly less misleading than the original.

The other point of interest in the discussion of language is the occurrence of one of Benjamin's more flamboyant assertions: "In my view every human evil comes about because men do not understand the significance of words." He illustrates this dictum by arguing as follows:

> Men living in communities have to make laws, and consequently to appoint someone to execute and administer them. This individual they call a governor. So that a governor is nothing other than an executor and administrator of the laws. And to the extent that this individual carries out his function, of putting the laws into practice, then he *is* a governor. If instead of this, however, he proceeds violently to appropriate people's possessions, he is far removed from being a governor: he is a brigand. In spite of this, men go on thinking of him not as he is but as he is not; if they didn't it would be impossible for him to carry on the process of pillage. The same sort of thing can be said about ecclesiastical authorities, and with regard to every other appellative. A husband, for example, is one who promises happiness to his wife. If, instead of treating her kindly and cherishing her, he beats her, then he is something other than a husband. But he himself, instead of thinking himself something different, goes on thinking himself a husband. The same sort of thing can be said about others: teachers, priests, princes, generals and so forth.[25]

Not knowing how to talk is Benjamin's civilized if inadequate equivalent of original sin.

Benjamin concludes his theory of knowledge with a series of considerations about necessity, possibility and impossibility and their various senses, laws of nature, criteria of truth, and different sorts of "knowledge." As to the nature of truth, to which a special chapter is devoted,[26] he adopts a correspondence account and uses this to give him another argument (a crude one) against idealism. Idealists, he suggests, cannot give a coherent account of truth, because if truth is the conformity of idea to ideatum (i.e., that item, etc., of which it is an idea), and if ideata, on an idealist analysis, are non-existent except when they consist of the thinking subjects themselves, or of God, the only second term of which our ideas can be true at all is God—philosophically an intolerable restriction.

He also uses his correspondence account to carry the notion of "general ideas" one step further. For in regard to such ideas (or universals) the question arises how any conformity between idea and ideatum can possibly be envisaged. The inventory of "real existence" contains no general entities for our ideas to conform to, but only individuals. Benjamin's reply to this difficulty is that general ideas are nevertheless not mere words. They are "attributes or means of recognition of substances or individuals."[27] (Benjamin's subjective theory of qualities may be recalled in this connection.) It must follow that "correspondence," as Benjamin understands it, is far from being a uniformly analysable relationship.

He turns next to a series of topics that belong rather more to moral philosophy than to metaphysics. The first is that of freedom, which Benjamin discusses under the heading of τὸ αὐτεξούσιον (responsibility, literally "self-authorization"). He remarks (not entirely accurately) that European writers lack this concept, and that they have become confused accordingly.[28] The way in which he himself puts it to use, and hence some indication of its meaning for him, can be gleaned from the following passage:

> Whether . . . a person does something voluntary or something compulsory, he does it on his own authorization . . . for it is always up to him, if he wishes, not to do it—except in so far as his very rationality makes it impossible for him not to. The difference between the compulsory and the voluntary consists in nothing but this, that in doing what is voluntary a man prefers the greater good, whereas in doing what is compulsory, he prefers the lesser evil. And since the choice of the lesser evil is an act of will . . . and the will is a power of self-authorization, it is clear that even what is done of necessity is self-authorized.[29] For although force, or an external cause, is present in what is thus done, the actual decision to do it belongs not to this factor but to the soul. In the light of this the problem changes form: instead of "which of two people is to have the money?" it becomes "which is preferable, life or money?" His *freedom* (ἐλευθερία) has been taken from the man concerned; only his power to act authoritatively remains.[30]

All that need be said in comment is that the distinction proposed by Benjamin, even if not as novel as he supposes, is a useful one.

Benjamin goes on to discuss the objects of will and desire, a topic which he treats as coextensive with that of good and evil. In this connection the main problem for metaphysics, he says, has been whether the will is always determined by the greatest good; he quotes at some length Locke's arguments[31] to the effect that it is not. For his own part, he prefers to dismiss the problem as a mare's nest, on the ground that it ignores the relativity of the good and bad involved (though this is fair only against a particularly crude statement of it, which Locke's is not). He is prepared to argue, however, that a man never does evil as such. Here, as elsewhere, one feels that he is wrestling with the problem for himself. Amongst his arguments, for example, are these:

(a) "If someone, in doing what was truly evil, reckoned it as such, what would be the point of his bringing forward reasons to show that what he was doing was not evil? And, to go further, why should he seek to persuade not only other people of the propriety of his doings, but his own conscience as well?" (Certainly there is a less obvious answer to the second question than to the first.)

(b) If a man does the bad as bad, why does repentance follow? That is to say, why does he experience "grief at having done evil when the situation is that, if he himself had previously recognized the things involved as being evil, he wouldn't have done them? It is clear, therefore, that only after the action did he recognize them as evil, and not while he was performing it." (The question-begging remark thrown into this argument leaves it with the force of a mere suggestion.)

(c) People say such things as "Bad though it be, I want to do it." "But this, I assert, is nothing but the tongue's swearing what the heart will not bear witness to; otherwise it wouldn't be the case that everyone wants to avoid evil—which is absurd."[32] (Again, unfortunately, the question is begged: but the setting of the argument might have provided Benjamin with another instance of "the embarras and delusion of words.")

In a discussion of the passions which follows this one, Benjamin suggests that it would be impossible for someone either to prefer what he takes to be good or to set aside what he takes to be evil, if what always moved him in the last resort were mere sensibility and not rational considerations or at any rate calculation. The three "principles" which, according to Benjamin, are at the basis of the passions are the avoidance of what is nasty, curiosity or the desire to learn, and the prospect of betterment of some kind; and these he classes as belonging to the rational element (τὸ λογικόν) in us. It is not that Benjamin would necessarily want to deny that some "passional" element is always at least part of what moves us to action, but he rather grandly puts this question in its place by asserting, in effect, that the passions are as little abstractible from reason or calculation as matter is from form.

After discussing instinct and sympathy, and before he treats of "The Soul," Benjamin inserts a curious chapter[33] on sleep, dreams, nyctalopia, and various kinds of frenzy, mania and dim-wittedness. Its philosophical content is small indeed, but these phenomena are all given a naturalistic (physiological) explanation, and the point of the chapter seems to consist precisely in the demonstration that this is possible.

The last two chapters bring us back to more orthodox metaphysical argument, about the soul and about God. We know the soul, he points out, through its effects, namely, sensations, ideas, thoughts, and desires. That the soul exists, no one can doubt. It is whatever in us senses, thinks and wills (alternatively, is the "cause" of our sensations, thoughts and wishes) and also reflects on itself. The real question is whether it is a body, a property of a body, or immaterial. Benjamin argues, at considerable length, that it is neither a body itself, nor a power or property of a body, but a "self-existent" entity, a substance in its own right. The style of his thinking on these topics can be seen to some extent from the following passages:

> The soul is not a body. For since the idea of body is a synthesis of those of extension, compositeness, inertia, and so on . . . and since the soul is possessed of diametrically opposite properties (that is, is non-composite, not in motion, not inert) it follows that it is essentially different from body . . . it is a self-existent entity, the subject of properties contrary to those of body.[34]
>
> Which of us ever doubts that he understands, judges, thinks, resolves, wishes, controls his own will and moves his own body? Doesn't all this represent the consciousness of activities which, as has been sufficiently shown, do not belong at all to the body? They necessarily, therefore, belong to something else, to which we have given the name "soul." We thus have a clear idea of the soul, just as we have of the body.[35]

Benjamin does take note of Locke's admission[36] that, for all our clear ideas tell us to the contrary, God might have endowed matter with the faculty of thinking. Just for once, Locke's speculations are too strong meat for Benjamin, and he cuts short the discussion by replying that "rational matter" is simply a contradiction in terms. He concludes by arguing that one in particular of the soul's non-bodily properties, namely its being simple or without parts, entails its indestructibility.

His proofs of the existence of God need no special comment. They are versions of the argument from design and the cosmological argument: and while, like much of Benjamin's writing of traditional arguments or points of view, they are put forward with a certain freshness, this quality of Benjamin's mind has been sufficiently illustrated already. The existential arguments lead into a discussion of God's nature, including his wisdom and providence. All that need be remarked in this connection is that Benjamin's pleasure in the argument from design, and in the concept of God associated with it, is connected fairly obviously with the enlarged (but perhaps unduly amiable) view of nature which late eighteenth-century science was providing.

I have described Benjamin's *Metaphysics* at such length because, while conventional enough in many of its lines of argument and conclusions, it is unconventional in others, and is the least doctrinaire philosophical work to have appeared in Greek literature up to the War of Independence—indeed, it might be argued, until well beyond it.

And, as in the case of Voulgaris, so in that of Benjamin, one can only admire the level of aspiration that is represented by the teaching out of which this work grew. The published *Metaphysics* is an extension and elaboration, but not an importantly different version, of what appears in the manuscript "schoolbook" version preserved in the Mytilene *gymnasion*.[37] When one considers that Benjamin was teaching ethics,[38] physics, and the various branches of mathematics up to a comparable standard, it is clear that here again we have a man of great versatility and a very great educator.

Unfortunately, like Psalidas's *True Happiness*, Benjamin's *Metaphysics* failed to establish its own tradition of thought and criticism. The general reasons for this, which I take to be largely the social and political upheavals associated with the war of liberation and Greece's subsequent attempts to make a new beginning in education, I shall discuss in due course. But Benjamin's personal history in its later stages already shows a thinning-out of his educational influence.

In 1812 he left Kydonies in consequence of feuds.[39] His next period of teaching was in Bucharest, where he went in 1818 to reorganize the Greek school on the model of a "European" academy. This spell, however, lasted for less than a year, again because of political and personal difficulties. In 1820 he became head of the Evangelical School in Smyrna, but by this time he was far more involved in secret political activity than in education. He had become a member of the revolutionary "Friendly Society" (Φιλική Ἑταιρία) in Iaşi after leaving Bucharest, and in 1821 he cut loose from educational work altogether. He traveled to the Peloponnese, where he became one of the Peloponnesian senators to the National Assembly, in December, 1821; in 1822 he became a member of the first provisional Governing Body, and in 1823 a member of the committee appointed by the National Assembly to draw up a provisional penal code. He died the following year.

The direct impetus which Benjamin gave to Greek education had ended, to all intents and purposes, in 1812. During the early stages of the war he achieved some importance as a man of affairs, but he did not live long enough to be the champion and exemplar of his educational ideals in free Greece, and he appears to have had no pupils with the capacity and the strength of mind to take his place.

Notes

1. *Metaphysics*, p. 52.
2. Ibid., p. η′.
3. Ibid., p. θ′.
4. Ibid., p. ιβ′.
5. Ibid., p. 13.
6. Cf. A. J. Ayer, *The Concept of a Person* (London, 1963), pp. 64 ff.
7. For the arguments discussed here, see *Metaphysics*, p. 46.
8. P. 49. He modifies this later (ibid., p. 296) to the extent of suggesting that where volition plays a part in deciding what sensations we obtain, the sensations are not utterly and absolutely "passive."
9. Ibid., p. 54.
10. Ibid., p. 52.
11. Ibid., pp. 81 ff.
12. Ibid., pp. 81, 82–3.
13. Ibid., p. 88.
14. Ibid., p. 89.

15. Ibid., p. 94.
16. Ibid., p. 147.
17. Ibid., p. 148.
18. See ibid., p. 144.
19. Ch. 9.
20. This is not the whole story about differences in sensation, according to Benjamin's own account. See pp. 122–3 above.
21. *Metaphysics*, p. 151.
22. Ibid., pp. 153, 154.
23. See Ch. 10 ("On Truth").
24. Ibid., p. 174.
25. Ibid., p. 178.
26. Ch. 10.
27. Ibid., p. 247.
28. Ibid., p. 307.
29. I read αὐτεξούσια here for ἑκούσια (which makes no kind of sense).
30. Ibid., pp. 308–9.
31. *Essay*, II, Ch. 21.
32. Quoted passages from *Metaphysics*, pp. 333–4.
33. Ch. 17.
34. *Metaphysics*, p. 416.
35. Ibid., p. 425.
36. *Essay*, IV, Ch. 3.
37. See Soterakēs, *op. cit.*, p. 46.
38. It is to be hoped that the *Ethics*, of which also there is a manuscript version in the *gymnasion* in Mytilene, will one day be published. This manuscript is a well-written, well-preserved copy. The Vatopedi Manuscript Catalogue records another one (item 778, 6).
39. Described in detail in Anghelou 3.

14

Adamantios Koraēs: The Classics as Humane Studies

The main thinkers whom I have considered so far, namely Voulgaris, Katartzēs, Moisiodax, Psalidas and Benjamin, were in a certain important respect one-sided in their educational outlook. If Greek thought were ever to become fertile again, it must first assimilate; it must first absorb itself in the material and attune itself to the rhythm of other people's thought and processes of discovery. The question was, whose? Voulgaris and the others mentioned agreed that it must be modern European scholars, scientists and philosophers. It must not be "the ancients." They agreed about this, in spite of a sharp difference between Voulgaris and the rest as to the propriety and profit of using an "ancient" version of the Greek language as a medium, and with varying degrees of emphasis on the fact that European culture could be regarded in any case as a refraction of ancient Greek. All of their writing is urgent—it seems to say that there is no prospect, for Greece, of entering the contemporary world if education begins again at its Greek beginning and retraces its slow way therefrom. It ought to begin, instead, with the knowledge, wisdom and scholarship that it finds developed around it, and to be content to think that only later, more or less, will it penetrate to the classic roots of that knowledge.

Hence, these writers, while they made considerable and explicit use of ideas and arguments drawn from many ancient authors, did not teach these authors' doctrines systematically, as continuous bodies of truth which could speak more or less immediately to the modern Greek intellect and supply modern Greeks with *a world* of learning. Consequently they never addressed themselves to the task of editing the Greek classics, of introducing and annotating them for the benefit of their own people; they did not even suggest that this was urgent work which others if not themselves should undertake.

Their outlook was thus one-sided in a clear enough—and, I must add, a non-pejorative—sense. What falls to be described now is that of a man who supplemented it by seeing for himself, and seeing for the first time amongst authentic Greek thinkers since the seventeenth century, the possible relevance to contemporary civilization and culture of a systematic study of ancient philosophy, history and literature. It was Adamantios Koraēs (1748–1833), probably better known to the world at large than any of the persons mentioned so far in this study, who was the first effective neo-classicist amongst modern Greeks, and his contribution to Greek educational thought was accordingly distinctive and powerful. Whether it was correspondingly effective is another matter, which I shall discuss in due course.

It ought first to be stressed that Koraēs supplemented—he did not in any accurate sense "correct"—the single-minded attitude to education which Voulgaris, Katartzēs and others preached and practiced. There was no question of correcting it, for he shared their views about the urgent relevance to Greeks of contemporary European culture, only without the obsession that this alone was relevant. He is continually talking about "the enlightened peoples of Europe"[1] and holding up their philosophical, literary and scientific achievements as a model for admiration and emulation. He urges the need to select teachers from amongst those educated in "enlightened Europe," or at least from amongst those who follow and are guided by such.[2] The battle-cry of education should be Μετακένωσις [meaning, literally, "pouring from one vessel into another"].[3] By what other method can the lack of 350 years of modernizing be supplied? Knowledge must be taken wholesale and ready-made, from those who have had a long time painfully to work it out.

In this connection Koraēs surveys the achievements of a recently founded Greek literary journal, the *Scholarly Hermes*,[4] and finds them largely beside the point so far as Greek reeducation is concerned. The journal, he argues vehemently, must be made instructive, and it should not be used as a forum for juvenile literary efforts by Greeks who really have nothing to impart. What it should print is translations, anthologies of knowledge and reviews. What it has to offer should be exercises in prose, rather than in poetry.

Koraēs wrote this hard-headed advice about the year 1814. It is very reminiscent of Katartzēs' injunctions in *Know Thyself* (1787) about the primacy of the instructive over the literary,[5] but Koraēs does not mention Katartzēs in this connection (he cannot, in any case, have read his views in print), and, it must be allowed, he would probably see more of an overlap between the two categories of writing than Katartzēs appears to do.

So far I have said nothing of Koraēs' supplementation of these points of view, or of his own contribution in detail to Greek letters and education. Before I do so I ought to remark on a certain isolationism of spirit with which Koraēs writes, even when what he has to say is in a tradition, or at any rate very much in accordance with what some of his (relatively notable) predecessors have argued or recommended. His discourses on education and language are lengthy, and, although they contain much that is new or at any rate freshly thought out, they accommodate lines of thought already quite well developed by various Greek educational theorists of the eighteenth century. I have mentioned a certain very strong affinity with Katartzēs, though again I must stress that Katartzēs' writings were not accessible to Koraēs in print. Other affinities might be remarked, with Moisiodax and even Voulgaris. But in the end of the day, apart from the general tribute to the unnamed Voulgaris which he paid in his *Mémoire*, Koraēs gives us little or no indication that there had been a Voulgaris, a Moisiodax, a Katartzēs (or, one might add, a Psalidas) to anticipate some of his own most strongly held doctrines.

Part of the explanation of this may lie in Koraēs' view that his own generation, in spite of its continuing need for "learning," could appropriately entertain higher educational ambitions and demand better standards of instruction than previous ones. He writes vehemently about this, and one senses in him the feeling that any educational principles adumbrated in the context of an earlier generation's educational needs and still, in general, relevant to the Greek situation, ought nevertheless to be written out in their new setting independently of what anyone made of them in the recent past.

Thus, learning must be imported, but not in the way that it has been. It must be distributed through more and narrower channels, as it were. Koraēs writes strongly against the "polymath," the man of varied, all-round learning who is essentially a mere collector or accumulator of knowledge.[6] The ideal of polymathy belongs, properly, he argues, to an earlier generation. The polymath is the social reflection of a need to learn combined with a general lack of means and resources for learning, otherwise, that is, than by consultation of himself and his like. His range and versatility, which are his conventional justification, are of relative and provisional value only. In the nature of the case he will not advance learning: he lacks the kind or degree of single-mindedness that is required. Unfortunately, he is unlikely himself to appreciate this shortcoming. A polymath too readily becomes a know-all.

And it is not just that he fails to advance knowledge and so to secure the end of education in that limited sense. Koraēs frequently couples with the advancement of knowledge the fostering of national prestige, the reputation of a people (ἔθνος) and its pride in itself. New discoveries "increase the range and forward the progress of science; they confer true fame upon the learned, and upon the whole nation in which they take place." But polymaths are constitutionally receivers rather than discoverers. There comes a time when "the nation, finding it intolerable that it should always be the pupil of [more] enlightened nations, will make it a matter of honour to reflect back at these its own discoveries." Men of learning, emulating those of enlightened nations, will then give up "illusory and vain polymathy" and specialize. The lesson is that those who make provision for Greek education must realize how radically its needs have changed, and must act accordingly.

Koraēs takes as an example of a now ludicrous ideal that of the person who, in many Greek communities thirty or more years previously, had been teaching grammar, rhetoric, and Aristotelian philosophy all together. He might have mentioned other, still more extensive, combinations of subjects that were taught conjointly by "one small head," and have given more recent examples (since these were his real ground of complaint) of the same deplorable virtuosity. It is not that the example which he does take is unfair; it is merely rather weak, and tends to illustrate the outdated nature of the material taught, more obviously than its excessive scope. Koraēs' general polemic, however, certainly had its grounds, and was not inept.

At the same time, one is entitled to observe that his "polymath" is so conceived as to be, by definition, not an advancer of knowledge; and that the label of "polymath" is applied to teachers of the past generation with perhaps less than due discrimination. Voulgaris at least would appear to deserve some special mention in this context. He was a "polymath," certainly, in one sense of that term, but he was also an innovator on a wide front and, though an eclectic, quite disposed on occasion to think for himself. It may be suggested that here we have one instance of a just-slightly lofty disregard on Koraēs' part for his predecessors. And another, I suggest, occurs in close proximity. In a speech which Koraēs puts into the mouths of the previous generation of teachers he conveys the far from accurate idea that they *all* wrote in a dead Greek of long ago and *all* left their "mother" as opposed to their "ancestral" tongue for use by hewers of wood and drawers of water. He could have noted at least one exception, namely Moisiodax, who, on precisely this question, had very strong views which put him completely beyond the pale of Koraēs' present criticism.[7]

If Koraēs suffered from spiritual loneliness, then, it was perhaps to some extent self-imposed. For we have not yet come to the end of the principles and beliefs that unite him with the line of radical thinkers who have been described already.

As regards Grammar, for instance, one sometimes gets the impression that Koraēs' twin enemies were Grammar and the clergy, and, while he could afford to criticize the clergy more openly and more pointedly than his predecessors, on the subject of "grammatical" education he is neither more nor less open and pointed than were several other "radicals" of his own or of a previous generation. Be that as it may, Koraēs does concern himself with this topic systematically and at length. The first and greater part of his *Impromptu Reflections*,[8] a collection of prefaces to some of his editions of the Greek classics, is devoted to it, both critically and constructively, in that he examines not only the need for reform in "grammatical" education but also new and more suitable methods of teaching the ancient language, which he never for one moment proposes to replace as the matrix of scholarly education. What Koraēs was contending against was a pernicious dryness and abstractness in the teaching of Greek—dryness, in an endless preoccupation with the ancient language as a set of forms of expression the learning of which was a goal in itself, obstructing the path towards a critical sense of values about what the ancient language might have to say, in terms of living truth; and abstractness, in a complacent lack of regard for what became of this language, in the neglect of comparative studies of Greek, ancient and more modern,[9] and in contempt, implicit or explicit, for the immediately-present "mother" tongue. What he wanted, to put it in crude terms, was to make "Hellenic," or ancient Greek, come alive and be serviceable—in less crude terms, to let it be the medium of "philosophical" education by being allowed continually to suggest *ideas*, expressive of practical as well as of theoretical wisdom.

These aims he states in a measured way in the *Reflections*[10] and elsewhere. On one occasion, speaking through the mouth of the amiable parish priest who figures in his narrative, "Papa Trechas,"[11] he puts them more flamboyantly:

> Not grammarians, please!—unless they are at one and the same time philosophers. Grammar without philosophy breeds not truly wise men but scholastics, that is to say, tyrants in another form, to whose advantage it is that the nation should *not* be very enlightened, so that they can govern it as they will. The reading of Byzantine history has taught me that a great part of the misfortunes of our wretched race are due to the scholasticism which then dominated our spirits.[12]

It is not that Koraēs wanted education to be exclusively classical. I have said enough about his devotion to the Enlightenment and his rapacity for instructional literature in general to show that this is not so. But if either or both of civilization and freedom of thought be its aim, then education must provide for classical studies. As Dimaras observes,[13] Koraēs' own editions of the ancient Greeks, far from representing a retreat from reality, were undertaken as the most opportune possible patriotic educational service. In ancient literature he saw a veritable network of principles from which not just general truths but lessons of considerable practicality could be drawn or inferred in the interests of present-day Greeks. A very good, if obvious, example of such a source-book is Aristotle's *Politics*, which Koraēs himself edited, with a Prolegomenon (called "Political Counsels"),[14] in 1821. The Prolegomenon is a representation, by Koraēs, of political truth in more or less Aristotelian terms, with special reference to the present state of Greece in which it is to be realized.

He begins by observing, prognostically, that the attainment of freedom is a great enough accomplishment, but the preservation of it through harmony a much greater one. In Greece's situation, divided counsel is a more serious enemy than the Turks. (He remarks elsewhere[15] that the "fatal disease" [θανατικὴ νόσος] of the Greeks for many years past has been clerical fear [arising from suspicion and jealousy] of taking education from abroad, but he also complains[16] that Greeks in general are at sixes and sevens in their views as to the nature and the means of obtaining education, and one infers from him that only in such a state of confusion about first principles could such a prejudiced attitude have the influence that it does.) How then is a harmonious freedom to be attained?

In the first place, Koraēs answers, by hard thought about the meanings of four concepts about which politics is fundamentally concerned, namely *happiness*, *virtue* (ἀρετή), *law* and *freedom*. The ideal is that, as exemplified in social life, these should be closely tied together; what ties them together is, for Koraēs as to a large extent for Aristotle, moderation in the pursuit of pleasure, regard for equality, and a spirit of cooperation. Thus, the pleasures on which happiness rests must be moderate, which means to say in effect that they must be mixed with toil and shared in due proportion with other people: or, that happiness depends on justice.

> What is the equal sharing of toils and pleasures but justice itself? And what is justice but a benevolent disposition in the citizen, a disposition to reckon that all his fellow-citizens, being men similar in nature to himself, have the same inclination towards and consequently the same right to the enjoyment in due proportion of all those goods which make for the citizen's happiness?[17]

The consequence of this is that neither community nor individual can be happy without virtue, which is to be defined as "love of and care for the common benefit."[18] "Good order" (εὐνομία) is clearly a function of virtue thus socially regarded; so, at a further remove, is freedom, which must be orderly. Freedom consists in "doing without hindrance not what one wants but what the laws grant (συγχωροῦν)"[19] (a restrictive-looking definition which would not have appealed to J. S. Mill). One's own freedom depends on a constant respect for the freedom of others; social freedom and justice are, to a large extent, overlapping notions.

Finally, as to *law*: to be worth the name, law "must be the enaction of the whole city [i.e., community]."[20] This means, in modern conditions, that there must be a representative system and men of sobriety and wisdom to act as representatives, as law-givers and guardians of the law. It also presupposes a community marked in general by public-spiritedness. Koraēs makes a point here of the dangers to such a community of excessive poverty and excessive riches (especially the latter); but more fundamental than this consideration is the importance of education, a theme which underlies all of his previous emphasis on social equality and public spirit, and which eventually becomes the main deliverance of his Prolegomenon. For he proceeds immediately to apply these Aristotelian lessons to contemporary Greece. In the light of them he argues against kingship and for the exploitation of that one advantage, at least, which the Turks have left their oppressed subjects, namely that these all start off relatively equal. From the very beginnings of their own political life Greeks must be preoccupied with justice, hence with education, on the powerful principle that habitual thinking about and well-formed respect for justice does more to restrain a citizen from ill-doing than fear of the law.

Education, which is important enough at its elementary level—where, Koraēs urges, the "reciprocal method" of instruction (ἀλληλοδιδακτικὴ μέθοδος) should be brought into common use—nevertheless has its nucleus at the more advanced. Essentially, education is "a new way of looking at things, with stress on the rational, a way which rounds off the other ways that we have of looking at things."[21] In this sense it is essentially principled or "philosophical," concerned with the rationale of whatever a man professes to know, or does. But it is education so understood that Greeks have most painfully lacked and, indeed, have been most prejudicially denied by their own spiritual mentors.

It is true that there have been wealthy patrons eager enough "to spread the enlightenment of philosophy amongst their kindred,"[22] but in the Greek situation the duty to educate lies very heavily upon clerics, and these most conspicuously need education themselves in the first place.

> Up till now we have put up with the lack of education of our priests and with the way in which some of their prelates behave, little different from that of the satraps of the barbarian tyrant. Very few of them have concerned themselves with the education of the race . . . . The majority

of them have shown themselves indifferent to education; some have actually displayed a quite unashamed hatred of it. The latter were responsible for the denunciations of philosophy heard a few years ago and for the advice to our young people to keep away from the schools and teaching of enlightened Europe: it was they who recently engaged in a campaign of persecution, at first concealed and afterwards quite open, against *gymnasia*, putting the teachers' very lives in danger.[23]

Koraēs concludes with addresses to the rich and powerful, the poor and weak, the middle class and the young, exhorting each class to serve the nation by cultivating the political virtues as circumstances allow. The young he advises most warmly to occupy themselves with "the science of Politics, this queen amongst the sciences,"[24] and to implant everywhere the hatred of injustice.

This Prolegomenon is a very fair sample of Koraēs' own method of doing and using "philosophy." So far as philosophical ideas are concerned, he is not at all an originative thinker; he is primarily an expositor, but with a lively and valuable sense of the social bearing of what he is expounding. I may cite, as one more example of his method, his discussion of the theme "Right and Wrong are by Convention" (Νόμῳ Καλόν, Νόμῳ Κακόν), part of which has recently been reprinted.[25] The approach here, too, tends to be oblique, and not of independent philosophical interest. The case against conventionalism is presented, for the most part, historically and rhetorically, largely in terms of the dispute between Socrates and the Sophists, with frequent references to Plato's *Republic*, *Laws* and *Gorgias*, and (again) to Aristotle's *Politics*. Shaftesbury, Hobbes and other modern writers are also cited.

Koraēs' systematic publication of the texts of ancient authors began in 1805. How he came to it and the circumstances that made it practicable may now be described briefly.[26] Koraēs was born in 1748 in Smyrna, of a "good" and well-doing family (his father being a merchant of Chiote descent[27]). His family intended Adamantios himself to engage in commerce, and it was not until 1782 that the unwilling son, who had spent the years from 1771 to 1782 in Holland in that pursuit, finally got clear of it. In 1782 he went to Montpelier to study medicine. Even medicine did not fulfil his primary interests, long since developed, in language and languages, literature, and the bearing of other cultures on modern Hellenism. But it did provide him with the opportunity to write a doctoral dissertation on Hippocrates, significantly enough one of the first of the ancient authors whom he edited (in 1800). Koraēs' knowledge of ancient Greek was profound; this much he owed to his own severe, "grammatical" schooling in Smyrna. He left Montpelier for Paris in 1788. From that time onwards he supported himself as a man of letters and in fact did not leave Paris for the rest of his life. It is a paradox that because of this fact he was committed to and involved in the Greek independence movement in a way which would hardly have been possible for someone living within the physical area of the struggle. His enormous output required that degree of detachment which Paris provided.

At the same time, it is safe to say, nothing which Koraēs wrote on his own account was unrelated, in his mind, to the needs of his countrymen, or of no account to them in their progress towards self-realization. To put it positively and more strongly, he applied himself to whatever he published or wrote about because it *mattered* to them. This is obviously true of the appeals, addresses, memoranda and other directly political and nationalist writings which he published between 1798 and 1805 particularly. But it is just as true, for reasons which have been indicated already, of the editions of ancient authors which included, as well as the Hippocratic *De Aere* etc., Theophrastus's *Characters* (1799) and the *Aethiopics* of Heliodorus (1804), before the main series began in 1805. The latter actually consisted of two series, a basic one known as the Greek Library (Ἑλληνικὴ Βιβλιοθήκη) and a secondary, parallel series (the Πάρεργα). Altogether, about twenty volumes of ancient texts, including works of Isocrates, Plutarch, Strabo, Aristotle, Plato, Xenophon, Arrian and Marcus Aurelius were published during the next fifteen years. Most of this material was far from being as directly applicable to the needs of early nineteenth-century Greeks as were the principles of politics according to Aristotle, but Koraēs believed nevertheless in its intellectually liberating effect and its general instructive value (not to mention its importance as showing models and paradigms of linguistic use), and in any case the directness of its applicability was a matter of degree.

Koraēs, for his part, left nothing of its applicability to chance. In a way, the most important features of his editions were the forewords. These take different forms, epistolary, narrative, or (in the main) straightforwardly protreptic, but a single great general theme runs throughout them, namely Koraēs' policy and program for Greek education and language. One long series of these forewords, a particularly notable one, was that named collectively Αὐτοσχέδιοι Στοχασμοί,[28] the *Impromptu Reflections* to which reference has already been made, and from which I have quoted.[29]

The point is that, in all these introductory writings, which occupy hundreds of pages, comment on or discussion of the text that follows either leads into or leads out of what may be called (if it is proper to use the epithet "philosophical" for anything so specific) philosophical considerations respecting Greek education or language, in relation to the Greek polity as Koraēs saw or foresaw it in these early nineteenth-century years. It would be true to say that all of Koraēs' own writing (and that is a very large corpus, of which a very large amount is available in print) was occasional, in the sense that it was called for by some specific project or happening or was called forth by some specific controversy; more concretely, it consists of a multitude of shortish pieces rather than of long, continuous works, but it is not "occasional" in its preoccupations. This is true even of the rather disparagingly-named Ἄτακτα, miscellaneous pieces on lexicographical and other matters which Koraēs proceeded to publish from 1829 onwards; but it is outstandingly true of his earlier publications, and particularly of the introductions I have been describing, where his educational theorizing is both freshest and best developed.

As I have indicated already, part and parcel of Koraēs' ambition for the development of authentic thought, scholarship and discovery amongst the Greeks was his concern that they should also develop their "mother" tongue as their medium for expressing ideas and knowledge of all sorts. In this respect they should *not* be receivers. That you can, as it were, "present" a people with a language, even one as perfect and accomplished in its way as ancient Greek, and even when that language is the ancestor of its own, is an absurd, unrealistic idea.

> Its language is one of the most inalienable of the people's possessions. Every member of the nation shares this possession in a, so-to-speak, democratic equality; and no one can sensibly believe either that he has or that he can procure the right to say to the people, "Thus do I bid you speak, thus write." Anyone who, professing to write in the common language, departs to a certain degree from the common mode of expres-

sion, is seeking to achieve something which not even the harshest tyrant is competent to bring about. The tyrant strips the citizen of his possessions; he may take wife and children from him, he can send him into exile or put him to death; but he cannot change that man's language: this, which is his at home, even accompanies him into exile. Only time has the authority to change the speech of nations. . . .[30]

Such is the thesis with which all else that Koraēs has to say about the language question must be made to come to terms. Its vehemence strikes the reader with surprise, for Koraēs has argued just previously that we must "correct and embellish our common language,"[31] and the question is how such a prescription can be consistent with recognizing that a people's language is inalienable. Is not Koraēs now recommending us to write just as the vulgar speak?

Koraēs himself does not write just as the vulgar speak. His is a scholar's Greek written with a scholar's care for syntax and for word-formation and with the combined fastidiousness and freedom of vocabulary that is (or ought to be) a scholar's mark. Also, he openly claims to be following a "middle road" (μέση ὁδός) in the choice of a written language, and he explains in great detail how, in the selection of words and phrases, one must avoid existing barbarisms as well as superfluous or otherwise misguided appeals to antiquity.[32] What then is his own answer to the question of consistency? He provides it explicitly.

If one departs so far from the common manner of speech as to make what one is saying obscure in sense and utterly odd-sounding, this is a piece of tyranny; but, on the other hand, to speak with the vulgar to an extent that is offensive to any educated person's taste, seems to me like demagoguery. When I say that the whole nation shares its language with democratic equality, I do not mean that it must abandon the formation and fashioning of that language to the ochlocratic fancy of the vulgar.[33]

A mob is a mob, he goes on, and under barbarian occupation especially it becomes stupid and insensitive. It is quite wrong to play up to it or to treat it as a repository of standards of speech. What we have to say is not, "Thus do I bid you speak," but rather, "Thus ought we in seemliness to speak."

Root out of the language the tares of vulgarity; not, however, all at once with the fork, but one after the other, little by little, with the hand; sow Hellenic [i.e., ancient Greek] seeds in it, but these too with the hand,

> and not by the bagful. And you will be surprised how in a short time your words and phrases have passed from books into the mouths of the people. A nation's men of letters are naturally the lawgivers of the language which the nation speaks; but they are (I repeat) lawgivers in democracy. To them belongs the correction of the language, but the language is a possession, a sacred possession, of the whole nation. Hence it must be renewed with piety and in tranquillity. . . .[34]

The upshot of Koraēs' "middle road" was a form of Greek which can best be identified, in more recent terms, as a simple *katharevousa*. It is "purified," and to some extent artificial. Koraēs' writing now looks old-fashioned in such matters as noun-endings, the formation of the passive verb, the employment of participles, and the use of prepositions with the genitive, and his syntax often has a stilted, contrived air. Yet the result is not as unnatural as *katharevousa* often appears in its later manifestations. His Greek remains recognizably what he would have claimed it to be, namely a development out of the language of the people. There is no doubt that by precept and example Koraēs did notable work on and in the Greek language. At the same time it has to be confessed that his subsequent influence on that language has not been altogether a happy one. Until very recent times the "demotic" side of his thinking has been greatly under-emphasized, and all too much attention has been paid to the side represented by the "tares of vulgarity" exhortation, with its encouragement to over-academicism in the writing of the language, and to mandarinism generally.

My account of his linguistic position may suitably be concluded, however, with a piece of down-to-earth sense which can speak for itself:

> From the point of view of Logic . . . no word is in itself good or bad, proper or improper. What makes it seem one or the other is the way in which, the place in which and the occasion on which it is spoken or written. And the fear of using an improper word, when its employment puts backbone into a piece of reasoning and strengthens its impact on those who hear it, is mere vulgar propriety (*vile décence*), as that illustrious exponent of the literary art, Rousseau, calls it.[35]

It is difficult to suggest summarily what was the extent of Koraēs' influence upon Greek educational thought and upon Greek culture generally. All of his productive life was spent in France—according to himself because life under the Turks became spiritually insupportable to him,[36] but more generally because a man of letters could flourish only in some cosmopolitan and civilized centre of affairs such as the homeland could nowhere provide. However, his perpetual exile did not cut him off from his own countrymen in the important sense that it prevented the transmission of his ideas from him to them. On the contrary, Koraēs not only poured out his theories in print but also argued for them in correspondence and contended about them in personal controversies on a large scale. There is no question whatever of his having been out of touch with his countrymen in this respect.

On the other hand, though, his influence was not concentrated in any compact, coherent, effective group; I mean a group which might have had the power, when a Greek state came into being, to realize some at any rate of the policies for which he had striven. It is possible that this kind of loss was the price which Koraēs had to pay for the spiritual richness of life in exile, and if so the cost was heavy. But without the resources which he found in Paris there might well have been less to strive for anyhow, and if *this* is so Koraēs' position in history can be represented by a neat dilemma.

The "tragic" view of Koraēs would be that, for all his great output and for all the correctness and importance of many of his views, he remained a voice crying in the wilderness. He continued the educational radicalism represented by an earlier stream of Greek thought, and he provided another channel through which this might issue and bring life to uncultivated plains. But the radicalism dried up and the new channel remained empty. Greek education after 1829 turned decisively enough to the writings of the ancients, but what it took from them was their romance and not their philosophy. It turned to their language, but with precisely the sort of abject devotion that Koraēs had condemned. The darkest of all the shadows which, from this point of view, lie across Koraēs is the suspicion that his neoclassicism was effective only in preparing the way for archaism and unrealism, and that the stress which he laid on relating both literature and language to life, in other words the main emphasis in all of his work, was the main feature of it to be ignored.

With this "tragic" estimate of Koraēs' influence I agree, at any rate in relation to the two or three generations immediately succeeding his own. That he contributed to the revival of Greek thought, and through this to the movement towards independence, scarcely needs saying. But with the coming of independence his influence was suspended rather abruptly (for reasons which I shall try to assemble later), and it is arguable that only in comparatively recent times has Koraēs begun to come into his own. As a result of the work of Dimaras and others it is probably true that at the present time more attention is being paid to Koraēs' specific linguistic and educational theories than at any period since the 1820's. If so, the "tragic" assessment of him is, as I have hinted, interestingly relative. In any case it is not surprising if his early "Martial Song" and "Martial Trumpet-Call"[37] continued to be heard more clearly in the 1820's and 1830's than the Spinozism of the following passage:

> It moves me to laughter . . . whenever I hear intelligent people praising tyrannicide as a heroic accomplishment. Some time or other you must have chanced to see a dog hit by a stone; you've noticed how angry it is with the lump of rock and how furiously it bites it, as if the stone and not the thrower of the stone were the cause of its hurt. Much the same is true of the victims of tyranny, when they consider their misfortune to be the work of some particular tyrant and fail to look for the real cause of them in their own souls which have been barbarized by ignorance—brutalized, rather—to such an extent that they no longer have the sensitivity to appreciate the just sceptre of equitable rule, but require a despot's iron rod.[38]

Notes

1. Cf. Dimaras 14, p. 37.

2. See Dimaras 4, p. 157.

3. Ibid., p. 162. The theme is developed on pp. 162–6.

4. Ἑρμῆς ὁ Λόγιος: published in Vienna from 1811 to 1821. (Koraēs is writing in 1814.) For details see, e.g., Dimaras 1, p. 203. Its first editor, from 1811 to 1813, was Anthimos Gazēs, of whom an account is given in Ch. 16. Koraēs explicitly includes Gazēs' editorship within the scope of his criticism (see Dimaras 4, p. 164).

5. See pp. 78–9.

6. The account which follows is based on Dimaras 4, pp. 145–9 (from which the quoted passages are taken).

7. Cf. ibid., p. 231, where, in some remarks on the progress of letters in the seventeenth and eighteenth centuries, he again ignores his "radical" predecessors.

8. Αὐτοσχέδιοι Στοχασμοί.

9. Cf. Dimaras 4, pp. 157–8.

10. Cf. ibid., p. 156.

11. Παπᾶ Τρέχας (printed in Dimaras 4).

12. Ibid., p. 200.

13. Ibid., p. 30.

14. Πολιτικαὶ Παραινέσεις. Ed. with abbreviations by Dimaras, 14. The account that follows is based on this edition.

15. Dimaras 4, p. 158.

16. Ibid., p. 157.

17. *Op. cit.*, pp. 42–3.

18. Ibid., p. 43.

19. Ibid., p. 47.

20. Ibid., p. 50.

21. Ibid., p. 67.

22. Ibid., pp. 75–6.

23. Ibid., pp. 69–70.

24. Ibid., p. 83.

25. Papanoutsos 2, pp. 211–33. The whole work was called Διατριβὴ αὐτοσχέδιος περὶ τοῦ περιβόητου δόγματος τῶν Σκεπτικῶν Φιλοσόφων καὶ Σοφιστῶν: «Νόμῳ Καλόν, Νόμῳ Κακόν». It was published pseudonymously in Leipzig in 1819. See also, on the circumstances of this work, Anghelou in Ἔρανος εἰς Ἀδαμάντιον Κοραῆν, Α΄ (Athens, 1956), pp. 185–6.

26. For fuller details see his own *Autobiography* (printed in Dimaras 4, pp. 240–50), as supplemented by Dimaras (ibid., pp. 28–34, and elsewhere). In this section my indebtedness to Dimaras is considerable.

27. Koraēs cherished his connection with Chios. The admirable Koraēs Library in Chios to which he persuaded the learned in various parts of Europe to contribute their works and to which he himself left some 3,500 volumes and many manuscripts, is sufficient evidence of this fact.

28. Collected and published separately in 1815 and 1833 (Dimaras 1, Suppl., p. 55).

29. See pp. 143–7.

30. Dimaras 4, p. 124.

31. As he admits, ibid., p. 125.

32. See, e.g., ibid., p. 214 (for the phrase) and pp. 215 ff. for details. Cf. pp. 118–24.

33. Ibid., p. 125.

34. Ibid.

35. Ibid., p. 222.

36. Cf. ibid., p. 242.

37. Ἆσμα Πολεμιστήριον (1800). Σάλπισμα Πολεμιστήριον (1801). Dimaras 4, pp. 88–91, 92–9.

38. Ibid., p. 200.

15

"Nomarchy": A Harsher Call to Reform

Koraēs once expressed himself sadly, through the mouth of his *Papa Trechas*, on the lack of insight amongst his countrymen into the real meaning of what they were about. "We are all calling for the resurrection (ἀνάστασιν) of Greece and talking about it in grand terms, but if we are asked what the word signifies and by what means the resurrection can be brought about, very few of us as yet have any idea."[1] Thus Koraēs in 1818, and of course the mood was natural. But at least part of what a "resurrection" implied was freedom, and it was not that "philosophies" of freedom had been missing in contemporary writing. On the contrary, Koraēs himself had explored that notion persistently, and he devoted virtually all of his protreptic writing to the means, namely education, by which freedom could be brought about. One of his ideas (which I have already quoted[2]) was that *freedom* and *law* cannot be understood apart from one another. This same theme had already, and not so long previously, been raised and supported in another context, vigorously and with a more polemical tone than Koraēs' own. Of course the mere existence of such discussions in print does not invalidate Koraēs' complaint, but it does at least show that the "very few" were not dumb.

The context mentioned was a longish tract of 266 pages called *Greek Nomarchy* (Ἑλληνικὴ Νομαρχία). The word νομαρχία in the sense of "rule of law" neither is nor was a common term and is best kept here in transliteration. The title-page of the original edition gives the book as being published simply "in Italy," in 1806, and the author simply as "an anonymous Greek."[3] It explains that the object of the work is to compare nomarchic with other kinds of government, to examine the nature of freedom, to show that nomarchy is the only safeguard of freedom, and to apply the principles so established to the contemporary condition of Greece.

There has been much speculation about the identity of the writer of this piece and about the exact place of publication,[4] but none of it has established anything definite enough to be worth recapitulating here. In its radical liberalism and the explicitness with which its political point of view is applied, as also in its anticlericalism, more direct and pointed than Koraēs', the tract is unlike any of the other regenerative Greek writings which I have described up to now. In sentiment and in the general bearing of its ideas it is closest to Koraēs, but it is harsher in expression and less urbane.

The tract proceeds by speaking as if there has been a historical transition amongst mankind from a state of nature through various unsuccessful forms of interreliance to some approximation to nomarchy. But the "historical" language employed is vague and is purposely non-commital as to times and places, so that the author can fairly be taken as indicating (like Plato in *Republic* VIII) a series of "natural" rather than necessarily actual transformations. In the original condition of mankind, he says, happiness became impossible, because men found themselves not independent of one another in their desires and their needs, and had to learn through bitter experience how to make provision for their wants by summoning one another's aid. Their experience can be typified. The transition from a state of nature, in which the will of each prevails, no person depends on another, and each seeks only his individual, immediate happiness, is through Anarchy (represented as, so to speak, the first failure in political organization), Monarchy and Tyranny (the ruler become slave to his own depravity—another echo of Plato) to Nomarchy. Nomarchy comes about inasmuch as men finally learn their lesson from the sheer unendurability of Tyranny. According to circumstances, Nomarchy can be realized in both Democracy and Aristocracy—if the spirit of law prevails it does not matter much, according to the writer, which of these systems a man lives under; but, for what it is worth, he observes that Democracy inclines (in its mode of corruption) towards Anarchy, and Aristocracy towards Oligarchy, which can be even worse than Tyranny. (He leaves it uncertain, however, which kind of corruption he finds the more deplorable.)

The four main states can be differentiated thus: in Anarchy freedom belongs to the strongest alone, in Monarchy to one, in Tyranny to none and in Nomarchy to all. In obeying the laws each is virtually obeying his own will and is free. Freedom *is* the rule of law, and is not the same as riotousness or indiscipline. In Nomarchy we must expect not absolute equality, but rather a coming-to-terms with various general kinds of human inequality, i.e., in natural endowment, in upbringing and in matters of fortune. Nomarchy, without making everyone equal in strength, education, riches and so on, moderates natural inequality and balances other kinds with a certain complete equality realized through justice, mutual respect and a general high-mindedness that sees a man's wealth, for example, as issuing from a plain coffer, not from a fount of honor. (The concept of *law*, which is exploited here without analysis, is a moral rather than a juristic concept—like Plato's "justice," which it often enough recalls—and it supplies a sort of Pandora's-box of all the virtues.)

The primary symptom of decay in a Nomarchy is the corruption of morals. The securing of private interests begins to preoccupy people, fear and mutual distrust arise, and those in authority become, in the bad sense of the term, oligarchs. Oligarchy itself, under those identical strains, gives place to Monarchy or Tyranny (which the author, at this stage in his argument, prefers to treat as one and the same thing). Some tyrannies, he goes on, are compounds of theocracy and oligarchy. (Again the author's imprecision of terminology and his tendency to conflate originally distinct concepts are confusing, but his meaning is roughly as follows.) It is not unusual to find states of affairs in which tyranny is exercised by "a lifeless inert statue,"[5] i.e., some stupid, insensitive brute of a man, working through a vice-tyrant with a group of ignorant, idle and socially parasitic followers (the so-called "nobility"), who provide in effect an oligarchic base for his rule. The theocratic element is provided by the clergy, who seal off and secure the tyrant and his retinue with popular ignorance and superstition: suppressing with the authority of their institutionalized religion any tendency on the part of the people to think for themselves. "Instead of calling the impossible false, they call it holy."[6] How can a people that they keep so abject develop a critical sense or bestir itself against the tyrant, monstrous and incredible though he may be?

The corruption of morals, a corruption from within, may result in the enslavement of a free community (like Rome, which has fallen under an unprecedented theocratic tyranny); for a community so enslaved it is difficult to regain its freedom by its own efforts. The author says rather hopefully and dogmatically that this is not so when it loses its freedom to assault from without, because then its moral qualities, and particularly its devotion to freedom, remain to be reckoned with. He makes it quite clear that he regards this as being true of Greece, i.e., as holding for the Greeks of his own day; but what he goes on to say represents a substantial blurring of the distinction which he has made between the corruption and the overwhelming of a people. It may be true that in the case of Greece freedom has been "perpetually at war with tyranny";[7] but while Greece was simply dominated, in a physical sense, by the Romans, the reasons why she did not recuperate so as to resist the Ottomans lay, in terms of the author's own account, in Byzantine tyranny, superstition and ignorance—surely, one may remark, a state of corruption if these terms are seriously applicable.

And the author is in no doubt that they are. He denounces the Byzantine empire and church with a severity achieved by probably no Greek writer before him. Byzantium, a triptych of tyrant, clergy and nobility, is the clear and obvious example of the "compound" type of tyranny that he has previously described in general terms. The decline of the Greek intellect and of the Greek spirit over eleven centuries are, he says roundly, to be blamed upon the common action of those three authorities, not least upon the corrupting work of the priesthood.

> Since, as I am saying, the clergy wanted to run together ecclesiastical decrees and political laws, so as to be reverenced in the very exercise of authority, it had no trouble in understanding that first it had to blind the people with ignorance. . . . So it tried to stifle every kind of study by Greeks and to act as ignorance's protector. The sciences which formerly flourished began to wither, schools were closed, teachers turned into morons, and truth with philosophy went into exile. No book was to be found but the works of priests. The student of literature could read nothing but the lives and miraculous works of the saints. Although they were lovers of freedom, the wretched Greeks, deprived of the light of philosophy, became virtually slaves by habit, and being stupefied by ignorance and superstition obeyed and dreaded their tyrants without knowing any sort of reason why they should do so.[8]

The author writes as if Greece's plight under the Ottomans was, essentially, very little different from its plight under the Empire. In the later phase he discerns the same combination of forces as in the former. Only the identity of the tyrant differs. The same demoralizing priesthood and the same complacent hangers-on and agents of government support him.

For the writer of *Greek Nomarchy* as for Koraēs the fact that Greece is subject to a foreign tyrant is, in a curious way, incidental to the situation. What is not incidental is the passivity of mind and spirit amongst the Greeks. What has to be attacked, directly, is not a military power, but inertia in thought, empty political ideas, superstition, and the sufferance of caste, hieratic or archontic. Greeks must not just contrive to expel the tyrant: they must be worthy to expel the tyrant. Liberation must be regeneration. Of the two authors, Koraēs writes on this theme the more broadly and philosophically and with the deeper insight, but the preoccupation of *Greek Nomarchy*, like his own, is with the Greek people's understanding of themselves and the creation of an *enlightened* resolution amongst them, rather than with the horror and frightfulness of the tyrant's rule and the sounding of a call to arms on that basis.

The writer's denunciation of the priesthood extends into circumstances and details that need not be entered upon here. Some of them are impressive, some trifling; and the style becomes more rhetorical and the tone rougher as he goes on. Whereas priests in their dealings with the people should instruct them in truth, virtue, freedom, concord, and all the means of human happiness, and should castigate tyranny, they teach none of these things and offer the people nothing but an opiate against tyranny.[9] "Give over just once your monotonous refrains. Don't always and in every circumstance tell us the same thing, to fast and give alms!"[10] He has a kinder word for those clerics who are teachers in schools, for whose virtue and wisdom he has some respect. But they are to listen to "the counsels of the young Hippocrates, that virtuous Greek philosopher, Mr. Koraēs in Paris"[11] for guidance in their task of extirpating superstition and ignorance; and they are to put no personal advantage in the way of the common good.

The writer does not have so much to say in detail about that other support of tyranny, namely a drone-like nobility, which he has described earlier in general terms. He does refer to "the wealthy ignoramuses of the Phanar,"[12] and he denounces the drag upon progress represented by "the unsavory rulers (βρομοάρχοντες) of Constantinople,"[13] meaning by this expression Greeks, not Turks. In the conditions of the time it would be hard, if not impossible, to find amongst Turkish-ruled Greeks any representatives apart from the Phanariots of a noble class which could play the part assigned to it in the author's scheme of tyranny–oligarchy. But the fact that this class was rather localized and rather small does not, from his point of view, diminish its perniciousness and its ability to fit his bill.

There are others, though, who on an extreme and unconventional interpretation of their activities might just come into this category: the writer seems half-tempted to put them there. These are Greeks living abroad, conventionally regarded as benefactors of the race, but who, although they are not within the Turkish empire, can nevertheless align themselves with some who are, in that, consciously or not, they are postponing the day of reckoning. For, the author argues, the absence from the country of its ablest nationals is itself, by now, a cause of injury to Greece. He contends that they have now done enough rekindling abroad of the fires of Greek learning; the time has come to return to their country and make their talents immediately available to it. Their motives for remaining abroad are either bad or (by now) mistaken, for their benefactions towards the homeland simply serve to keep at bay that near-despair which, it is to be feared, Greeks must experience before they take the road towards freedom—the sort of intensification of misery, one might remark, to which Marx would have given his theoretic approval. The parallel with what the author was saying about the placebos of the clergy is pretty clear. Exiles should return, then, and their young people in foreign academies should study politics, law and military tactics, which are of use to their own country, instead of medicine or literature. This represents a very curious prohibition indeed, in the light of the author's attachment to Koraēs, and one might wonder how that conspicuous exile contrived, as it seems he did, to escape from all censure in the present connection.

The author next casts a disapproving eye on marriages of Greeks with foreigners: there is a sort of logic in some of the things he says (such as that many a woman would marry a Greek for his money and at the same time despise him for remaining an exile), but generally the discussion is a silly one, xenophobic and occasionally even fascist in sentiment.[14] The author is on perhaps safer ground when he remarks that the return of educated Greeks would serve to keep the paralogisms of the archbishops in check. And he says wisely (in view of the lack of direction and the political uncertainties which marred the subsequent struggle for independence) that if they do not return, but leave those who are in Greek lands to free themselves, "greater rivers of blood will be shed"[15] than if they are present. One illusion in particular cannot be held, that any real liberation is to be looked for from foreign powers.

Towards the end of the tract, in addressing himself to the question whether the liberation of Greece is possible, the author takes comfort from (amongst other things) the educational progress made by Greece during the preceding ten years. He now writes more benignly. He remarks (surely with exaggeration) that there is no town (πόλις) which does not now have two or three schools. Superstitious reverence for "grammatical" education and learning by rote have begun to be supplanted by the acquiring of useful knowledge. Logic and Physics have opened people's eyes. Teachers use improved methods and pupils both attend well and study seriously. He pleads in this connection that "the simple mode of speech"[16] and not Hellenic should be the medium of instruction. Hellenic should be a separate study on its own account. He echoes not-so-ancient controversies when he says that pupils, after reading Xenophon, Plutarch and other classical "philosophers," are no longer afraid to pronounce the name of Liberty, afraid "lest governor or prelate hear them and proclaim them atheists, as once they did."[17]

The author of *Greek Nomarchy* is, in an obvious sense of the term, a rationalist. The emblem of his book, prominently printed at the outset, was Στοχάσου καὶ ἀρκεῖ ("Think, and it will be sufficient unto you"). It has been held against him[18] that this very rationalism was productive of historical unfairness in his account of the part played by the Church during the Turkish occupation. The Church's admittedly elementary and rigid educational standards, *and* her inculcation of the faith through marvel, tradition, and so on, did (it is argued) what rationalism could not have done, and held the foundations of Hellenism together. This sounds an interesting argument, but it does not amount to very much. If the Church and "rationalism" had been competitors for the heart and mind of Greeks, given the low level of existence and subsistence of that people during the seventeenth and eighteenth centuries, then there is no question but that the Church would have won. Part of the argument of *Greek Nomarchy*, however (as it certainly is part of Koraēs'), is that such competition, if it ever was inevitable, had become far from inevitable by the beginning of the nineteenth century; and that the perpetuation of the narrow, "safe" standards in education which the Church generally supported had become, in fact, deplorable.

It can be admitted that the author fails, unaccountably, to name the many individual clerics past and present, Voulgaris, Anthrakitēs, Benjamin and others, who could have been excepted from his general thesis about the inertia of the priesthood. But, as I have already indicated, he does exempt from his general censure those clerics who, at the time of his writing, were concerned with education; and if he had specified individual teachers like those mentioned, he could also have told a long story about the ecclesiastical impediments and persecutions to which more than one of them was subjected.[19]

As to the Greeks abroad, the author has been accused[20] of ignoring the fact that Greek culture reassembled itself, so to speak, in the Greek communities abroad, and that these communities were in some ways pilot schemes for the future Greek state. This accusation, like the previous one, is justified only to the extent that the author of *Greek Nomarchy* projects too undiscriminatingly over the past complaints that are more or less valid for the present. The author in fact concedes that up to now Greek communities abroad have properly justified themselves by bringing about a renaissance of Greek thought, but (as I have mentioned already) he holds that this task is now, for them, of diminishing importance. However, it is fair to complain[21] that there are other functions of these communities which the author ignores or fails to anticipate, notably their provision of money, men, and moral assistance during the War of Independence and their encouragement, then as previously, of philhellenism and European philanthropy. The importance of these for a revolutionary Greece he certainly did underestimate.

The antiecclesiasticism of *Greek Nomarchy* may be compared with that of another anonymous revolutionary publication, issued in 1819, called *Reflections of Crito*.[22] This is a much shorter work, being a pamphlet of some 16 pages, and it concerns itself specially with conditions in Thrace, and to some extent Constantinople. But, like *Greek Nomarchy*, it descends to the particular from a rather elevated, theoretic beginning, shares some of its themes, and very obviously belongs to the same liberal, free-thinking school. There is no firm evidence as to the author's identity. His concern for and knowledge about Adrianople and its inhabitants is held[23] to rule out Koraēs, who in other respects could conceivably be the author.

The introductory theme of the *Reflections* is the decline in true learning, in both intellectual and moral wisdom, seen as causing the destruction of individuals and nations alike. Coupled with it is the cessation of "the sacred authority of law."[24] Wisdom and respect for law are easier to lose than to regain. When they are absent, so is patriotism or "zeal for the common interest."[25] We must create and call upon a high-minded spirit of freedom (ἠθικὴ ἐλευθερία), a "peaceful improvement" which alone is capable of contending with and overcoming tyranny.[26] In this connection a particular responsibility belongs to the Patriarch, to bishops, to presidents and to other representatives of communities. The pamphlet then attacks the Bishop of Adrianople and others for their failure to assume such responsibilities, for showing zeal only for such schemes as the completion of an episcopal palace when it is schools and their teachers to which energy and money should be directed. When priestly rule prevails, says the author, it slows, restricts, or even prevents altogether the advancement of happiness such as comes from education at the hands of modest-living, humane teachers. Where (as in Chios) the priesthood is confined to its proper, churchly functions, we find justice and philanthropy—school, library, printing press, hospitals and courts of law. "The bishop, instead of drawing the social spirit along, is drawn by it."[27]

There is no need to enter upon further details. Enough has been said to show the affinity of the *Reflections* with *Greek Nomarchy* and with Koraēs' protreptic writing. The point of describing these works at such length as has been attempted, and of comparing them, is to show that they represent an interestingly self-conscious style of writing which we do not meet in modern Greek didactic literature before the beginning of the nineteenth century. Koraēs and the writers of the two tracts described all begin with general principles (stated simply as more or less self-evident truths or as truths invested with the authority of some classic writer), and having displayed their connections with one another and having explained to some extent (usually rather sketchily) the significance of the principal notions which they contain, the writers then proceed to apply them to the present state of Greek society. This is where they are self-conscious, or at any rate explicit, by comparison with other writers on and on behalf of education whom I have mentioned. They see exactly where and how their principles need to be worked out, they say this in detail, often mentioning names and having no hesitation in telling people, collectively or individually, where their duty lies. Moisiodax, Katartzēs, Benjamin and others whom I have mentioned previously contended vigorously for new studies, new methods, the recognition of new sources of influence or a certain style of literary expression; and in so doing they raised up opposition enough. But the precise national bearing of what they were doing or recommending they made less explicit than did Koraēs, for example. They tended to remain on the level of principle, certainly to apply their principles less pointedly and personally than he did. In this respect they were not controversialists, as were each of the three writers just described. Nor did they "preach" as each of these did. Hence we must recognize in the writers just examined a more impatient concern for educational and for political principles than has been evident before, a concern to bring about the more-or-less immediate application of those principles to Greek society, the feeling being obvious in the writing of all three that time is no longer on the side of those who would qualify Greece for her destiny.

Notes

1. Dimaras 4, p. 205.
2. P. 148.
3. A second edition, edited by N. B. Tomadakēs, was published in Athens in 1948.
4. For a summary and discussion see Tomadakēs, *op. cit.*, pp. η′—ιγ′.
5. *Op. cit.*, 2nd ed., p. 74.
6. Ibid., p. 75.
7. Ibid., p. 78.
8. Ibid., pp. 83–4.

9. The phrase is not the author's, but the sentiment is.

10. *Op. cit.*, pp. 142–3.

11. Ibid., p. 148.

12. Ibid., p. 129.

13. Ibid., p. 172.

14. Cf. the following: "Don't you know that the marriage which makes a man completely happy is one which has no aim but to produce so many citizens and rulers (διαυθεντευτάς) for the Mother Country?" (Ibid., p. 159.)

15. Ibid., p. 165.

16. Ibid., p. 176 n.

17. Ibid., p. 178.

18. By N. B. Tomadakēs in *op. cit.*, pp. ιδ'—ιστ'.

19. For further discussion of this and related themes, such as that of the venality of the higher clergy, see Theodore H. Papadopoullos, *Studies and Documents relating to the History of the Greek Church and People under Turkish Domination* (Brussels, 1952), pp. 131–58. Papadopoullos quotes at length from *Greek Nomarchy* and takes the author's charges against the higher clergy as being fairly serious evidence.

20. Also by Tomadakēs, in *op. cit.*, p. ιστ'.

21. As Tomadakēs does, *loc. cit.*

22. Στοχασμοὶ τοῦ Κρίτωνος. Republished with introduction and notes by D. Ginēs in Ἔρανος εἰς Ἀδαμάντιον Κοραῆν, Α' (Athens, 1956), pp. 140–56.

23. See Ginēs, *op. cit.*, p. 142.

24. *Op. cit.*, p. 147.

25. Ibid.

26. Ibid., p. 148.

27. Ibid., p. 149.

16

Philippidēs, Konstantas, Gazēs: The School of Melies

Possibly the most symbolic of Greece's educational institutions in the early nineteenth century was the school of Melies in Thessaly; most symbolic, that is, of a time when educational ambition and political nationalism were pressing on together more and more closely. Melies is a small village situated at a height of 360 meters on Mt. Pelion. In the comparative security of this place educational ideas and ideals germinated, and some of them, in interesting ways, contrived to develop. A certain Anthimos Papapandazēs, a monk, had taught there and collected books there from the 1770's, or earlier, until his death in 1811. One of his pupils was Gregorios Konstantas (1758–1844), who published geographical and philosophical work, and himself returned, in 1812, to Melies, where he taught for two long periods of years. Associated with Konstantas in his geographical writing, and himself a native of Melies, was Daniel Philippidēs (1755–1832)—Philippidēs, too, was a philosophical author and he interested himself in Konstantas's educational work in Melies, although, apparently, he did not teach there personally. The third of the principal figures associated with the place was Anthimos Gazēs (1758 or 1764–1828). He published work on geography, physics and ancient Greek. He was not himself born in Melies, but he may[1] have received his elementary education there, and in any case he collaborated with Konstantas in a plan for establishing, in Melies, what they themselves called "a regular school."[2] The plan was put in train in 1814.

Their program was that Konstantas would do the teaching and would supervise the building of the school. Gazēs was to provide money and books to let the work begin, but, more importantly, he was to undertake the collection of further sums, to pay for building, books and teaching equipment, from his fellow countrymen in Vienna, where he himself had lived for many years. In the event, Gazēs seems to have done little or nothing to carry out his part of the agreement: he came to Melies himself in 1817, but by that time he was preoccupied with the affairs of the "Friendly Society" and seems to have seen Melies rather as a center for its political activity than as the nucleus of an educational revival. At any rate the whole labor and expense of founding the school fell on Konstantas, though it is fair to add that at some stage, or perhaps over a period, a large collection of books provided by Gazēs was added to the school's library.

How large the school actually became I do not know. Konstantas continued to teach in Melies until the outbreak of the War of Independence (1821), and he returned eventually in 1834, to work there until his death ten years later. But by this second phase free Greece had been constituted, and Melies was still in unredeemed territory—Thessaly did not become Greek until 1881. The idea (which had been current) of making the school of Melies an Academy of Hellenism lapsed.

Nevertheless, the school, small though it must have been and short though its history was, did represent a meeting place of the ideas and ambitions of three energetic, productive and talented men: the school library, which has survived through severe hazards of wars and earthquakes, still suggests the intellectual and patriotic excitement that went into its foundation and growth. The greater part of approximately 1,120 items which make up the principal, and older, section of the printed collection consists of books given to the library by Konstantas, Gazēs and Philippidēs; some of them, indeed, have descended from the collection of Anthimos Papapandazēs and his brother Zacharias; and at least some of the 120-or-so manuscript items which the library also contains are due to the same group of benefactors.

The school at Melies, like the Athonite Academy, was a failure, at any rate in relation to the ambitious plans that lay behind it. Still less than the Athonite Academy did it become a source of educational progress in its own right. Nevertheless the project was of great interest as an expression of educational idealism and energy. The range and quality of the library do still evoke in one's mind the Academy that might have been. What one has to be content with, however, in dwelling on its unfulfilled possibilities, is really just the history and achievements of those who came together to found or develop it; but this itself is worth some attention, because the three men concerned represented, in what they wrote or otherwise worked at, every trend in contemporary Greek thought, save one.

They were, that is to say, collectively translators, commentators, editors, linguistic theorists, book collectors and educational philosophers (in a broad sense of this term)—transmitters and exponents of ideas in very varied fields, from the study of ancient Greek, through geography and physics to logic and general philosophy. They were knowledgeable and could on occasion write authentically and with vigor. What they did not undertake was the production of pioneering, systematic intellectual work for its own sake. In this respect they differed from their contemporaries, Benjamin and Psalidas. Whatever the shortcomings of the systems of philosophy which these two produced, and whatever patriotic or nationalistic pride they themselves may have taken in their work, that work does also suggest the fascination of ideas developed for their own sakes (a *sustained* authenticity), in a way not characteristic of other Greek writers at the time, even—be it said with all deference—of Koraēs. So that the virtues of Konstantas, Philippidēs and Gazēs are largely those of intellectual collectors, of unstuffy ones, all the same.

These remarks can perhaps be given point by reference to a work of Philippidēs. This is his translation of the *Logic* of Condillac, published in Vienna in 1801,[3] twenty-one years after the first appearance of the original. The translation happens to be one of the few works alluded to specifically by Koraēs in his *Mémoire sur l'état actuel de la civilisation dans la Grèce*[4] as being emblematic of an intellectual regeneration amongst the Greeks and as an example of their awareness of and readiness to exploit modern Western thought in varied fields.

Philippidēs believes in philosophy both because it teaches us about the intellectual powers of man and because it is itself the art of developing and exercising those powers. He begins his Preface to the *Logic* by appropriating educational theory for metaphysics. It is not grammarians, rhetoricians, historians, physicists, or mathematicians who are competent to lay down methods of learning for children, he suggests, but metaphysicians, like Locke, Condillac and Kant, who have made a systematic study of the human mind. (The suggestion that Kant's architectonics are so readily adaptable is new to me.)

The general method which Philippidēs takes to be sanctioned by "metaphysics" is a combination of very common-sense, empirically-based didactic moves with high theory. As a general principle, he advises us, it is most important to keep on proceeding from the known to the unknown. (Initially, we must build on what a pupil "knows" at age six or seven at the latest; this will then be as little as possible obfuscated by bad influences, teaching or habits.) The "known," to begin with, is the child's mother tongue (i.e., the spoken language), and the child's first study must be "the similarities and dissimilarities of words, the agreements and disagreements that subsist amongst them."[5] This is an obscure remark, which Philippidēs does not trouble to explain, but he appears to have in mind comparisons of the functions or roles of words in different kinds of discourse rather than etymological considerations. His point is that we must begin by getting the child to arrive in his own way at some notion of *kinds of expression*—one is tempted to say "categories," in the Rylean sense—and that only subsequently must we try to teach him the meaning of terms such as "noun," "adjective," "case," "declension," "number," and so on.

With obvious Cartesian overtones, and anticipating Condillac's own emphasis, he describes this recommended method as "analytic," in opposition to "synthetic," which latter he describes as the practice of proceeding *from* formal principles *to* acceptable discourse, and so putting first what should come last. He attaches very great importance to the analytic, the "natural" method of cultivating in the child an appreciation of linguistic analogies and distinctions; he marks it by insisting that the observation of word-use in the spoken language *is* the metaphysics of language; and he appears to mean by this that sensitivity and reflectiveness in thought come through well-directed practice, merging into skill, in the use of language for this, that and the next purpose, rather than through rule and rote.

Philippidēs returns to this general theme in an Address, "On Teaching," which he appends to his translation of the *Logic*. Again he pleads for the introduction of the analytic method, emphasizing that it is to be applied not only in linguistic but in other studies as well: in this connection he complains that language has been taught in Greek schools up to the present time by the wrong methods, and that mathematics has been neglected almost entirely. As regards language, teaching must proceed on a basis not of definitions or rules, but of "the simplest sort of metaphysics."[6] The reader cannot but be puzzled once again by the occurrence of the term "metaphysics" in this context, and the author gives him little assistance in elucidating it. The stress which it marks on moving from the known to the unknown, i.e., on the analytic method, suggests that the whole phrase, "the simplest sort of metaphysics," signifies an awareness of the articulation of ideas which is not derived from, though it can be registered by, general rules; which depends, that is to say, on the imaginatively guided use of words and not upon theorizing or laying down the law about them. (Practice in the use of words includes, as Philippidēs explains, the reading of the best authors.)

Clearly, the regimen which he prescribes for the first phase in education could be a very free and undoctrinaire one, if suitably interpreted. To call it "metaphysics" is perhaps an over-dramatic piece of naming, but the word does contrive to suggest that what the pupil should acquire, even at the earliest stages of his education, is a set of authentic "relations of ideas." The development of our ideas and the use of words go hand in hand. Philippidēs does say once [7] that the range of our ideas overlaps on all sides that of the words we have at our command to express them; but he immediately corrects himself by declaring that unless ideas can be put clearly into words they are not really "ideas." The verbal point is unimportant. What matters is the implication that ideas are to be developed by reliance on use, not on mention.

So far, so good. The next stage in education, according to Philippidēs, is that the child should be brought to see the force of the maxim, "Know Thyself." Once he has mastered the fabrication (τέχνημα[8]) and relationships of words he must study the arts of thinking and reasoning; that is to say, he must undertake the study of "metaphysical man," [9] or, the mind and its workings, and in the process learn *to* reflect, *to* reason, and so on. The study of the active (ψυχικάς [10]) and intellectual powers of man is so crucial and so urgent that it must precede such studies as those of geography, history and foreign languages. The point of logic, Philippidēs firmly states, is that it should teach us to reason, and it pursues this end best by teaching us what is the foundation (ἀρχή [11]) of our knowledge, how knowledge is acquired, and so on.

One assumption of such a policy (if I may paraphrase Philippidēs rather freely at this point) is that the categorization of discourse has already been accomplished sufficiently by the type of exercise in language-use that has been recommended for the previous stage in education. At any rate, the *Logic* which he is introducing does not include, and is commended for not including, the doctrines of the five φωναί, or the ten categories, or definition, division, propositional structure, the syllogism, epicheiremata, sorites, dilemmas or sophisms, but instead tells us positively how (in various ways) we think and reason, and how we may do these things methodically and retentively.

It will be clear that the study so foreshadowed observes no more than a perfunctory distinction between knowledge-how and knowledge-that. The logic so envisaged is a considerable mixture of rules of thought with general theses in psychology and epistemology. Philippidēs does not, in this respect, obey his own injunction to keep the idea of analysis distinct from that of synthesis, and to prefer analysis. But neither does the author he is translating, and the "logic" presented is itself in a tradition.

What is of more interest about Philippidēs' advice is his opinion about the power of "mental philosophy" (let us call his "logic" by that more appropriate term) employed at what must be a very early stage of education. (He does not specify ages.) No fear is expressed by him of developing in the child an unseasonably critical disposition, exercised, as some might say, before he has enough to bite on. The present work, Philippidēs points out, is specifically suited to "children, uneducated people, and women"[12]: in any case, he holds, it is on philosophical soil that knowledge of other kinds will flourish and proliferate. Philippidēs' trust in philosophy is certainly not in doubt. I do not know of any other eighteenth- or nineteenth-century Greek writer who recommends the subject as the very first variation on the educational theme.

Philippidēs himself displays a quite considerable acquaintance with general philosophical literature. He supplements his translation with notes, often lengthy and frequently learned. For example, he acknowledges in Locke the doctrine of the sensory origin of all our knowledge, but he also traces it back to Aristotle, and even, conjecturally, to Anaxagoras. He recommends Locke's teaching on the origin of our ideas of space and time. He gives a long account of Cheselden's findings on visual discrimination, which he says were intelligently anticipated by Locke and Berkeley. He is very interested in the deaf-and-dumb "grammar" of the Abbé de l'Épée, praising his work as being truly philosophical, "metaphysically-imbued." He expounds the views of Descartes and Gassendi about innate ideas, in the existence of which he does not believe. He discusses Descartes's and Leibniz's theories about the relation of mind and body, but dismisses them finally as "quite unfounded hypotheses"[13]; for his part, he professes a blunt agnosticism on the subject. He is acquainted with the system of Malebranche. Amongst older writers he refers to Plethon, Georgios Trapezountios, Vessarion, Theodoros Gazēs and Gennadios, and amongst older still cites Aristotle and, from time to time, Pythagoreans, Peripatetics and Stoics in general.

He propounds an argument for a First Cause and explains various theological consequences of this notion, but he keeps the argument matter-of-fact sounding, and even here expresses himself as an empiricist rather than as a rationalist. He revives the expression "sound philosophy" (ἡ ὑγιεινὴ φιλοσοφία)[14] as a term of praise for the style of philosophy which he is introducing and practicing. It is characteristic of such philosophy, he remarks, not to make use of the five φωναί of Porphyry or of other such accoutrements.[15] "Genus," "Species," "Difference," "Property," and "Accident," he says, are nothing but "common appellatives (ὀνομασίαι)."[16] In general, he thinks, nominalists have been nearer the truth than realists, but he does not go further than merely to indicate this preference. The one notable empiricist of the previous generation or two of whom he takes no account is Hume. His own empiricism is eclectic and not completely radical. The general impression which his work leaves, nevertheless, is of a lively mind, and of an engaging enthusiasm, allied with common sense, outspokenness and educational zeal.

Philippidēs wrote or translated other work, in physics, chemistry and history; but, next to the *Logic*, his best-known production is probably the *Geography*[17] which he compiled in association with Konstantas and which was published in Vienna in 1791. The book was striking in two ways: first, that it was written in an extreme demotic; and, second, that its scope and outlook were so "modern," taking into account not only the material conditions but also the social characteristics of life in the regions described; at the same time, historical considerations were not neglected.[18] Who wrote which parts of the book is apparently not known. In a work of collaboration it seems odd to find the first person singular used, as in the following piece of national self-castigation:

> The regime does not impede us at all in *this* [i.e., the renewal of the language]; we ourselves with our ignorance and with the habit of faction which we have inherited from our forefathers are responsible for our evils. Some time or other, perhaps, the progress of instruction will force us to abandon this ruinous failing by exhibiting to us the many examples of it provided by our ancestors, all of whose ills I ascribe to divided counsel; but so long as we despise our own language we shall remain ignorant and wretched and a common victim, a common pasturage for others.[19]

Gregorios Konstantas was, like Philippidēs, a philosophical empiricist and, like Philippidēs, he tried to turn certain educational implications of his empiricism to account; this can be seen in his general insistence that we must build, in one way or another, on what a pupil *has*, and must not confront him with either principles or a language taken from some alien domain, over against his own experience, so to speak, and radically unconnected with it. Like Philippidēs, Konstantas was a translator of philosophical work. In 1804 there was published in Venice, in four volumes, a version by him, entitled *Elements of Logic, Metaphysics and Ethics*, of the system of Francesco Soave, himself an exponent of the ideas of Locke and Condillac.[20] Konstantas, too, provided explanatory notes along with his translation. Speaking of innovations in Soave's work, and especially in the Logical part of it, he says, very much as Philippidēs might have done:

> Do not take it as an imperfection in the book or as a mark of ignorance in the author that he gets rid of superfluities, and particularly the verbosities of wisdom-lacking Sophists concerning the so-called syllogistic figures. By the common verdict of the wise in Europe these have been adjudged vain and useless, indeed positively harmful, and as such have been ostracized from the sacred precinct of Philosophy; and if some celebrity appears in their defense, then he is moved by sentiment and not by consideration of their usefulness.[21]

Like Philippidēs, again, Konstantas is preoccupied by questions about the linguistic medium in which educational literature is to be presented. In translating the *Logic* itself, Philippidēs had kept to a comparatively colloquial form of Greek, fairly simple and generally clear (his policy in doing so was appropriate to the directness and lucidity of the original), but he also offered an example of a more literary style in a brief appendix translating part of Condillac's *Traité des sensations*, as also in the language of his Address, "On Teaching," likewise appended. Theory and inclination both move him to the side of the "spoken" language, but he does confess to the difficulty of settling upon a grammatically standard version of this, and, particularly, of providing it with the series of more or less technical vocabularies that it needs for scholarly and scientific purposes. The choice, he seems to say,[22] is between persevering with the spoken language and flying to another one more or less discontinuous with the spoken; and just as a "synthetic" logic is included in his book for consultation if the reader must have it, so also is a "literary" style of writing exhibited at sufficient length to be a paradigm or deterrent to the reader, as the case may be.

Konstantas, for his part, offers the reader no choice, but he, too, adverts to the difficulty of adapting the "common" language—in which he writes—for sophisticated, in this case philosophical, use. He explains his own method. Where the "common" language lacks the special terms required to express his author's ideas, he has tried so far as possible to take them from Hellenic (i.e., ancient Greek), but to express novel (νεοφανεῖς) ideas he has had either to borrow from Italian or else to coin his own terms. In the formation and declension of words he has kept (sometimes with reluctance) to Hellenic forms, except in a few instances in which he feels that this would look absurd.[23] He is diffident about his success in following these rules—success, that is, in terms of the consistency and felicity of the results achieved—but he is confident enough that the rules themselves are sound. His general style of writing, he explains, he has striven to make "plain, lucid and smooth,"[24] as befits a piece of work written for instruction and not for diversion. A modern reader may well agree that his style is indeed, for its period, unusually direct and measured; that it reads evenly and far from disagreeably; in short, that Konstantas made an interesting contribution towards the forging of a modern, scholarly Greek.

Over and over again, in the authors I have been considering, one finds this intense preoccupation with the *means* whereby the powers of comprehension of the people for whom they were writing might be married with the works of wisdom that they desired to bring before them. From one point of view, namely the democratic empiricist view adopted by both Philippidēs and Konstantas (and Katartzēs and others before these), the problem is to be expressed in terms of "cultivation" (καλλιέργεια), the cultivation of those means already latent in the people's very power to talk. "The cultivation of a people's language is the cultivation and enrichment of the people's spirit—Locke says this, and so does Condillac; it is said by all the wise in Europe. . . ." Thus Konstantas.[25] But then he comes down to practicalities. What is needed urgently is works of reference, dictionaries, grammars, and linguistic manuals of all kinds, and the publication of the whole corpus of literature that would support and supply them.

In this connection he makes a proposal which other scholars besides himself had been discussing for some time past,[26] for the institution of an Academy to act as both provider and legislator for the language.

> The only means, then, by which our own race too can be improved, is a small—for the time being—Academy, instituted in a suitable place; that is, a council (σύστημα) of educated men, experts both in Hellenic and in other, foreign, languages; not to give lessons and to be transmitters of knowledge . . . but to cultivate our language . . . that is, to compose its Grammar, to make its lexicon, to compose the necessary books of instruction, to translate from the cultivated languages those works of method which are required for the upbringing, if I may so put it, of the race; proceeding by degrees from the most elementary primer to the higher learning; to sift the Hellenic authors, in some instances to translate them into our own language and in some to annotate and elucidate them, so that in future whoever wishes to do so may apply himself to them with profit; and after that to compile a full and accurate lexicon of the Greek language. . . .[27]

The Academy so envisaged was not the same as the Academy of Hellenism which Konstantas originally wished to create in Melies. In fact, the first of these projects, at the time at which he was writing, was even more visionary than the second. But I mention it because it was emblematic of concern and discussion amongst people (Katartzēs and Philippidēs must be counted in this connection, as in so many others, along with Konstantas) who saw how much effort the resolution of the language issue was to involve; who nevertheless felt, to a peculiar degree, the urgency of the problem, and who were beginning to delineate the nature of the work and the arrangements required in order to make progress with it. What was visionary about Konstantas's idea was not so much the prospect of finding individuals competent or willing to undertake the sort of work required—Koraēs was absorbed in it at that very time and Neophytos Doukas was then just beginning his long career as an editor of classical texts and a philological teacher—as that of creating and maintaining an *institution* to do so, particularly an institution having as its motif an appropriate philosophy of language. The difficulties preventing this were many, and obvious.

It is not that there was no corporate support to be found anywhere, in these times, for letters and for education. Anthimos Gazēs, the third of the personalities associated with the school at Melies, names one society the activities of which bore fruit to some extent. Gazēs was the first editor of the periodical called *The Scholarly Hermes*,[28] which was published in Vienna and ran from 1811 until 1821; and in the Advice to the Reader which prefaces its first volume, he refers to "The Philological Society of the Greek Lyceum" in Bucharest as having sponsored and to some extent financed the journal.[29] The society's aim was to promote the advancement of learning on a wide front, and the range of its interests is reflected to some extent in the editor's invitation to contributors, who are asked to send in "observations" in Geography, Astronomy, Natural History, Archaeology, and Epigraphy, including information about such matters as the location of ancient cities, and coins and early manuscripts. It is true that the journal did not flourish greatly under Gazēs' editorship—or for that matter under anybody else's—and that Gazēs' editorial policy was soon called in question by Koraēs[30]; but at least here was a definite effort assisted by a body which, if its aims were less coherent and single-minded than those suggested by Konstantas for his Academy, was thinking ahead in quite an enlightened way. The fact remains, however, that this Society is the only one of its kind, existing prior to the War of Independence, of which I have found mention.

Gazēs' editorship of the *Scholarly Hermes* came to an end in 1813. His previous output had been distinguished for its range and variety rather than its quality or importance. Suffice it to note that it included philological work (in ancient Greek), the reissue[31] with notes and supplements of a very old-fashioned *Geography* by Meletios, Metropolitan of Athens (originally published in 1728), and a translation, published under the title, *Grammar of the Philosophical Sciences*,[32] of a compendium of physics by the Englishman Benjamin Martin.[33] Gazēs' work for the education of his time was busy enough, but his views and his writing lacked the sprightliness and interest to be found in those of Philippidēs and Konstantas. He himself, as has been noted, failed to persevere with the scheme for the school at Melies upon which, with Konstantas, he had agreed in 1814; or, rather, he allowed his enthusiasm for education in the particular, scholarly sense to be absorbed in general political, liberationist campaigning. I have taken account of him here nevertheless, because his importance in the revival of Greek letters was not negligible, and because his activity complemented that of the two others whom I have described. Through those three the village of Melies controlled, in a manner, an impressively large educational field.

Notes

1. According to Dimaras 4, p. 56. For biographical and other factual details given in this chapter I am indebted partly to Dimaras 4 (introduction, *var. loc.*), partly to miscellaneous sources of evidence seen in the library of Melies itself.
2. Dimaras 4, p. 27.
3. Ἡ Λογική, ἢ αἱ πρῶται Ἀναπτύξεις τῆς Τέχνης τοῦ Στοχάζεσθαι. Σύγγραμμα στοιχειῶδες.... Συγγραφὲν παρὰ τοῦ Κονδιλλιὰκ καὶ μεταφρασθὲν... παρὰ Δανιὴλ Δημητρίου Ἱερομονάχου τοῦ Φιλιππίδου τοῦ ἐκ κώμης Μηλιῶν τοῦ Πηλίου ὄρους, παρ' οὗ προσετέθησαν καὶ σημειώματα.... The original was entitled *La Logique, ou les premiers developpemens de l'art de penser, ouvrage élémentaire.* It was published at Paris in 1780.
4. [Paris, 1803], p. 55.
5. Philippidēs, *op. cit.*, p. ιγ'.
6. Ibid., p. 329.
7. Ibid., p. 327.
8. Ibid., p. ιστ'. Cf. p. 330.
9. Ibid., p. ιστ'.
10. Ibid., p. ιζ'.
11. Ibid., p. κ'.
12. Ibid., p. ιη'.
13. Ibid., p. 117.
14. Ibid., p. 50.

15. In these circumstances it is distinctly odd that he should think it worth while appending to his translation, as he does, a compendium of the "synthetic" logic which contains these items. His own explanation is that he does so for the historical record and also for the benefit of anyone who thinks he needs such logic and cannot find it elsewhere (see pp. κδ′—κε′).

16. Ibid., p. 50.

17. Νεωτερικὴ Γεωγραφία, I. No sequel was published.

18. Excerpts from the part of the *Geography* concerning Greece have been reprinted by Dimaras in 4, pp. 75–81. Dimaras has stressed the importance of this work, in several places, e.g., 13, pp. 91–2.

19. Dimaras 4, p. 79.

20. Στοιχεῖα τῆς Λογικῆς, Μεταφυσικῆς καὶ Ἠθικῆς. . . . Soave (1743–1816) was a professor in the University of Parma. The work translated was his *Instituzioni di logica metafisica ed etica* (Milan, 1791).

21. Dimaras 4, pp. 85–6.

22. His motives for exhibiting *two* styles are left to be inferred.

23. These explanations are given in the Address to the Reader (reprinted in Dimaras 4, pp. 82–6), prefacing the translation of Soave.

24. *Op. cit.*, p. 83.

25. Ibid., pp. 84–5.

26. Cf. Dimaras, ibid., p. 17.

27. Ibid., p. 85.

28. See p. 156, n. 4.

29. Dimaras 4, p. 327.

30. See p. 143.

31. Venice, 1807.

32. Γραμματικὴ τῶν Φιλοσοφικῶν Ἐπιστημῶν (Vienna, 1799).

33. His *Philosophical Grammar*, first published in London in 1735.

17

Doukas and Koumas: Archaism and Liberal Education

It is a far cry from Philippidēs and Condillac to Parios and the Church Fathers. Athanasios Parios (1725–1813) was a contemporary of Philippidēs over a long period. I take note of him here in order to indicate how complete a contrary to the broad educational liberalism of Koraēs' type there could in fact be, and to use this example as a yardstick by which to assess another, in itself more important, divergence from Koraïsm. Parios's attitude and work are an expression of the completest archaism and conservatism in matters both of language and of general education; from a social point of view, they represent the "philosophy" of fear and of obsession with security, as against that of enquiry, experiment and enlargement. Parios, who had been a pupil of Voulgaris on Athos, pursued a career as teacher and preacher in Salonika and other places, before becoming head of the school in Chios in 1786. He remained in that position until 1812. His teaching was "grammatical" and religiously instructive, though it did apparently include some logic and metaphysics along with rhetoric and theology.[1] His opposition to the philosophical outlooks associated with, for example, Psalidas, Benjamin and Koraēs was complete; I mention these men in particular because Parios was involved in controversy against all three.[2]

He was a celebrated-enough teacher, but he is best remembered for a book called *Response* (Ἀντιφώνησις), published pseudonymously in Trieste in 1802. The full title of this work reads as follows:

> Response to the phrenetic zeal of the philosophers who come from Europe; exposing the vanity and folly of their lamentable efforts exerted upon our Race and teaching what is the real and true philosophy. To

which is added a salutary admonition to those who recklessly send their sons to Europe on business. Both constructed and composed by Nathaniel Neokaisareus.[3]

This declaration speaks for itself. The only important indication of the spirit or contents of the book which it fails to give concerns the Greek classics. Parios's aim was in fact the restriction of education, on its whole theoretical, doctrinal (or ideological) side, to the teachings of the Church Fathers. Even the philosophers of antiquity were not acceptable. The form which his opposition to them takes is personal, and in this way oblique, but it represents one important trend in his polemic.[4] They are featured (all the most important of them) as men not worthy of being taken as models and authorities, because their lives and deeds fail, grossly and outrageously, to match their words and professions.

That this judgment is quite beside the point need not concern us here. Anghelou remarks[5] that Parios was in an impossible position, in that he was unable directly to deny the validity of ancient philosophical modes of thought without thereby reflecting criticism upon the Christian philosophy to which these made their contribution, and to which he was committed. What matters for present purposes, however, is simply that the neo-Classicism which Koraēs was introducing could be feared, by one not-uninfluential teacher, for those very features in it, the authenticity and force of its ideas, which others were ready to regard as vital to the intellectual regeneration of "the Race."

One of those who did so was, of course, Koraēs himself. Another, in a rather different way, was Neophytos Doukas (1760–1845). In his instance one might add to the terms "authenticity" and "force," "authority," for he believed that it was as repositories of actual, as it were *ex cathedra*, truth that the ancient writings must be re-presented to the Greek people. He claimed that if he had done a service to philosophy it was through "introducing good Grammar, and the literature of the ancient Greeks, in whom reside true philosophy and the very perfection of mankind."[6] His work as an editor of and commentator upon classical texts was on a scale similar to that of Koraēs, beginning well before the War of Independence and continuing well after it.[7] His respect for ancient wisdom was fundamentalist in various ways, but notably in this, that he regarded its linguistic form as of its essence; so that to broach that wisdom required of his contemporaries both the recognition of ancient (Attic) Greek as their linguistic ideal and the energizing of themselves to master it. His own philosophical style tends to be, accordingly, extremely artificial and archaistic; the pains of construing Doukas's philosophical writing are, by general consent, second only to those involved in reading Voulgaris. He went so far as to hold that any philosophy worth the teaching—and it has to be realized that he regarded philosophy as an important part of general education for senior pupils [8]—should be presented in the ancient language. The most concrete of his arguments for this point of view is worth quoting:

> A person philosophizing in the modern language (by which is to be understood this loosely arranged and unconnected style of writing [with which we are familiar], bad in presentation and full of foreign turns of phrase), and treating matters of expression so brashly as he does, will proceed through matters of substance carelessly and superficially, passing from period to period and jumping about from idea to idea haphazardly, without proper relationship and linkage. The ancient language, however, because of the tautness with which it is bound together by its transitive and connective particles, expressing *vis-à-vis* one another the carrying-on of a relationship or the introduction of a contrary notion, everywhere demands consequentiality; and this means that in their whole extent ideas are presented connectedly and as holding together in terms of ground and consequent. Thus there is no excuse for a philosophical student to go through a series of ideas superficially, with indifference as to how he tackles them. [9]

The objection that to demand the study and presentation of philosophy in ancient Greek is to put the subject into a straitjacket is dismissed by Doukas for the curt reason that philosophy is, in any case, formal and considered discourse. The objection that the demand is just too difficult for students to meet is received with equally little sympathy. If prephilosophical education in ancient grammar and ancient literature is as thorough and comprehensive as Doukas believes it must be, then no unreasonable strain will be put upon the student's linguistic aptitude when he finally turns to philosophy. It is part of the purpose of insisting that earlier education be in "good Grammar" that this should be so. [10] For the question affects everyone who gets to a certain stage in the educational curriculum, and not just a specialist few. Doukas never doubts that philosophy, in more or less our familiar academic sense of the term, is the coping stone of general education. It follows that his demand for the teaching of philosophy in the ancient language amounts to the introduction of that language into contemporary Greek education and culture on a far larger scale than might at first appear. As we shall see shortly, the demand is in fact one facet of a somewhat strained vision, embracing the conversion of Graecism into Hellenism, which Doukas entertained.

It might be objected, further, that there are other sources of wisdom, namely mathematics and science, upon which school education could draw and which represent just as good a way of preparing philosophical soil as do grammar and literature. Doukas denies that they have this virtue and insists that they should not be allowed to compete with, or apparently even to complement, grammar (and its associated literary study). He finds or thinks he finds himself in agreement with Koraēs in the following sentiments:

> Who does not know that neither the symbols of Algebra, nor the solutions of Chemistry, nor the experiments of Physics engender the love of learning, but the divine art of speaking and writing correctly? And what could this be, but the study of good grammar? For grammar is precisely the art of thinking, speaking and writing correctly: activities wherein literature and true philosophy, as study of the mind, are founded. . . . The sagacious Koraēs advises us, that teachers should be in no hurry to let their pupils go on to study science—as Doukas [*sic*] for his part has said many times already—before they become good scholars (γραμματικοί) and have perfected their reasoning powers in the divine art of speaking and writing correctly, that is to say in the philosophy of Socrates.[11]

There is some sense in this, but Doukas is undoubtedly very one-sided, in a dogmatic, assertive sort of way.

> The young, thinking that philosophy can be picked up on the cheap and without scholarly toil, and at the same time horrified at the labors involved in the study of literature, will neglect that best and most useful lesson, the very one that leads the nation into philosophy. . . . I shall never stop declaring this truth, seeing that good scholars simply and solely as such become excellent philosophers, and that many philosophers unendowed with scholarship lapse into unreason. . . . I have never at any time spoken a word against philosophy, or even uttered it in my thoughts, persuaded as I am that good scholarship and philosophy are in reality inseparable.[12]

(Doukas puts this last point curiously. It is as if philosophy could be the condition of good scholarship just as much as good scholarship of philosophy. For what it is worth, he does remark in another context that the language of the ancient Greeks is still more a sacred and divine thing than their philosophy.[13])

Even if we set aside the claim (rejected by Doukas) that mathematics and science represent an authentic approach to philosophy, there remains the claim (modest, it would seem) that they have a part to play in general education, both as giving variety to the pupil's work and as enlarging his comprehension of reality. Doukas will not allow even this. Replying to his contemporary Konstantinos Koumas—who did, admittedly, put the point forward in rather provocative terms[14]—he asserts:

> It is absolutely plain that only the writings of the Greeks contain philosophy and reason at every stage; the vain and foolish wordlets [to exploit Koumas's terms] are the symbols of Algebra.

And he thinks that physical experiments in schools have an entertainment value only.

From this series of declarations it would be a natural inference that ancient Greek is to emerge from its grammatical and philosophical base in the schools and to become the medium at least of all formal communication and of all serious culture in the state. (We need not, for present purposes, define those vague phrases.) Yet at one point Doukas reminds us, as is correct, that he himself maintains two "literary" languages, and one wonders whether his own practice is not testimony against the idea that ancient Greek might become current to the extent suggested.

> Some say, that I differ from the sagacious Koraēs, in that he wants us to write in modern, I in ancient [Greek]. They are wrong. It is only with regard to philosophy that I am so minded. My own writing, past and present, in modern Greek is more extensive than anyone's, and that gentleman (ἐκεῖνος) has not ruled Hellenic out of philosophy.[15]

This disclaimer is, nevertheless, misleading. Doukas does undoubtedly envisage the modern literary language as conforming, steadily, more and more closely to its ancient matrix. Words and phrases from ancient Greek already in the modern language are to be kept, he urges, and their number augmented in every suitable way. Ancient Greek, in being spoken or written in schools, is to be regarded as a paradigm for modern. There is to be no intrusion, into the modern language, of "foreign" idioms. A periodical, he proposes, should be founded to serve as a practice-ground and testing-ground for the writing of the ancient language, and he gives most explicit instructions how contributions to it are to be organized and encouraged.

These, however, are but hints of the prospect that Doukas sees, and he does not leave us without a more definite indication of it. The fact is that he takes seriously (against Koraēs, Koumas and other theorists) the idea that all educated people might one day be speaking, quite naturally, ancient Greek. The conditions required are, first, Doukas's own kind of shame at his countrymen's inability to *display* their linguistic inheritance in word and thought; secondly, his own kind of vision of the perfectibility of Greek mankind which its re-absorption in ancient molds of thought would entail; and, thirdly, the practical rules which he gives for easing and improving the learning of the ancient language and for schooling people to regard it as their linguistic aim and end. "We must learn the language of our ancestors more and more completely, if we wish to remain Hellenes."[16] Hellenes, that is to say, as distinct from lowly and despised Γραικοί.

Doukas's own philosophy is set out for the most part in his *Tetract*, from the preface to which I have been quoting. This is a compendium of Rhetoric, Logic, Metaphysics and Ethics which, although first published in Aegina in 1834, dates in fact from 1817–18.[17] At the time of its composition he was teaching in Bucharest (where the greater part of his career, prior to the liberation of Greece, was spent), and the manner and arrangement of these pieces is purely didactic. They were compiled, indeed, for the benefit of some of his pupils who asked him to give them logical and philosophical lessons, and accordingly the book makes no claim to originality. On the contrary, what gave Doukas difficulty was the question where to take his material from. Not surprisingly, he rejects the offerings of "the moderns"—vaguely described and unidentified, but evidently his own countrymen, whose crime is that they have adulterated both philosophy and the language in which it is written. Very surprisingly, in the light of all that I have been saying about Doukas's romantic classicism, he rejects the ancients, including even Aristotle, on the grounds that in a didactic manual he could not accommodate such a confluence of streams of thought.[18] The upshot is that he allows himself to be freely and widely eclectic; but it turns out that most of his indebtedness, by a long way, is to three sources, namely "Heineccius,"[19] Eugenios Voulgaris, and the Italian philosopher, Francesco Soave, whose work had already been translated into Greek (as I have already noted) by Konstantas. The teachings of Voulgaris are, at many points, sympathetically followed, and of the three sources mentioned he is, except in the Ethics, the main one.

There is no point in trying to give an "internal" account of Doukas's philosophy. It is, as might be expected, very much of a patchwork and mostly superficial, educative only after a doctrinaire fashion. The Ethics contain a great deal of direct moral and religious teaching. The Theology (part of the Metaphysics) gives various forms of the argument for a First Cause with a kind of flat absoluteness. Doukas often retails the arguments of the philosophers for or against a certain thesis, but without making an attempt to come to a decision about the matter. His unwillingness to play the Solomon is not, perhaps, indefensible in every possible set of terms, but Doukas, one feels, sometimes just gives up. Thus, in the course of his Cosmology (which is also part of the Metaphysics) he discusses the questions of the beginning of the world and the degree of perfection which it may be held to possess. As regards the first, his own and only recourse from the arguments of the philosophers (the impasses reached by which are fairly enough indicated) is the literal Genesis account of creation. In recounting what philosophers have said about the second, he is scornful both about those who support the view that the world is perfect (or, the best of all possible worlds) and those who pronounce it imperfect in various respects. He thinks that the former view is theologically (and hence philosophically) insupportable because it circumscribes the power of God to make the world better if he should choose so to do, and the second insufferable because of its presumption. In discussing neither of the two problems does he take up the question what it is about them that makes them into philosophical "aporiai."

The general air of didacticism in these writings, however, can best be indicated by a brief quotation from one of the catechisms, on

Ontology, Cosmology, Psychology and Theology, which are appended to the Metaphysics:

Q. What is Psychology?
A. A science which provides a rationale of the soul, and of the actions and passions of the soul.
Q. What is the soul?
A. A substance, free of all matter, simple, indivisible, incorruptible and immortal.
Q. Tell me first of all, whence comes your knowledge of this substance?
A. From that power that we have within us, to think of a continuous variety of things in a variety of ways.
Q. How then do we arrive from this at the idea of the existence of the soul?
A. By considering that no power and no activity subsists in and through itself, but only in a subject; there is therefore a certain subject, in which these properties have their subsistence.[20]

Except for the language in which it is couched, all of this is a far cry from any Rylean–Platonic "eristic Moot."

It would be misleading, however, to represent Doukas as a sheer conservative or a sheer, rigid traditionalist. The propriety of doing so depends entirely on what traditions are in question. One is apt to judge his arguments for a return to the ancient language in terms of their success, of the fact that nineteenth-century language developments in Greece did Doukas all too much justice, and that the inheritors of his romantic classicism were indeed conservative in their educational outlook. But, in his own way, Doukas is as much an exponent of "right reason" (ὀρθὸς λόγος, a phrase he is fond of using) as those whose language creates less of a prejudice against them. If one realizes that he was looking back to a *classical* tradition of rationalism—and, incidentally, that he was by no means a mere continuator of Greek seventeenth-century Aristotelianism but was a scholar of much wider classical interests—then one can allow that he was enough of an "original" to make a partisan labeling of him unsatisfactory. (He represents nothing like the dead-end conservatism of Parios.)

It is quite true that even classical rationalism comes to us through Doukas didacticized, or, what is partly the same thing, cribbed, cabined and confined by a simple, rather dogmatic piety. But even Doukas's piety is, in its fashion, a return to first principles, for it is unmediated by ecclesiasticism. He is against both superstition and the submissive, unexamined elaborateness of traditional religiosity.

For example, he ascribes to virtue or virtuousness three aspects, a self-regarding one which he calls "prudence," an other-regarding one which he calls "justice," and a third, namely piety, or reverence towards one's Creator. But this reverence is, so to speak, direct. Doukas emphasizes that he wishes to exclude from his conception of virtue everything adventitious and accidental, like extreme bodily asceticism and self-imposed tribulations, obsession with the Church calendar, fasting and "vain repetitions" (βατολογίας).[21] He directs shafts against the ecclesiasticism which sneers at philosophy and is, in effect, a vested interest; he contrasts a theology "of the senses" with a theology "of the intellect," and ritualism with effective works.[22] In writing about "Justice" and "Nobility" he expresses, though in a more sophisticated and urbane manner, sentiments about freedom and equality reminiscent of those found in *Greek Nomarchy*.[23] The only counter to both superstition and atheism, he holds, is "the true philosophy." It is this which imposes a mean, alike between deficiencies and excesses in qualities of character, and between submissiveness and outrageousness in matters of belief. Philosophy, which is really recollection (as Plato held), *is* proper education, and proper education is the way to piety.[24] Piety itself, as the companion of reasonableness of mind, will take us as near as we can get to the supreme good for man.[25]

Doukas's opposition to education in mathematics and science, and his linguistic idealism, were neither of them out of line with the course followed by Greek education in the remainder of the nineteenth century. His faith in philosophy perhaps was. But, for obvious reasons, it would be unfair to the Greek people to complain that they, any more than anyone else, failed to realize that faith, at any rate if we take it as represented by what Doukas wrote in 1810 or 1811:

> Philosophy, of which I am speaking, is that whose presence will naturally disperse the gathered cloud of misfortune and bring to us the clear sky of fair living, will scatter the darkness of ignorance, of lawlessness and of barbarity, and bring in the light of wisdom, good order, and moderation; philosophy which knows how to scan the culture of old (τὰ ἀρχαῖα) with critical exactness, and to see the future in the light of its lessons; whose presence teaches what is pleasing to the Lord; admirable educator in things good and excellent corrector of things bad,

she is ruler over all our progress towards virtue; she is the art which is the perfection of all arts, and of sciences the supreme science; and, finally, she instils in us love of our neighbor and teaches us our duty towards our motherland. . . .[26]

After the liberation of Greece Doukas became the head of schools, first in Aegina and then in Athens. If one considers the length of his teaching career plus the fact that he was the author or editor of something like a hundred volumes, one supposes that no one of his generation can have had anything like his influence in determining the course of Greek education in the later part of the nineteenth century. But what was his influence? His ideas were, at one and the same time, narrowing and retrogressive, and rationalistic and liberal. His romanticism, one suspects, prevailed; the equable scepticism that sometimes tempered it was overlooked (though it is fair to ask how far Doukas himself had it at heart). In any case, it comes as a considerable surprise to the student of nineteenth-century Greek intellectual history to find that the following statement is by Doukas:

Humanity is always accustomed to despise what belongs to the present, however great and admirable this may be: to admire, rather, what they hear of as being far distant from them, even though it be minor and less noteworthy. The further away things are in space or in time the more exaggeratedly they tend to praise them.[27]

Let us turn now to someone who did believe in the value of a scientific element in education. Konstantinos Koumas (1777–1836) probably argued more explicitly in favor of that element, and wrote material for it and taught it more energetically than anyone else I have mentioned in this study, including even Benjamin. He was very much a follower of Koraēs, whose influence is to be seen both in Koumas's devotion to didactic activity, including the translation and compilation of instructive work on a very large scale in many branches of knowledge, and in the development of Koumas's views about the language in which this instruction is to be presented, as of his own writing of it. Most of all, it is to be seen in his liberal philosophy of education.

It was Koumas, as I have mentioned, who provoked Doukas by daring to appeal to a sense of reality in pupils' minds which might make them eager to receive some knowledge about the actual non-linguistic world. He carried the provocation further[28] by looking to this knowledge, and generally to a sensitive awareness of the distinction between words and what they relate to, as conditions of incisive and pointed discourse. The underlying thought is quite simple, and, if applied *ad hominem* to views on education like Doukas's, also a sharp reminder. If speech (or language) be the "end" of education, it says in effect, let speech be knowledgeable; there are more ways of talking well than talking in flowery fashion about nothing. Furthermore, if you are teaching language, it eases the process considerably as you go along if the meaning of every term you come across does not have to be dispensed by *you*: in any case, what exclusive rights do you, as grammarian, have vested in the meanings of words, like "atmosphere," "light," or "attraction," which science for its part is able to use with such authority?

The *Synopsis of Physics*,[29] in which the point of view thus described is expressed, was compiled for the benefit of *gymnasion* pupils in Smyrna, where Koumas taught, with interruptions, from about 1809 until the beginning of the War of Independence; and it was eventually printed in order to satisfy a public interest and demand which Koumas's own teaching had stimulated. He describes how on Saturdays, days which were free of other teaching, he conducted public-education classes in physics, for the benefit of all comers, of any age, who cared to attend, provided only that they had a minimum grammatical education.

One wonders again (the question having arisen already in connection with Benjamin's work) how Koumas, especially in extending his teaching in this way to large and mixed audiences, was able to provide apparatus and materials for experiments. But he implies that in Smyrna he is not too badly off. He uses equipment bought in Vienna by contributions from progressively-minded Smyrniote citizens. As to materials (for chemistry, but also to some extent for physics), one way of getting hold of them is to make a good enough friend of a well-provided doctor. . . . Koumas adds, interestingly enough, that at the time of writing the Greek schools in Bucharest, Constantinople, Smyrna, Chios, Kydonies and Ioannina are all reasonably well provided with the apparatus necessary for the teaching of experimental physics. Nevertheless, because his book is likely to reach pupils in small communities where no such equipment is available, he carefully includes in it sketches of all the more complex types of physical instrument used in the experiments described.

There is no doubt that Koumas was a very considerable laborer in the cause of scientific education. He produced, as well as the *Physics* mentioned and other physical and mathematical work, an *Epitome of Chemistry* (Vienna [1808]), a two-volume translation of a work by P. A. Adet.[30] In introducing it to the reader he pleads, just as he does in the *Physics*, for a certain concreteness and definiteness in the subject matter of education. In this instance his complaint is not against grammarians, but against those who rest content with logic and pure mathematics as ends in themselves.

> What profit is there in logic when it teaches us to reason, but when we are then denied every other scientific subject matter which could serve us as a point of application for its rules? What good do the abstract ideas of mathematics do us, when we fail to use them for that purpose which forced men into becoming arithmeticians and geometers in the first place?[31]

Another truism to which Koumas gives some life is that education is for the good of society; and he believes that the good of society is staring his countrymen in the face, in the shape of the *natural* philosophy (in the broadest sense of the term) so highly developed amongst the nations of enlightened Europe. There is nothing *ad hominem* in this justification, but a plain belief that the time has come for Greek education to think in terms of material progress, and a conviction that a purely literary education, imposed all round, will but make dreamers of us all. The contrast with Doukas's ideas is complete. Piquantly enough, the two of them make use of the same secondary argument in support of their views, namely that the culture towards which they see education as working will redound to the honor and adornment of the race; but in Doukas's case it is because, he thinks, Greeks can do what no other people can do (and what so many of those others expect of them), namely re-present themselves in the image of Hellenes, their own ancestors; in Koumas's, it is because Greeks can do what others can, and that is present themselves to the world of learning as sophisticated, scientifically-minded Europeans.

Koumas does make what might appear to be a prospective concession to Doukas. In the same Address to the Reader he puts forward a plea for the reconciliation of Philosophy and Grammar.

> Philosophy, if it is not to be barbaric and uncouth, must take Grammar [or, grammatical scholarship] as its partner: just as Grammar, if it is not to lose direction and vacuously and senselessly trifle with words, must everywhere have Philosophy as its guide. . . . The Philosopher without Grammar is an eye without a foot. The Grammarian without Philosophy is a foot without an eye; so it is obvious that whoever wants to walk, that is, to prove himself useful, must have eyes and feet.[32]

However, he obviously would not allow Doukas's claim that "good scholars (γραμματικοί) simply and solely as such become excellent philosophers." Also, we must remember that Logic, which he counts as the first part of "Philosophy," is not to remain forever on its airy perch. And that Metaphysics teaches truths, albeit general ones, about the world. And that Ethics, the third part, teaches some quite definite rules for the conduct of life. The point is that Koumas here, too, though less explicitly than in the other contexts which I have mentioned, is stressing his concern that education, in every possible way, should be in gear with "reality."[33]

The most majestic in scope of Koumas's many works is his twelve-volume *Histories of the Acts of Mankind*[34] (Vienna, 1830–2), but the only part of it that is non-derivative to any extent is the final volume, which contains an account of the revival of learning in Turkish-dominated Greece, up to and including his own times. Majestic enough is his four-volume Σύνταγμα Φιλοσοφίας (Vienna, 1818–20), the title of which can perhaps best be rendered, in paraphrase, as *Philosophy Drawn Up and Constituted.* Here we find systematic philosophy in the grand manner. The first volume begins with a sketch of the history of philosophy and then proceeds through Empirical Psychology to what Koumas calls the Groundwork of Philosophy, considerations relating mainly to the scope, limits and classifiability of different kinds of knowledge. The second volume provides a system of Logic, to which is appended a Universal Grammar, this phrase being defined by Koumas as meaning "a science exhibiting the parts of speech in their pure and necessary forms together with the rules that are indispensable for combining them so as to reveal human thought."[35] Volume three consists of Metaphysics and Aesthetics. Volume four consists of Practical Philosophy, which is divided into Philosophy of Law, Ethics, and Ethical Theology (this last being a consideration of the existence of God, the immortality of the soul and related questions, from the standpoint of "practical reason") : and there is a long appendix on Pedagogics (interesting from the point of view of the history of education). This formidable body of doctrine is presented on the title-pages of the four volumes as having been composed by K. M. Koumas, "Headmaster of the Philological Gymnasium in Smyrna, and Teacher of Mathematical Sciences and Philosophy. For the use of his pupils." The eye may rest respectfully on this last phrase.

Koumas's philosophy is interesting simply as a specimen of didactic material, and not as originative work. The influence of Kant is manifest in it at many points. Surprisingly, in the light of this fact, his writing is plain and easy to understand, within its philosophical limits. Each section of his work represents a useful-enough outline of the terminology and the main distinctions appropriate to the branch of philosophy concerned, but the limitations are that the subject tends to be treated as if it were a corpus of agreed doctrine and that questions are left less open than they should be. In presenting philosophy as a subject to be learned rather than as a series of disputable problems, Koumas does not differ much from Doukas. But with how much heart can one criticize either of them for this? Any considerable stress upon the eristic side of philosophy, in the historical conditions in which these teachers found themselves, would have represented at best an educational luxury and at worst a waste of educational time. There is something to be said (I put it mildly, and with the admission that this itself is a disputed point of view) for letting the pupil or student find his way around the history of philosophy and be taught some of the "bread-and-butter" aspects of the subject before he is given the choice of devoting himself entirely to the life of a gadfly. The precocious eristic can operate as distastefully as the premature dogmatic. Anyhow, if there ever was a period when philosophical teachers might be excused for exhibiting their subject rather than trying to duel with it, then it was surely one in which striving, toil and sacrifice were required in order that anyone should catch sight of that subject at all.

In this context it seems appropriate to mention one more pre-War philosophical work. I take note of it not because it itself is particularly redolent of the classroom, but because it was written by a man whose later output was only too much so, and whose authority, educationally, became pretty far-reaching.

Neophytos Vamvas (1770–1855), who was professor of philosophy in the University of Athens from its foundation in 1837, published in 1818 an essay called *Elements of Philosophical Ethics*.[36] In it he discusses such matters as moral "first principles," the sources of "moral" truth and error, the real and non-conventional difference between virtue and vice, virtue as a mean, happiness and conscience. The discussion is on an Aristotelian pattern, but with Christian theological threads, and the philosophy, accordingly, is unventuresome. Numerous definitions, which are insufficiently supported, give the work an air of confidence which it hardly earns, and the appeal to divine revelation or to common sense is never very far away. Nevertheless, Vamvas's writing at this stage has a certain freshness which is not to be found in it later. His *Elements of Philosophy*,[37] for example, published in Athens in 1838, is, in some of its parts, quite outrageously secondhand. Both in his educational outlook and in his literary style, Vamvas after the War moved steadily further away from the standpoint of Koraēs, whose most trusted pupil he had at one time been. It is to be feared that he contributed his part to the comparative dullness into which Greek speculative thought settled in the early decades of the Greek state.

Notes

1. According to K. N. Sathas, Νεοελληνικὴ Φιλολογία (Athens, 1868), p. 634. Sathas (p. 639) ascribes to Parios an anonymous translation of the *Metaphysics* of Genovesi (Στοιχεῖα Μεταφυσικῆς, Trieste, 1802). Voulgaris's translation (mentioned on p. 46) was published in Venice four years later (cf. Sathas, *op. cit.*, p. 571).

2. See, e.g., Anghelou 3, pp. 52–4, 72–3.

3. "Neokaisareus" means "of New Caesarea" [in Asia Minor, near the River Lycos].

4. See 'Αντιφώνησις, pp. 15–6.

5. 4, p. 96.

6. From 'Αργώ, a preface to his edition of Herodian (Vienna, 1813). Dimaras 4, p. 264.

7. See Dimaras 4, pp. 34, 251.

8. See, e.g., his essay Περὶ Γλώσσης 'Ελληνικῆς, prefacing his Τετρακτύς (Aigina, 1834), p. ιγ'.

9. Ibid., p. ιζ'.

10. See ibid.

11. Dimaras 4, p. 268.

12. Ibid., p. 265.

13. Τετρακτύς, p. λβ΄.

14. In the Address to the Reader in his Σύνοψις Φυσικῆς (Vienna, 1812), p. 4. The whole Address is reprinted in Dimaras 4, pp. 347–60. Doukas's reply is quoted (without exact reference) by Soterakēs, Βενιαμὶν Λέσβιος, p. 27.

15. Τετρακτύς, p. κγ΄, note 2.

16. Ibid., p. μγ΄.

17. The constituent parts are thus dated.

18. Τετρακτύς, Prologue, p. [ii].

19. J. G. Heinecke (1681–1741), German jurist. The book on which Doukas draws is presumably the *Elementa philosophiae rationalis et moralis* (Frankfurt, 1728), but Doukas does not refer to it explicitly.

20. Τετρακτύς, p. 223.

21. See his dialogue, "On Virtue" (1823), published in his Σοφιστής, I (Aegina, 1835), esp. p. 87. On βατολογίας cf. *St. Matthew's Gospel* VI, 7. (I owe the reference to Dr. E. P. Papanoutsos.)

22. In a dialogue on "Supplication," ibid. See esp. pp. 68–77.

23. Ibid., pp. 93–126.

24. Ibid., pp. 148–60.

25. Τετρακτύς, Ethics, *ad fin.*

26. Dimaras 4, p. 262.

27. Ibid., p. 261.

28. See the Address mentioned in note 13.

29. Σύνοψις Φυσικῆς (Vienna, 1812). Koumas states that its sources were, exclusively, works by Haüy [R. J. Haüy, 1743–1822], Gren [F. A. C. Gren, 1760–98] at Halle, and Grimm [J. K. P. Grimm, 1768–1813] at Breslau, Gren being the main one (Dimaras 4, pp. 353–4).

30. Χημείας Ἐπιτομή. The original was *Leçons élémentaires de chimie* (Paris, 1804). Koumas's Address to the Reader is printed in Dimaras 4, pp. 341–6.

31. Dimaras 4, p. 343.

32. Ibid., pp. 345–6.

33. It should be remarked that in the present context Koumas uses the term "philosophy" in its relatively narrow, academically familiar sense. In the Address which prefaces the *Physics* he uses it much more broadly so as to take in Mathematics, Physics and even Geography (Dimaras, *op. cit.*, p. 351).

34. Ἱστορίαι τῶν Ἀνθρωπίνων Πράξεων.

35. Vol. II, p. 228.

36. Στοιχεῖα τῆς Φιλοσοφικῆς Ἠθικῆς (Venice).

37. Στοιχεῖα Φιλοσοφίας.

18

Epilogue:
Liberalism not Victorious

I begin this chapter with what amounts to a caricature of the intellectual options facing the Greeks just before the War of Independence. It occurs in an Encyclical issued by the Patriarch Gregory V in 1819.

> What is the advantage of having our young people glued to these lessons [i.e., in mathematics and the sciences] and learning about numbers, and algebras, and cubes, and cubes of cubes (κυβοκύβους), and triangles, and triangulated squares (τριγωνοτετράγωνα), and logarithms, and calculations with symbols, and problems about ellipses, and atoms, and voids, and vortices, and forces and attractions and masses, and properties of light, and the *aurora borealis*, and bits of optics, and acoustics, and tens of thousands of similar things, and other prodigies, so that they may count up the grains of sand in the sea and the drops of the rain and may move the earth, provided only that, like Archimedes, they are given a fixed point on which to stand—and then have them barbarians in their speech, solecists in their writing, ignorant in matters of religion, in morals perverted and corrupt, irresponsible in affairs of state, and backward in patriotism and unworthy of their ancestral calling?[1]

The "sound philosophy" of Moisiodax, Benjamin and Philippidēs is thus put in its place. At best it is no more than a supplement to "grammatical" education and is useful only for special purposes. Grammatical education itself must not be just a matter of attaining correctness in speech and writing; it must also be the matrix in which correct moral and religious instruction is conveyed, from the very earliest stages. At its apex is the ancient language. The devout, the controlled, the learned and the patriotic character are all nurtured by the study of ancient Greek. This is the language employed in the writings of the Fathers and teachers of the Church, and in all the sacred laws and ordinances. Consequently we need it in order to profit from their inspiration, and to learn through them the meaning of reverence towards God and right conduct towards men. We need it, also, to learn from the moral wisdom of old: how modes and fashions in behavior are to be contemned, virtue is to become fortified and resolute, and justice to be brought about between rulers and ruled. It is the means by which the learned may undertake the translation of all that is worth translating. It is an orderly medium for epistolary exchanges on all sorts of subjects. And it is the proudest possession of the Race.[2]

Although Gregory V was executed by the Turks in 1821, he was, to all appearances at any rate, antirevolutionary; and the tone of his Encyclical indicates clearly how reactionary were his educational principles and his general cultural outlook. He was, unfortunately, the mouthpiece of the only educational point of view that, in prewar Greece, could be called corporate.

What was ranged against him was something serial rather than solid: a succession and series of individuals, homogeneous enough in their educational, linguistic and philosophical outlooks, but physically rather remote from one another, and collectively having no authority save that which the sheer force of their ideas could lend them. In certain places, Kydonies, Chios and Smyrna perhaps most of all, these ideas aroused great popular interest and caused the first stirrings of a "movement" towards up-to-date, all-round, academically serious, secular education. But in none of these places did the movement become well-enough established to continue beyond the presence of that particular individual who gave it impetus.

It was not, however, a case of the Church and conservatism fighting a succession of battles, one after the other, against modernism and secularism, and winning them. What brought the "enlightenment" to a halt in all these places was, naturally and inevitably, the war which broke out in 1821, and which either destroyed the schemes or diverted the energies of the reforming educators. No "body" existed to carry on their work, even where that might otherwise have been possible. They had not persuaded the all-important, ethnarchic Church of the value of their liberalism, but rather had engaged it in a dialectic which tended to accentuate its own obsession with the traditional and the safe. That obsession was reinforced powerfully by the Church's alliance with the ancient language (if not always, as in the instance of Athanasios Parios, with ancient modes of thought), and by the romantic nationalism of which linguistic archaism was one aspect.

The War, then, in effect left the Church in possession. For reasons I have suggested, classicism and its archaistic extreme were in a relatively strong position by the 1820's; after the war a "Hellenic" direction was given to Greek education which would not have controlled it so rigidly had the work of men like Psalidas, Benjamin, Philippidēs, Konstantas and Koumas not been cut short by events.

Did these men not, however, contribute to the production of those very circumstances that overwhelmed them? The answer must be that they did, by contributing to the revival of Greek thought which it has been the object of this study to trace. They, together with all whom they taught and influenced, were agents in an intellectual recovery, which *was* a rediscovery by the Greeks of their own capacities, needs and ambitions. Through their teaching and writing, that consciousness of their identity and their powers, which the Greeks as a whole had never entirely lost, became more explicit. The sheer labor that these men performed, whether in the assimilation of knowledge or in the production of more authentic thought, and especially their great and strenuous, if not always harmonious, efforts at linguistic re-creation, revived their own and others' confidence, and made them realize that it was by transforming themselves in the first place that liberation would come.

"We live, then, in slavery, my dear Greeks, not because our tyrant is strong, but because *we* are insensitive and indifferent, and thus intensify the shame that is upon us from being slaves of the most cowardly and indolent tyrant."[3] These sentiments were expressed in 1821, but they were far from new and had already been taken to heart in many ways. The ideas of nationhood and independence had been fortified by the consciousness of an educational renaissance which had become widespread amongst Greek writers in the generation before the War of Independence.

> In the renaissance of Greece which has already, with God's help, begun, the Muses with their immortal voices laud those patriotic Greeks who, in all sorts of ways, are endowing their country with benefits.

> The zeal for education has been kindled in the breasts of Greeks everywhere. The people of Smyrna, I hear, have this year collected a considerable fund for the foundation and support of their Philological School. The people of Kydonies, at their own expense, are sending many young men to study in Europe. The Chiotes are erecting an excellent library for their High School. Many patriots in various parts are contributing generously towards the publication of books and the institution of many benefits for their country.

This is the testimony of Konstantinos Oikonomos, then a follower of Koraēs, in 1816.[4] Koraēs himself, in his *Mémoire sur l'état actuel de la civilisation dans la Grèce*, had put the same optimistic point of view, at greater length, thirteen years before. But the whole manner of activity of people like Koraēs himself, Konstantas and Koumas, for example, was evidence enough on its own of that hopeful resoluteness which the recent progress of Greek thought could support.

Thus there is no question of the Greek eighteenth and early nineteenth-century Enlightenment's having been hollow. For particular political reasons its impetus may have lapsed and its ideas may have been left in abeyance, but not before they had changed the scene in the way just suggested. *Were* its ideas then left in abeyance? Could some of them, at least, not be said to have had a continuing influence upon the educational and cultural developments and controversies of the later nineteenth century?

Take, for instance, the greatest of all the educational questions upon which the War of Independence irrupted, namely the language question. Whereas Voulgaris and Doukas had taken it that serious and progressive thought could be accommodated only in an imitation of the ancient language, the consensus of the other Greek *savants* was that thought could live vigorously and be fertile only in a living language. When the War broke out, the question, as a controversy, was unresolved,[5] but the main lines of argument about it had been clearly laid down. The philosophy of language, so far as language answers or should answer to the needs of education, was set out by Moisiodax, Katartzēs, Philippidēs, Konstantas, Koraēs and others (sometimes in answer to the archaists) with comparative unanimity and satisfactory fullness. They tried to lay down the fundamental principles involved in the re-forming of their language as a vehicle of knowledge and discovery, and to establish more than a casual or a sentimental connection between progress and expansion in thought and naturalness in the grammar and syntax of the language available for its expression. The debate in which they took part was nothing if not emphatic. Consequently, although in the early years of the Greek state the palm might appear to have been awarded to classicism,[6] it is difficult to believe that the "simple"-language philosophy quite lost its influence.

For one thing, the philosophers had not been altogether alone in their defense of a simple language—in arguing, for example, that to express ideas in the language of the people is far from vulgarizing them. "Condillac said that words are signs of ideas, but it never entered his head to think that sharing the same words is *ipso facto* sharing the same thoughts." It was a poet, Dionysios Solomos, who made this observation,[7] and he declared that it was indeed an absurdity to think of the one sort of sharing as involving the other. Coins have the same value throughout the country in which they are current, he pointed out, but this does not mean to say that they may not yield the most enormously varying profit to their possessors. Why then should using the same words as simple and uncultivated people condemn us to thinking the same poor, undeveloped thoughts? The robust and commonsense attitude to the language question which Solomos shared with Philippidēs and other philosophers was overshadowed for a generation or so by one that was much nearer to the romantic classicism of Doukas. Yet Solomos lived until 1857, and, although he was an Ionian Islander, his influence reached into Greece as such.

There is another consideration which might seem to favor the idea that the philosophers of "simple" language had spoken so as to be heard by their descendants. The language which in fact emerged during the middle part of the nineteenth century as "official" Greek, the language which it became the aim and object of the higher schools to perfect in their pupils, and which the University of Athens adopted as its medium of instruction, was not, after all, a version of ancient Attic. It was the so-called καθαρεύουσα, the "purified," formal language which became the language of the State, and which has set itself over against "demotic" from the mid-nineteenth century until the present day. True, the καθαρεύουσα was a very artificial creation, but it did represent *some* recognition of a need for compromise with the existing spoken language, *some* coming-to-terms with the view that that language is the essential substance in any linguistic development. It did depart in this way from the fanatical view that nothing would be satisfactory even in the fairly short term but the relearning of the ancient language.

Did this, however, represent a real compromise in the sense that it took account of any of the principles for which the philosophers of "simple" language had argued, and that it acknowledged their validity up to some point? The answer must be that it very probably did not. It was in the nature of things that some such "compromise" as the καθαρεύουσα should have come about anyhow, independently of all the arguments of the philosophers. Doukas's optimism about the revival of ancient Greek must soon have seemed utterly unrealistic; in practice one could not just disown the existing language. It would take an extended study, however, to discover to what extent Greek philologists in the mid-nineteenth century, or later on when the language controversy really came alive again, took into account the linguistic debate of the eighteenth and early nineteenth centuries. My own impression is that they took little or no notice of it, and that Giannēs Psycharēs and Emmanouel Roïdēs, for example, who revived the controversy late in the nineteenth century, did so in their own terms.

In any case, so far as the generation or two immediately after the War were concerned, it seems that the pre-War philosophy of language, as put forward by the *philosophical* exponents of simplicity and naturalism, became virtually a lost body of literature. And if this is true of their philosophy of language, it is true also of the many less immediately-engaging subjects which these thinkers discussed: other aspects of education, theories of morality, of law and society, and so on. The setting for and the idiom of discussion of all these topics altered after the War, academically and politically.

What was the basis of this general change, however? Why did the sturdy philosophical, scientific and educational thinking of the eighteenth and early nineteenth centuries weaken so much in the atmosphere of political independence? Three reasons, at least, may be suggested. The first has been indicated already. It is that the intellectuals of the earlier nineteenth century suspended their educational efforts during the War and either failed to renew them afterwards or did so ineffectually, and without a following.

The second possible reason is closely connected with this first one. It is true in general that originative and enterprising thought does not flourish in an atmosphere of haste and improvisation, and this is true in particular of the early Greek state. The effort and excitement of the years of war were succeeded in the 1830's and later by the consciousness of all that was entailed in the building-up of that state and the development of national institutions—including an educational system—from the beginning. That these tasks had to be undertaken in conditions of political confusion and with a very great poverty of resources discouraged rather than stimulated "higher" educational thinking. In the circumstances, a tendency in education towards an unambitious didacticism in general, and ancestor-worship in particular, was understandable enough. The only safeguard against total bewilderment and confusion of purpose was to look, so far as possible, to the past and the well-tried.

The third reason for the loss of intellectual impetus is complex. The confinement of political Greece into so small a state as was set up in 1832 meant that the main centers of contemporary Greek educational activity were still in Turkish or other foreign hands. One might expect, therefore, that books and scholars would have continued to emerge from the non-liberated lands once the issue of the war was seen. There was no prospect of a wholesale migration of their people into free Greece, and if political and social dissatisfaction is any stimulant to thought, as it had been for their predecessors, the conditions providing that dissatisfaction remained in many places unchanged from those of the eighteenth century.

In fact, only the Ionian Islands continued to flourish intellectually. Even the Greek mercantile centers in Italy and other non-Greek lands became educationally inactive. It was as if there had been an implicitly acknowledged transfer of responsibility for the keeping of Greek culture from "outer" Greece and beyond to "inner" Greece, with inner Greece, for reasons which I have outlined, unable to do much to nourish that culture for the time being. The fact that there was a recession of Greek thought from many places where it had thriven before the War is undoubted. Of the reasons for this, some are particular, differing according to different places. Others are general, and more speculative.

One that seems probable, however, is the rise of Athens in prestige and attractiveness, and its possession of the only university in Greek lands. One would expect Athens, even in the absence of a general migration towards free Greece, to have drawn in many students and potential men of letters from outside. This would account for the removal of one line of influence in the production of Greek intellectual work, and, perhaps, for the somewhat tardy replacement of it by another.

One must not forget, too, the distracting and irrelevant influence exerted in Athens by the Bavarian court of the first Greek (Othonian) dynasty. The classicistic romanticism of Munich left its not unattractive mark on the buildings of Athens, but it contributed little to the intellectual advancement of the Athenian people; and the Greeks themselves who hung around Otho's court, particularly the Phanariots who came to Athens seeking places and influence, represented no more than a pseudo-aristocracy of the intellect; pen-pushers (καλαμαράδες), as I have heard them called, rather than thinkers and scholars.

After the War the watchword of education was no longer "philosophy." As the nineteenth century went on, philosophy in Greece became more professional, more compartmentalized, to a large extent Germanic in style and outlook, and, in short, one academic pursuit amongst others.[8] Taken as a body of literature it lacks the sense of urgency, of educational purpose and of general relevance that unites and vivifies the work of most of those writers whom I have been examining.

As regards this earlier work in general, it cannot be claimed that there is much novelty, except in points of detail and in style and manner of treatment, in its purely doctrinal content. Formally regarded, the ideas and arguments contained in the writings of the earlier Greek *savants* echo to a very large extent what is to be found elsewhere, either in more or less contemporary Western European thought or in Greek classical sources. To insist on this aspect of the matter alone, however, would be to miss the fascination which these ideas and arguments reacquire when collected and directed towards a particular social situation: to miss, in other words, the interest and significance of an educational movement the ultimate principles of which, whatever their origin, were intensely held, and which were re-expressed, transformed or combined as emblems of an educational and political reawakening. Voulgaris on toleration, Moisiodax on liberal education, Koraēs on political virtue and Philippidēs on the unappreciated significance of our very power to talk, are examples of a humanistic concern which maintained itself like a tough plant, amid the bleak rocks of ecclesiastical conservatism, in the rough desert of political oppression and corruption. The humanistic concern often enough merges into patriotic exhortation, and general principle into political precept: but this is simply a sign of the life that these men's writings contain: they do not all have to be galvanized by a historian's interest, even though history lends them so much significance.

Notes

1. Dimaras 4, p. 302.
2. These sentiments may be found ibid., pp. 301–3.
3. From Konstantinos Nikolopoulos's Προτροπὴ Πατριωτική (Paris, 1821) (Dimaras 4, p. 307).
4. From the prefatory address in his Ὁ Φιλάργυρος κατὰ τὸν Μολιέρον (Vienna, 1816) (Dimaras 4, p. 322).
5. It still is.
6. On this see Dimaras 4, pp. 61–2.
7. In his Διάλογος, composed about 1824. (Quoted from Παιδεία καὶ Ζωή, no. 55 (Jan.–Feb., 1957), p. 4).
8. Its course can be followed in the selections published in Papanoutsos 3.

Index

Academy, Athonite, 44–49 *passim*, 51 n.9, 52 n.26, 89, 92; arrangement of classes in, 45; instructional material in, 45–46

Academy, Greek, 179–80

Academy, Ionian (French), 115

Academy, Ionian (Guilford's), 115

Academy, Patriarchal, 5, 21, 38, 49, 193; curriculum in, 2, 13

Adet, P. A.: *Leçons élémentaires de chimie*, 194

Aegina, school in, 192

Alexander (scholiast), 16

Ali Pasha, 114, 115

Analytics, *Prior* and *Posterior*. See Aristotle

Anaxagoras, 65, 175

Anaximenēs, 65

Anghelou, Alkis: on Platonism, 25, 26 n.21

Anthrakitēs, Methodios, 17, 33–38 *passim*, 39, 56, 63 n.23, 166; and Peripateticism, 33, 36, 37; career of, 33–34, 36–38; differences with Church of, 34, 36–38; *Introduction to Logic*, 34–36, 40 n.22; other work by, 34

Anticlericalism, 146, 149–50, 160, 161, 162–63, 166–67, 169 n.19

Apology. See Moisiodax

Aristotelianism: revival of, in Padua, 7, 12–13; unproductivity of, 14

Aristotle, 12–14, 16–17, 20–21, 33, 54, 58, 60, 62, 65, 67, 120, 151, 175–76, 189; *De Interpretatione*, 14; *Physics*, 17; *Politics*, 147, 150; *Posterior Analytics*, 14; *Prior Analytics*, 14; restrictive influence of, 17, 32

Arnauld, A., 56

Arrian, 151

Atakta. See Koraēs

Athanasios, Saint: Greek Catholic College of, 12

Athens, school in, 192

Athens, University of, 197, 203, 206

Atomists, the, 65

Aurelius, Marcus, 151

Bacon, Francis, 56

Balanaian school (Ioannina), 113–14; curriculum in, 114

Benjamin. See Lesvios, Benjamin

Bergler, Étienne, 23

Berkeley, George, 175

Bibliotheca Graeca (Fabricius), 22

Book of Duties. See Mavrokordatos, Nikolaos

Bucharest, Philological Society in, 180

Bucharest, school in, 140, 188, 193
Byzantine tradition, 3

Carlyle, J. D., 52 n.26
Catherine the Great, 50, 69, 103
Chantzerēs, Samuel (Patriarch), 49
Cheselden, William, 175
Chios, school in, 10 n.5, 48, 117, 124, 183, 193, 202
Chrysanthos (Patriarch), 36–37, 40 n.26
Church, the Orthodox: as supporter of humanism, 7; conservatism of, 2, 8–9, 101, 165–66, 200–201; differences with Anthrakitēs, 36–38
Clarke, Samuel, 66–67
Claudius (Κλαύδιος), 89
Clémence, Joseph-Guillaume (Abbé), 77–78
Condillac, Étienne Bonnot de, 9, 111, 127, 177, 183, 203; *La Logique*, 172, 181 n.3; *Traité des sensations*, 178
Coste, Pierre, 46, 90
Cremonini, Cesare, 12
Cyril V (Patriarch), 44, 47–48

Damodos, Vikentios, 29–33 *passim*, 38; career of, 29; on "right reason," 29–33, 55; *Synopsis of Moral Philosophy*, 29; other works by, 29
Definitive Harmony of Things, The. See Vlachos
De Interpretatione. See Aristotle
Demokritos, 65
Descartes, René, 8, 14, 33, 55–56, 58–59, 62, 63 n.15, 65–67, 79, 111, 127, 176
Dialogue on Life and Death. See Mavrokordatos, Nikolaos
Dimaras, Constantin Th.: on numbers of schools, 10 n.6; on output of Greek books, 10 n.7
Doukas, Neophytos, 9, 180, 184–92 *passim*, 193–96; ambivalent intellectual position of, 190–92; influence of, 192; literary activity of, 184, 192; on "good grammar," 184–86; on language problem, 184–88, 202–203; on philosophy and grammar, 185–88; on philosophy in education, 185–86, 191–92; on psychology, 190; on virtue, 191; respect for Classical culture of, 184–188; *Sophistēs*, 191, 198 n.21; *Tetract*, 188–90
Du Hamel, J. B.: *Logic and Metaphysics*, 46

Education: general content of, 142–143, 199–200; nature of higher, 5, 10 n.5; post-war problem of, 205; progress of, 165; science as part of, 9, 192
Eleatics, the, 65
Elements of Logic, Metaphysics and Ethics. See Konstantas
Elements of Metaphysics. See Lesvios
Elements of Philosophical Ethics. See Vamvas
Empedoclēs, 65
Épée, Charles Michel de l' (Abbé), 176
Epicurus, 65
Epitome of Chemistry. See Koumas
Euclid, 89

Flanginian Institute (Venice), 29, 39, 51 n.3
"Friendly Society," the, 140, 171

Gassendi, Pierre, 65, 67, 176
Gazēs, Anthimos, 170–72, 180–81; editorial work of, 143, 180; *Geography*, 180; *Grammar of the Philosophical Sciences*, 180–81
Gazēs, Theodoros, 176
Gennadios (Scholarios), 176
Genovesi, Antonio: *Elements of Metaphysics*, 46, 197 n.1
"Georgantes," 117
Giounma, Emanuel, 39
Giounma school (Ioannina), 39, 43
Gordios, Anastasios, 38–39
Gracián, Baltasar, 92
Gravesande, G. J.'s, 43, 56, 66; *Introduction to Philosophy*, 46, 49
Greek Library. See Koraēs
Greek Nomarchy, 159–68 *passim*, 191; anticlericalism of, 160–63, 169 n.19; comparison of, with Koraēs, 160; on forms of government, 160–61; on law and freedom, 161; on political corruption, 161–62; on progress of education, 165; on the nobility, 162–64; on unjustifiable exile, 164–66; rationalism of, 165–166
Greek Orthodox Church. See Church, the Orthodox
"Greek thought," meaning of, ix–x
Gregory V (Patriarch), 199–200
Gren, F. A. C., 198 n.29
Grimm, J. K. P., 198 n.29

Hamilton, Sir William, 12
Hartley, David, 122
Haüy, R. J., 198, n.29
"Heineccius." See Heinecke, J. G.
Heinecke, J. G., 198 n.19
Heliodorus: *Aethiopics*, 151
Herakleitos, 65
Herschel, Sir William, 118
Hesiod, 65
Hippocrates: *De Aere*, 151
Histories of the Acts of Mankind. See Koumas
Hobbes, T., 56, 150
Horváth, K. J., 115, 116 n.18
Hume, David, 176
Hunt, Dr. Philip: on Voulgaris, 50

Iaşi, school at, 76, 89, 95
Impromptu Reflections. See Koraēs
In Praise of the Philosopher. See Katartzēs
Intellectuals, as rationalists, 4; characterization of, 4; persecution of, 4
Introduction to Aristotle's Categories. See Porphyry
Introduction to Logic. See Anthrakitēs
Ioannina, schools in, 33, 39, 43–44, 113–15, 193
Isocrates, 151

Kallonas, Gavriel, 48, 92
Kalokinēmata. See Psalidas
Kant, Immanuel, 9, 104, 111, 113, 115, 196
Kaplaneian school (Ioannina), 113–114; curriculum in, 114–15
Kapodistrias, Ioannēs, 115
Kastoria, 33
Katartzēs, Demetrios, 9, 78–85 *passim*, 118, 142–43, 168, 179; career of, 81, 84, 86 n.18; comparison of, with Koraēs, 142, 144; comparison of, with Moisiodax, 96; influence of, 84–85; *In Praise of the Philosopher*, 82–84; *Know Thyself*, 78–81, 84;

linguistic theories of, 80–81, 84, 86 n.14, 202; on instructional literature, 78–79; on philosophy and Christianity, 82–84; on Voltaire, 85 n.9; self-contradictory position of, 81
Katephoros, Antonios, 39, 51 n.3; teaching of Voulgaris by, 42–43; works of, 42
Katharevousa, 154, 203–204
Kausokalyvitēs, Neophytos, 44–45
Keill, John, 66
Know Thyself. See Katartzēs
Konstantas, Gregorios, 84–85, 170–172, 177–81, 189, 201–202; *Elements of Logic, Metaphysics and Ethics*, 177–78; *Modern Geography*, 176–77; on language problem, 177–79, 202
Koraēs, Adamantios, 9, 142–56 *passim*, 159, 163–64, 166, 172, 180, 183, 186–88, 192, 202, 207; anticlericalism of, 146, 149–50; career of, 150–51; comparison of, with *Greek Nomarchy*, 160; comparison of, with Katartzēs, 142, 144; influence of, 154–56; isolationism of, 144–46; "middle road" of, 153–54; on Classical studies, 146–47; on divided counsel, 148; on education, 143, 146–47, 149; on Greek apartness, 10; on Greek language, 152–54, 202; on Greek "resurrection," 159; on law and freedom, 148–49, 159; on polymathy, 144–146; on *The Scholarly Hermes*, 143; on Voulgaris, 103; professionalism of, 8; scope of writings by, 150–52. Works: *Atakta*, 152; *Greek Library*, 151; *Impromptu Reflections*, 147, 152; *Martial Song*, 156; *Martial Trumpet-Call*, 156; *Mémoire*, 7, 10, 103, 172, 202; *Papa Trechas*, 147, 159; *Parerga*, 151; *Political Counsels*, 147–150; *Right and Wrong are by Convention*, 150, 157 n.25
Korydaleus, Theophilos, 12–18 *passim*, 20, 28, 33, 37, 56, 87; as head of patriarchal academy, 13; as humanist, 13; as transmitter of Aristotelianism, 7, 12–17; career of, 12–13; combined antiquarianism and radicalism of, 16; contrast of, with Nikolaos Mavrokordatos, 20; deference to Aristotle of, 14; influence of, 16–17; manuscripts of, 17; neglect of Byzantines by, 16, 19 n.10; on nature and method of logic, 15; on rhetoric, 15–16. Works: *Notes and Problems Pertaining to the Entire Logic of Aristotle*, 14, 16, 19 n.4; *Preface to Logic* (from *Notes and Problems*), 14, 35; *Treatise on Rhetoric*, 15–16, 19 n.9; works (other), of, 16–17
Korydalism, 7, 16–17, 87
Kosmas (the Aitolian), 48
Kosmas Balanos. See Vasilopoulos, Kosmas Balanos
Koumas, Konstantinos, 188, 192–96, 201–202; as educational "progressive," 9; controversies with Doukas of, 187, 192–95; on Anthrakitēs, 34; on philosophy and grammar, 194–195; teaching of experimental science by, 193–94. Works: *Epitome of Chemistry*, 194; *Histories of the Acts of Mankind*, 195; *Philosophy Drawn Up and Constituted*, 195–96; *Synopsis of Physics*, 193
Kozanē, school in, 43
Kydonies, school in, 117–18, 124, 193

La Caille, J. A. de, 95, 98 n.23
Language, Greek: renewal of, 2–3, 8–9, 85, 95–96, 202–204
Lavoisier, A. L., 120
Legrand, Émile: *Bibliographie Hellénique* (for eighteenth century), 10 n.7
Leibniz, G. W., 55–56, 62, 65–67, 111, 176
Leisure Thoughts of Philotheos. See Mavrokordatos, Nikolaos
Lesvios, Benjamin, 27 n.23, 96, 117–140 *passim*, 142, 166, 168, 172, 183, 199, 201; career of, 118, 139–40; comparison of, with Psalidas, 118; on abuse of words, 135; on evil-doing, 136–38; on existence of God, 139; on freedom, 136; on idealism, 133, 135; on mathematics, 118–19; on perception, 130–31; on qualities of bodies, 132–34; on science and philosophy, 118–19; on scientific explanation, 120–22; on sensation, 122–23, 128–30; on the soul, 138–39; on "universal motive element," 121–23, 127, 129; on Voulgaris, 68–69; professionalism of, 8; scientific teaching of, 124; theory of ideas of, 128, 131–32, 134–36. Works: *Elements of Arithmetic*, 118; *Elements of Euclid's Geometry*, 118; *Elements of Metaphysics*, 118, 127–39 *passim*; *Ethics*, 141 n.38; *Physics*, 120–25 *passim*; works (other) of, 118
Levkas, school in, 115
Libraries, 5, 157 n.27, 170–71, 202
Locke, John, 8–9, 43, 56–57, 62, 92, 115, 122, 127, 137–39, 175, 177; *Essay*, 46; *Some Thoughts concerning Education*, 48, 90–91
Logic. See Philippides
Logic (Voulgaris): catalog of Greek philosophical achievements, 17, 22, 32. See also Voulgaris
Loukaris, Cyril (Patriarch), 13, 18

Maignan, Emanuel, 65
Makolas, Ioannēs, 51 n.3
Malebranche, Nicolas, 33, 56, 127, 176
Manos, Iakovos, 40 n.30
Marlianus, Ambrosius: *Theatrum Politicum*, 22
Maroutsaian school (Ioannina), 39, 43, 113
Martin, Benjamin: *Philosophical Grammar*, 180–81
Mavrokordatos, Alexandros (1636–1709); career of, 21; *Meditations*, 21, 26 n.5; *Opinions*, 21, 26 n.6; other writings of, 21
Mavrokordatos, Alexandros (1742–1812), 26
Mavrokordatos, Alexandros (1791–1865), 26, 115
Mavrokordatos, family of, 40 n.26, n.30; as educational writers, 7–8, 18, 20–26 *passim*
Mavrokordatos, Konstantinos, 25–26
Mavrokordatos, Nikolaos, 21–26 *passim*, 38, 40 n.26, 81; career of, 22; conservatism of, 23–25; contrast of, with Korydaleus, 20, 22–23; on moderation, 23–24; Platonism of, 25. Works: *Book of Duties*, 22–24, 26 n.12; *Dialogue on Life and Death*, 22, 26 n.9; *Leisure Thoughts of Philotheos*, 22, 25, 26 n.10; works (other), of, 22

Meditations. See Mavrokordatos, Alexandros (1636–1709)
Meletios (of Athens): *Geography*, 180
Meletios (of Vatopedi), 44, 47
Melies, school of, 170–81 *passim*
Metzburg, G. I.: *Arithmetic*, 103, 115
Modern Geography. See Philippidēs and Konstantas
Moisiodax, Iosepos, 9, 48, 52 n.16, 87–97 *passim*, 118, 142, 144, 146, 168, 199, 207; career of, 89–90; comparison of, with Katartzēs, 96; debt to Locke of, 90–91; on Aristotelianism, 17; on ethics, 93; on language question, 85, 95, 102, 202; on metaphysics, 93; on traditional logic, 93–94; on Voulgaris, 46–47, 69, 75 n.12, 87–89, 99; radicalism of, 89–92. Works: *Apology*, 88–90, 92–95; *Moral Philosophy*, 88; *Theory of Geography*, 95, 102; *Treatise on the Education of Children*, 90–92, 97 n.13
Monboddo, Lord: on Voulgaris, 41–42, 51 n.1, n.2
Moral Philosophy. See Moisiodax
Muratori, Lodovico Antonio: *La filosofia morale*, 88
Musschenbroek, Petrus van, 65–67
Mytilene, school in, 139

Newton, Isaac, 65–67
Notaras, Chrysanthos. See Chrysanthos (Patriarch)
Notes and Problems Pertaining to the Entire Logic of Aristotle. See Korydaleus

Oikonomos, Konstantinos, 201–202
Opinions. See Mavrokordatos, Alexandros (1636–1709)

Padua, University of, 7, 12–13, 21, 29, 43, 89
Palamas, Panagiotēs, 47
Papapandazēs, Anthimos, 170–71
Papapandazēs, Zacharias, 171
Parerga. See Koraēs
Parios, Athanasios, 48, 70, 117, 183–184, 197 n.1, 201; *Response*, 183–84
Phanariots, 20, 81, 164, 206; educational influence of, 7–8
Pheraios, Regas, 84–85
Pherekydēs, 65
Philippidēs, Daniel, 84–85, 170–79 *passim*, 181, 183, 199, 201, 207; on analytic method, 173–75; on language problem, 173, 177–78, 202; on "metaphysics," 172–74; on power of philosophy, 175. Works: *Logic*, 172–76; *Modern Geography*, 176–77; works (other) of, 176
Philosophy, as apex of education, 3–4, 206; scope of, 3–4
Philosophy Drawn Up and Constituted. See Koumas
Photios, 42
Physics. See Aristotle
Physics. See Lesvios
Plato, 20, 54, 65, 150–51, 160–61; teaching of, 25
Plethon, 1, 176
Plutarch, 64–65, 79, 151, 165
Political Counsels. See Koraēs
Politics. See Aristotle
Porphyry: *Introduction to Aristotle's Categories*, 14, 176
Port Royal Logic, 53
Pourchot, E.: *Logic*, 46
Preface to Logic. See Korydaleus
Presses, Greek, 7, 50
Principles of the Philosophers, The. See Voulgaris

Proclus, 89
Prokopiou, Demetrios, 22
Psalidas, Athanasios, 96, 99–116 *passim*, 117, 144, 172, 183, 201; career of, 103–104, 115; comparison of, with Benjamin, 118; empiricism of, 101, 107, 109–10, 112–13; Kantianism of, 101, 104; on ideas, 110–11; on revelation, 99–101, 104, 106–13; on Voulgaris, 87, 99–104; professionalism of, 8; teaching of experimental science by, 114–15, 124. Works: *Arithmetic*, 103; *Kalokinēmata*, 99–103, 105 n.1; *Logic*, 104; *True Happiness*, 100, 103–104, 106–114 *passim*, 115–16, 139; works (other) of, 103–104
Psycharēs, Giannēs, 204
Pythagoras, 65

Reflections of Crito, 166–68; anticlericalism of, 166–67
Refutation of Voltaire. See Theotokes
"Religious humanism," meaning of, 13
Religious Toleration, On. See Voulgaris
Response. See Parios
Right and Wrong are by Convention. See Koraēs
"Right reason," 29–33, 54–55, 82, 123, 190
Rohault, Jacques, 65
Roïdēs, Emmanouel, 204

Scholarly Hermes, The, 143, 180
Scholastics, the, 65, 67
Schools, Greek, 39, 51 n.7; distribution of, 5–6; number of, 10 n.6; patronage of, 5–7; provision of books for, 6–7; scientific equipment in, 6, 115, 124, 193
Science, general educational importance of, 9, 192
Segner, J. A. von: *Treatises on the Elements of Mathematics*, 46, 88
Shaftesbury, 3rd Earl of, 150
Siatista, 33
Simplicius (scholiast), 16
Smyrna: *gymnasion* in, 193, 196, 202; school in ("Evangelical"), 117, 140
Soave, Francesco: *Instituzioni di logica metafisica ed etica*, 177, 182 n.20, 189
Socrates, 150
Solomos, Dionysios, 203
Sophistēs. See Doukas
Sophists, the, 150
"Sound philosophy," 82, 86 n.22, 92–96, 176, 199
Spinoza, Benedict de, 116 n.4
Strabo, 151
Synopsis of Moral Philosophy. See Damodos
Synopsis of Physics. See Koumas

Tacquet, A.: *Elements of Geometry*, 46, 89, 95
Tatakis, Basile: on continuity of Greek thought, 10 n.1
Tetract. See Doukas
Thales, 65
Themistius (scholiast), 16, 73
Theophrastus, 60; *Characters*, 151
Theotokēs, Nikephoros, 76–78, 80, 88, 102; career of, 76; condemnation of Voltaire by, 77–78; *Elements of Physics*, 76; *Refutation of Voltaire*, 76–78
Thought, Greek: history of, 1–2; post-war recession of, 205–206;

recovery of, 201–202; secularization of, 4–5
Thucydides, 79
Toleration, religious, 70–73
Translation, general problems of, 78–79, 87
Trapezountios, Georgios, 25, 176
Treatise on Rhetoric. See Korydaleus
Treatise on the Education of Children. See Moisiodax
True Happiness. See Psalidas
Turks, indifference to Greek education of, 6

Universal System, The. See Voulgaris

Vamvas, Neophytos, 196–97; *Elements of Philosophical Ethics*, 197; *Elements of Philosophy*, 197
Vasilopoulos, Balanos, 43, 113–14
Vasilopoulos, Kosmas Balanos, 113–114
Vatopedi, Monastery of, 44
Vessarion, 176
Vlachos, Gerasimos, 18; *Definitive Harmony of Things, The*, 18, 19 n.23
Voltaire, F. M. A. de, 8, 60, 69–70, 73–74, 76–78, 85 n.9; *Essai . . . sur les dissensions des églises de Pologne*, 50, 69; *La Bible enfin expliquée*, 76–77
Voulgaris, Eugenios, 29, 39, 41–74 *passim*, 87, 92, 99–103, 139, 142–44, 166, 183, 189; attitude to Voltaire of, 60, 70, 73–74; career of, 42–50; eclecticism of, 53, 62–63; formal logic of, 61; linguistic archaism of, 8, 80, 95–96; on Aristotle, 17, 32; on Cartesian physics, 65–66; on criticism, 59–60; on doubt, 58–59; on elements of body, 65–66; on freedom in philosophizing, 54–55; on ideas, 56–57; on Korydaleus, 17; on method, 61–62; on nature of body, 65; on philosophical language, 54, 202; on revelation, 100–101; on solidity, 66; on toleration, 70–73 *passim*, 207; on Tychonian system, 68; transmutation of Western thought by, 8. Works: *Elements of Metaphysics*, 46, 49; *Logic*, 8, 17, 22, 32, 42, 46, 49–50, 53–63 *passim*, 69–71, 73, 95–96, 98 n.26, 99–103; *On Religious Toleration*, 70–73 *passim*, 75 n.14; *On the Dissensions of the Churches in Poland*, 69–70; *Principles of the Philosophers*, 46, 49, 64–69 *passim*; translation of Voltaire's *Essai*, 50; translations (other), 45–46, 50, 52 n.14, n.31, 102–103; *Universal System*, 46, 49, 68

War of Independence, effect of, 139, 204
Western Europe, transmission of ideas from, 6–9
Whiston, William, 89
Wilson, Rev. S. S., 115–16
Wolff, C. F. von, 56, 65; *Elements of Arithmetic and Geometry*, 46, 89
Wucherer, J. Fr.: *Physics*, 46

Xenophon, 151, 165

Zaviras, Georgios, 34
Zenonians, the, 65
Zerzoulēs. See Zortoullios
Zortoullios, Nikolaos, 88, 97 n.3
Zosimas (brothers), 50